Private Sector, Public Wars

Private Sector, Public Wars

Contractors in Combat— Afghanistan, Iraq, and Future Conflicts

James Jay Carafano

The Changing Face of War

PRAEGER SECURITY INTERNATIONAL
Westport, Connecticut • London

Library of Congress Cataloging-in-Publication Data

Carafano, James Jay, 1955-

Private sector, public wars : contractors in combat—Afghanistan, Iraq, and future conflicts / James Jay Carafano.
    p. cm.—(Changing face of war, ISSN 1937-5271)
  Includes bibliographical references and index.
  ISBN-13: 978-0-275-99478-5 (alk. paper)
  1. Defense industries. 2. Contracting out—United States. 3. Defense contracts—Iraq. 4. Defense contracts—Afghanistan. 5. Civil-military relations—United States. 6. United States—Armed Forces—Civilian employees. 7. Private security services—United States. 8. Mercenary troops—United States. 9. United States—Armed Forces—Procurement. I. Title.
  HD9743.A2C24 2008
  355.6—dc22   2008010128

British Library Cataloguing in Publication Data is available.

Library of Congress Catalog Card Number: 2008010128
ISBN-13: 978-0-275-99478-5
ISSN: 1937-5271

First published in 2008

Praeger Security International, 88 Post Road West, Westport, CT 06881
An imprint of Greenwood Publishing Group, Inc.
www.praeger.com

Printed in the United States of America

The paper used in this book complies with the Permanent Paper Standard issued by the National Information Standards Organization (Z39.48-1984).

10 9 8 7 6 5 4 3 2 1

Contents

Acknowledgments

The work would not have been possible without my colleagues at the Heritage Foundation—past and present. Working with them on joint research projects has been a unique privilege. Much of that work informed and contributed to this project. They are all outstanding professionals—generous with their time, serious in their work, and dedicated to keeping America safe, free, and prosperous. No one could be blessed with better colleagues. My thanks go to Bill Beach, Peter Brookes, Ariel Cohen, Helle Dale, Dana Dillon, Mackenzie Eaglen, Alison Acosta Fraser, Kim Holmes, Oliver Horn, Tim Kane, Alane Kochems, Daniella Markheim, David Muhlhausen, Diem Nguyen, Jim Phillips, Jack Spencer, Baker Spring, and Jan Smith.

Prologue   **A Farewell to Arms**

It all started in paradise.

On April 9, 2003, U.S. Marines storming downtown Baghdad entered *al-Firdos*—Paradise Square. Down came the massive 40-foot bronze of Saddam Hussein. Cameras rolled. The era of Saddam ended.

Weeks would follow before the now infamous declaration, by President George W. Bush, from the deck of the aircraft carrier *USS Abraham Lincoln* (under the banner "Mission Accomplished") that marked the formal completion of combat operations. Nevertheless, for many the presumptuous belief that the war was over and cheaply won will always be captured in the iconic images of liberation and the tumbled statue, played and replayed on televisions around the world in the wake of a seemingly effortless American triumph.

Enraptured with shaky videos of the felled Saddam bronze, butchers in Chicago and car salesmen in California knew little and cared less about the role played by contractors in supporting ground wars in Iraq or Afghanistan that followed in the wake of the September 11, 2001, terrorist attacks on New York and Washington. As the wars became long wars, as the images of paradise square became more ironic than iconic—things changed.

LONG WAR COMING

The fall of Saddam marked only the end of the beginning of the American adventure in Iraq. As the occupation, troubled from the start, only got more difficult, Americans became increasingly anxious. They had lots of questions, and they wanted answers. One pressing concern focused on the place of private contractors in supporting public armies. As the course of conflict appeared more intractable, suspicion grew about companies that went to war to make a buck.

At first, as coalition forces streaked toward Baghdad, media reporting critical of contractors in combat garnered little attention. Journalists who cared at all (and these were few) turned to Peter W. Singer, whose *Corporate Warriors: The Rise of the Privatized Military Industry* had been published only months before the invasion. The book had more to do with a now defunct sketchy British company immersed in African civil wars than the contract support provided to today's U.S. military. Still, Singer had published a solid work on a subject few reporters knew anything about—and he was quotable.

Corporate Warriors received generally positive reviews, though only a trickle of interest, even after the start of the war. Singer was a certified Washington expert (a scholar at the respected Brookings Institution, a Washington-based think tank), articulate and knowledgeable. Reporters looking for a different take on Iraq turned to him. He, in turn, frequently reminded that for every ten soldiers in Iraq, there was one contractor. At the time, the statistic seemed mostly just interesting trivia.

The role of the private sector in the public's war was, in fact, newsworthy. Contractors had become ubiquitous on the battlefield in Iraq and Afghanistan. The U.S. government issued contracts for everything. Contract employees washed dishes, drove trucks, built facilities, and even guarded Jerry Bremer, the appointed head of the Iraq Coalition Provisional Authority, who ran the first year of the occupation.

As the American engagement in Iraq stretched on, as the battles and roadside bombings became increasingly bloody—both correspondents and war critics more frequently revisited the issue of how and why fighting public wars had become so dependent on the private sector.

In October, six months after the war ended, the Center for Public Integrity published a list of companies doing business in Iraq and Afghanistan with a record of their political donations. Their report, "Windfalls of War," matched $49 million from 70 companies doing about $8 billion in government business to political contributions that went almost two to one to Republicans over Democrats. President George W. Bush pulled in the most of all. The fourteen biggest contractors doing work in Iraq and Afghanistan alone kicked in $23 million—almost half of the total. The biggest contributor from that elite group was Kellogg, Brown, and Root, a subsidiary of Vice President Dick Cheney's former company, Halliburton.

The media took notice. With prospects for a swift and effortless occupation looking increasingly glum, a disturbing report from a Washington-based center like the Center for Public Integrity piqued the interest of the press. Staffed by investigative journalists with well-earned reputations for reporting on corruption and influence peddling, the center's report proved a tempting story.

Six months later, another of the Iraq war's iconic images, a picture of the limp, blackened bodies of four contractors killed in an ambush and hung by a mob from a bridge in Fallujah (a city in central Iraq's Al Anbar province), shocked Americans. For Singer, Fallujah offered grim confirmation of his complaints. In *Salon*, an online news magazine, he scolded, "just because we can turn something over to the private market does not always mean we should.... Unfortunately, our

CEO-filled defense leadership has forgotten Economics 101 and brushed aside basic issues of public accountability. Instead, it has outsourced first and not even bothered to ask questions later."[1] This time when Singer spoke, he had lots of company. A legion of journalists turned their attention to how the Pentagon had outsourced the war.

In the weeks that followed, perhaps the most disturbing of the war's icons appeared—a hooded figure draped in faux sackcloth, with arms extended like a bizarre recreation of the crucifixion—an amateur photograph staged by American soldiers.

After the war, the U.S. military had taken over one of Saddam's most notorious prisons, Abu Ghraib, employing the facility as a holding and interrogation center. Apparently, for some of the guards guarding included taunting, humiliating, and abusing prisoners—and then keeping souvenir photographs.

An Army investigation of the incident at Abu Ghraib was well underway when CBS obtained the pictures and broadcast them on the evening news. Days later, investigative journalist Seymour Hersh, who had gained recognition and a Pulitzer Prize writing one of the first stories on the My Lai massacre during the Vietnam War, published details of the scandal in the *New Yorker*. A media blitzkrieg followed. Among the first revelations—the soldiers had not acted alone. Attention spread to the role of a shadowy defense contractor who served as an interrogator, Steven Stephanowicz.

Only a year after the invasion of Iraq, everything looked different. Each day, Baghdad became a more violent place. Each day, it became more apparent that biological, chemical, and nuclear weapons were not going to be found stuffed in secret bunkers (undermining what many considered the most compelling rationale for the war). Each day, the country became more ungovernable. Each day American soldiers looked less like liberators and more like occupiers. Even the joyous scene in *al-Firdos* came into question. A *Los Angeles Times* story suggested the whole event had been staged.[2]

A short, successful good war had turned into a long, troubling bad one—and in the course of the campaign, contracting on the battlefield had evolved from an interesting footnote to a contentious and controversial concern. Americans began to wonder whether profit had trumped patriotism—and not for the first time in modern memory.

Understanding why we worry about contractors requires turning the clock back half a century.

IKE'S DILEMMA

In his final address as president, Dwight David Eisenhower warned his fellow Americans that "in the councils of government we must guard against the acquisition of unwarranted influence, whether sought or unsought, by the military industrial complex." Eisenhower feared that excessive defense spending might lead to a cabal of collusion among defense industries, the Pentagon, and big government that would make decisions that suited them best, undermining democracy. In short, they might use the pursuit of making Americans safer as cover for all kinds of ill.

After eight years of readying Americans to prepare for a protracted Cold War facing off against the Soviet Union, "Ike" recalled in his memoirs that "I began to feel more and more uneasiness about the effect on the nation of tremendous military expenditures."[3] Throughout most of American history, when not at war, the United States spent only about 1 to 2 percent of its Gross Domestic Product (or GDP, a measure of everything bought, sold, made, and traded) on defense. The Cold War was different. Even when not engaged in armed conflicts, spending by the Pentagon averaged about a whopping seven and half percent of GDP.[4] That spending represented 50 percent or more of the entire federal budget. Writing checks that big troubled Eisenhower (at his core a Midwest fiscal conservative), a thrifty man raised in a dirt-poor family that had counted its nickels and dimes.

Ike delivered his farewell address from the oval office in the White House on January 17, 1961, only days before he passed the torch of presidential leadership to John F. Kennedy. Few expected the speech to include a warning of American liberty in peril. But that was what they got. "The potential for the disastrous rise of misplaced power," the President ominously declared in his last speech from the Oval Office, "exists and will persist."

The discordant note in Ike's remarks did not go unnoticed. It was true that the Cold War had become a cold cash business, the idea that democracy was for up for sale was an odd and unexpected comment from someone who, before being president, had been a lifelong soldier (forty years of military service) with businessmen for brothers—a president who over eight years had practically built the Cold War establishment. Generals and the corporate elite were openly offended.

Even critics who agreed that corporatism in Cold War America had trumped the capacity of Congress and the president's ability to manage big business found the declaration odd. *Time* magazine called the speech "schmaltzy" and the public response "piebald." It was not so much that Washington skeptics disagreed with Ike's dilemma. They were just surprised that the outgoing president not only shared their concerns but actually acknowledged them in such an openly public manner; and they were puzzled that he waited till his opinion mattered little anymore to make his point.

Eisenhower's statement was anything but unstudied. In the summer before he left office, Ike concluded that he wanted to make a last personal address to the nation. Preparations for drafting the speech took at least three months. And while historians still debate who originally proposed the idea of including a presidential indictment of the private sector and the Pentagon, there is no question that it was Eisenhower's heartfelt expression. Ike's speechwriters would deliver him, as one recalled, "completed staff work: the whole thing laid out, tailored to the audience with everything in there."[5] And although a passage on the military–industrial complex was in the draft presented to the president, he treated it as he did so many of his other speeches, reading and rereading the text, changing it, asking others to comment on it, and changing it again until, in the end, it was his speech. His speechwriters may have coined the "complex," but Eisenhower made the term a coin of the realm.[6] When he spoke those words, he forever changed how Americans talked about the ways of Wall Street and the halls of the Pentagon.

GUNS VERSUS BUTTER

Historians also generally agree on what might have prompted Eisenhower to caution against the collusion of soldiers and suits. Scholar Martin Medhurst notes that Eisenhower, the first Republican president since the New Deal, "was deeply concerned about the growth of the federal government and the systematic loss of state and local autonomy. He was concerned about a government that spent more than it took in, a government in which the twin threats of spiraling defense spending and an ever larger federal largess threatened to turn the country into a garrison state where individual liberties might be easily lost."[7] Ike always felt he had to walk a tight rope between being tough on the Russians and tight on the purse strings. There were plenty of people trying to upset the balancing act by pulling him one way or another.

Throughout his presidency, Ike endured innumerable battles where he felt forces had tried to do an end run around the Oval Office, out-"hawking" an administration full of hawks. One of the most notable incidents was, in part, the president's own doing. Eisenhower chartered a blue ribbon commission under H. Rowan Gaither, chairman of the Ford Foundation and the RAND Corporation to assess the need for a civil defense program. The commissioners knew the president would not be pleased with their findings. They wanted to vastly ramp up defense spending. Ike would not approve. Then something happened that they thought might change his mind.

On October 1, 1957, shortly before the committee's report was due to be presented to the President, a flicker of light reached into the sky above the Baikonur Cosmodrome in Kazakhstan. Aboard was 184 pounds of metal called "Sputnik." The Soviets had managed to launch the world's first satellite. Although all it did was circle the globe and beep at the world below, the launch shocked Americans. If the Soviets could throw a satellite into space, it was feared, they could drop a nuclear-tipped missile on a U.S. city.

Sputnik hysteria set the stage for equally hysterical warnings from the Gaither committee. The report, authored by a who's who of defense policy experts from the ranks of the military–industrial elite, vastly overestimated Soviet capabilities, calling for a $32 billion civil defense program as well as a huge Pentagon spending spree.

Though the Gaither report itself was classified, news leaks whipped up a nervous public. Eisenhower, predictably, proved skeptical of the commission findings. He refused to endorse a national shelter-building program, despite the public clamor to do "something" in response to Sputnik.[8] It was neither the first nor the last time that the president had to fend off near-hysterical cries from political allies and adversaries, the armed services, and security experts, all pushing for more guns (spending on defense and foreign policy) than butter (funding domestic programs). Ike felt that he had spent eight years combating nothing less than "a distorted use of the nation's resources."[9] After two terms, he was a tired warrior.

A REPUBLIC OF VIRTUE

That Eisenhower waited until the end of his administration to reveal his misgivings about the course America was on, and used the occasion of his farewell to give it voice, does not give historians much pause either. It was, in fact, typical of Ike.

A formal farewell address to the nation—hardly a norm in modern American politics—was nevertheless exactly the kind of speech that folks had come to expect from Eisenhower: a throwback to the practices of the early republic. That was just Ike.

Eisenhower thought of the Founding Fathers more as a band of his brothers. He had, after all, graduated from West Point, established by Thomas Jefferson to provide an egalitarian officer corps that put the needs of the nation ahead of glory and power. The academy's motto, "duty, honor, country," could well have been Ike's personal credo.

The American colonial tradition held that the purpose of military power was to protect, not usurp, democracy, that large standing armies had a corrupting influence and too easily became instruments of tyranny. The Founding Fathers accepted anti–standing army ideology as a matter of faith. These ideas still held sway, even in the age of Eisenhower.

In particular, the president idolized George Washington. "Washington was my hero," Ike recalled in a folksy memoir, At Ease.[10] Little wonder he would mimic the leadership style of the first commander-in-chief. First among the founding fathers, Washington had delivered the nation's first farewell presidential address. In doing so, he in turn drew on an even older and deeper tradition, harkening back to the practices of the Roman Republic where soaring oratory was emblematic of political discourse.

In the Classical Age, a speech served as an occasion to awaken the conscious of the people, elevating the speaker and his audience, putting principles above partisan politics. Early eighteenth-century political thought, in which Washington and other colonial leaders were deeply steeped, considered Rome the model of republican virtue. The first president was often compared to the Roman general Cincinnatus, who had left his fields to serve the people, and then, mission accomplished, relinquished power to return to the plow. Washington and fellow revolutionary heroes were so enamored with this image that they established a veterans' society in his homage. Little wonder that when

Eisenhower looked for a model of civic leadership, he drew on general and president George Washington.

Ike, however, had a foot in the future as well as the past.

In the Cold War world, a presidential address from the White House was more than just following the rhetorical form of Roman republicanism or letter writing from Mount Vernon. Presidential speechmaking had been transformed by the advent of television. Eisenhower had the power to sit with millions of Americans in their own living rooms and have a grainy, black-and-white, one-way conversation. Television offered an unprecedented opportunity for the chief executive to shape his public image without any intermediary filters from press or pundits. Unlike radio, on TV citizens could look into the eyes of their leader as if they were sitting in the Oval Office, peering into the windows of the president's soul and measuring his demeanor.

For Eisenhower, television offered a definite advantage. At the end of his administration, Ike was still a popular figure: trusted, the liberator of Europe, and a successful two-term president. In his final days in office, the president understood how to exploit the theater of a final televised address, reinforcing the image of a principled leader offering a sobering warning with no alternative motive other than promoting a safe, free, and prosperous nation.

He succeeded too well.

BETTER THAN DEATH

Eisenhower wakened a deep unease within the polity, particularly among the far left. He gave a name to their fears, and one that resonated as had nothing before. As a moniker of distrust, the "military–industrial complex" quickly surpassed the notoriety of "merchants of death," the term then used in slandering defense industries.

Popularized by the 1934–1936 Congressional hearings on the practices of arms manufactures in World War I, the "merchants of death" label rested on a premise that big business had a vested interest in promoting war to drive up profits. The Senate Munitions Investigating Committee, led by Senator Gerald Nye, echoed a popular explanation for the outbreak of World War I and served as a caution against advocates clamoring for American engagement in the looming war in Europe. Nye organized a show of ninety-three hearings and 200 witnesses to make the case that there was a link between lobbying by munitions manufacturers and Washington's decision to enter the First World War.

While Nye railed in the committee rooms of Congress, Major Eisenhower labored in the War Department. Ike may have been influenced by the inflammatory hearings. Eisenhower would no doubt have been disturbed about the implications of Nye's assertions. The future president firmly believed that industry had a vital role to play in modern war and helped draft the Army's war mobilization plan which relied heavily on the participation of the private sector.[11] If the private sector could not be trusted, that would be a problem. Many shared Eisenhower's unease.

By the outbreak of the Cold War, however, "merchants of death" was an idea that had long gone stale. The success of World War II led many Americans to believe that big business had served the nation well. When the "good war" ended, millions of returning veterans joined the ranks of General Motors and other captains of corporate America. Americans liked big business. At the same time, "merchants of death" seemed old-fashioned, like a reckless pirate gang—out of place in the twentieth century. On the other hand, the "military–industrial complex" sounded like something new. It had an authentic "techno" ring to it that seemed much more appropriate to the nuclear age—a new danger for a new era.

A STRANGE LOVE

In the end, Eisenhower certainly did Nye one better. Debates over defense policy in the last half century have peppered with rhetoric recalling a presidential warning of cabals with contractors. The military–industrial complex quickly became an enduring component of American popular culture, the dark nemesis that explained why freely elected governments nevertheless undertook apparently very self-destructive acts for the sake of a few dollars more. No cultural icon exemplified the danger more than Stanley Kubrick's iconoclastic film *Dr. Strangelove* (1964), released only three years after Ike's speech.

Serving both as screenwriter and director, Kubrick started out writing a script for a serious film about the Cold War. He found the subject of the standoff between East and West just too preposterous. *Dr. Strangelove* became a comedy. When a scuffle breaks out during a White House briefing, the president screams, "Gentleman, you can't fight in here! This is the War Room!"

In the movie, U.S. and Soviet efforts to forestall nuclear war through the threat of mutual assured destruction spiral out of control until the two sides wind up contracting to build weapons that in the end obliterate everyone. The president's scientific advisor, Dr. Strangelove, works for the Bland Corporation—a clear reference to the RAND Corporation, a federally funded research development center established during the Cold War which for many came to epitomize the merger of academia, government, and business symbolized by the military–industrial complex.

Kubrick's nightmare satire was the ultimate expression of the fear of government and industry run amuck. It was not, however, the only one. In Hollywood, as well as Washington, and universities, in films, speeches, and textbooks, Eisenhower's warning became an integral part of America's political language.

The boy from Abilene, Kansas would no doubt have been stunned to learn that of all public pronouncements made in decades of public service, coining the term military–industrial complex would prove his most memorable and enduring comment. The phrase first used by the president easily outlived the Cold War. Even today, it is as popular as ever. In a June 18, 2006, broadcast of the news show *60 Minutes*, columnist Andy Rooney, lamenting about excess in current military spending, declared, "Ike was right. That's just what happened."[12] Eisenhower established the cultural icon Americans still use to complain about what happens when Washington mixes the military and money.

FATE OF THE STATE

Eisenhower's predictions turned out to be wrong. The irony of the president's last warning was that the threat of the military–industrial complex overwhelming liberties never occurred—in good measure because of the efforts made during his administration to forestall turning America into an armed camp.

Historian Aaron Friedberg convincingly makes the case, in his study on the early Cold War years, that a consensus emerged on how to deal with the Soviet Union, striking a balance between maintaining military strength and preserving domestic freedoms. Absent that self-restraint, he argues the United States could well have dedicated 15 percent or more national wealth on defense, installed universal military conscription, a centralized government planned economy, much higher taxes and tariffs, and other controls over civil society.[13] All these proposals were on the table in the 1950s. None of them were put into effect.

Leaders like Eisenhower had held the line in the early years. There was, however, more to it than that. Turning a republic into a permanent garrison state ran against the grain of American political culture. At their core, during the Cold War's coldest early days, Americans never forgot that freedom was one the nation's greatest competitive advantages, never to be casually sacrificed for the promise of security or the absence of inconvenience.

While generals and suits never hijacked democracy, it is true that during the Cold War military industries did grow to constitute an unprecedented component of the peacetime political economy. In turn, there was a fair amount of government engagement with top-tier defense contractors—and some collusion between official customers and their suppliers. By the time the Soviet Union collapsed, the Pentagon had bought supplies from more than a quarter of a million companies. Corporate leaders routinely swapped their conference table chairs for desks at the Pentagon, and retired generals signed on to corporate boards.

At times during the Cold War, contractors really cashed in. In the mid-1980s, when most American manufacturing stagnated and U.S. trade ran deficits, defense companies grew at a healthy clip, and net exports of military hardware tripled. The earnings of the ten largest military contractors were three times higher than the manufacturing industry average.

On the other hand, there were also many periods during the standoff with the Soviets when military spending retrenched instead of climbing, eras when defense contractors fell on relatively hard times. From 1958 to 1966, in the years preceding and following Eisenhower's speech, military outlays, as a percentage of the whole economy, dropped significantly. There were other tough times as well. After a spurt of increased spending during the height of the Vietnam War, from 1969 to 1975, defense giants of the time McDonnell Douglas, Boeing, and Lockheed dropped 40 percent in size.

Additionally, whatever military–industrial complex that did endure during the Cold War is long gone. Not long after the Berlin Wall came down, so did defense industries. In a 1993 speech glumly referred to as "the Last Supper," Deputy Secretary of Defense William J. Perry warned industry leaders that big defense companies would have to contract, consolidate, or diversify to survive. His rationale was simple. Pentagon budgets were not going to get any bigger. In fact, the fall of the wall saw the start of fourteen years of continuous decline.

Even now, defense spending is not what it used to be. During the Cold War, the federal government funded about two-thirds of all U.S. research and development. Today, it pays for only about a third. The rest comes from the private sector.

When Ike left office, defense spending was about half the federal budget. In 2007, even including the swelling of defense contracting, the Pentagon's bills represented about of fifth of government spending.

Overall, in 2007, defense outlays hovered at about 4 percent of GDP (pumped up a full percentage point to pay for the wars in Iraq and Afghanistan). In the absence of the long war, Pentagon annual spending would amount to about half the Cold War average.

In the post–Cold War world, defense businesses are no longer close to being the industrial giants of the private sector. Companies like the Bank of America and Home Depot could buy and sell the defense sector several times over. According to the *Fortune* list for 2007 of the largest U.S. corporations, the biggest military contractor, Lockheed Martin, even with the flush of spending for the war on terrorism, ranks only fifty-seventh. Halliburton, the parent company of Kellogg, Brown, and Root, the largest contractor in Iraq, ranks one hundredth. Indeed, corporate giants have far deeper pockets to use to sway government officials. The health care industry—with Medicare, Medicaid, and Social Security now accounting for half the federal budget—has a much bigger stake in what Washington does than do companies that cash in on the Pentagon's business.

ICONS AND IRAQ

Despite the fact that there was more myth than material threat from a corporate Cold War takeover of American foreign policy (and even that ephemeral danger is long past), the old bugbear persists. The troubled occupation of Iraq and the attention paid to the issue of contractors in combat fueled a resurgence in the belief that conspiracies between government and contractors are axiomatic. The military–industrial complex remains the default explanation for many American ills.

Ike is a pop icon once again. In 2005, the popular documentary *Why We Fight* argued that corporate interests and a militarized economy fueled the war in Iraq. Eisenhower is the film's prescient hero, his picture plastered on the front of the DVD jacket.

There is little question that Eisenhower bequeathed a handy, recognizable, and credible mantra for criticizing government. Ike's icon has set the tone for talking about the role of the private sector in the public's war. It has made all too easy the task turning a pile of photographs from Fallujah, Abu Ghraib, and other scenes of heartbreak and hardship into a flipbook that narrates the excesses of corporate greed and manipulative politicians.

When the popular conception of contractors lapsed so quickly into metaphors reminiscent of the military–industrial complex, Washington ought to have taken pause. Defaulting to pop culture explanations for how and why wars are fought was not the message Eisenhower intended for the Republic in his farewell address.

Arguably, the emotion, politics, ambiguities, and confusion surrounding the large-scale employment of contractors in combat and the sketchy performance of the Iraqi occupation have colored popular perceptions, and that has engendered a sharp and acrimonious debate. That is to be expected. That is the way America fights. Democracies argue, and rightly so, about when, where, and how to go to war before, during, and for decades after. And free debates often ring with shrill and discordant tones.

Icons sharpen debate. That is why they are so popular in political rhetoric. "Political rhetoric creates the arena of political reality within which political thought and action take place," notes Ted Windt, an expert on the use of language in politics.[14] But, a political "reality" based on a faulty premise puts freedom in peril. There is no room for cheap shots in learning serious lessons that affect national security. Iconic images are no substitute for sober analysis.

Reality, not rhetoric, should drive long-term public policies.

CONTRACTS IN AMERICA

There are few subjects in which bringing the debate over the future of public policy back to a calm and reasoned discussion will be more difficult than that of contractors in combat. Contracting is big business and a big part of the war. By 2007, there were over 100,000 individuals signed onto U.S. contracts in Iraq. By contrast, there were only about 160,000 U.S. combat troops. By some estimates, contractors account for about 40 percent of the costs of running operations (compared, for example, with operations in the Balkans only a little over decade earlier, in which contractors accounted for about 10 percent of military costs). The cost of contracting has gotten Washington's attention.

Debating the role of contractors in combat is certainly fair game, but it is hard to hold a fair debate. The rise of contractors from footnote to headline in less than a year is illustrative of the scope of the challenge. Getting to a reasonable discourse on any topic that gets that hot that fast (spawning a cottage industry of instant experts, sensational books, exploitive documentaries, and Congressional investigations in a New York minute) is not going to be easy. It is, however, a task worth tackling.

The emerging role of contractors on the battlefield reflects a deeper and deeply significant transition in the nature of armed conflict: a significant rebalancing between the roles the private and public sector play in war. This change is the most significant upheaval in the nature of warfare since the rise of the nation-state in the seventeenth century. It represents a transformation started long before the invasion of Iraq. Absent a dramatic change in the evolution of the global marketplace, the role of the private sector in public wars will continue to increase long after the Iraqi conflict ends, regardless of the course of American domestic politics.

At the same time, the challenge of harnessing the growing capacity of the market place to market combat capabilities creates new and daunting responsibilities for government that cannot be addressed by business as usual practices. Washington was not prepared for the scope, scale, and complexity of managing contractors in combat. Government will have to change to keep up.

Private Sector—Public Wars asks and answers some basic questions for beginning an informed discourse: looking at why the "companies" on the battlefield are looking increasingly more like Microsoft and Wal-Mart than infantry, armor, and artillery, asking how these changes are changing us, and asking how the United States can manage and exploit these companies to maintain its competitive edge well into the future.

Understanding why the private sector has come to play such a prominent role in public wars requires tracing a story as torturous and, at times, as mysterious as the search for the Holy Grail, a tale filled with deceit, greed, courage, selflessness, stupidity, misdirection, and myth. It includes following a surprising, winding path from Medieval Tuscan hills, through England, colonial America, and the sands of Iwo Jima to the sands of Iraq, the mountains of Afghanistan, the corridors of Wall Street, and the halls of the Pentagon. It demands walking through the cross sections of military, political, social, cultural, economic, intellectual, and business history. At the end of the journey lies the story of contractors in combat. That is the story that *Private Sector—Public Wars* tells.

Looking at the facts argues that the heated rhetoric over contractors in combat does match reality. *Private Sector—Public Wars* finds that contractors

- make sense—they have been used for centuries and their roles on the battlefield will likely only expand.
- are not a threat to the public good—good governance and the appropriate use of contractors in combat go hand in hand.
- could have been employed much more effectively in Iraq and Afghanistan—the principal problem was the U.S. government's lack of capacity to get, oversee, and manage large-scale contracts in combat. Government can sometimes be a pretty lousy customer.
- can be improved—operations can be made more efficient and effective by creating military and other governmental institutions, doctrines, and practices that will better enable the public sector to tap the capabilities of the private sector in wartime.

If the United States does it right, the use of contractors in combat can become one of its greatest competitive advantages in the twenty-first century.

Many will find the answers that are provided wholly unexpected. This is a book guaranteed to please almost no one in Washington. Much of what people in Washington think they know about contractors in combat is simply wrong. Many don't care—but then Washington thrives on controversy. Washington prefers playing the blame game. Partisan bickering is the preferred method for resolving deeply divisive political issues cared about by many people in Washington and those who care about them. Such efforts are certainly understandable. War, after all, is a lot about politics, and contractors are a part of war. It is difficult to talk about contractors in combat without descending into partisan scorekeeping. *Private Sector—Public Wars*, however, is not about the politics of the long war. This story is about the business of fighting wars and what must be done to prevail in a manner that, as Eisenhower had wished for the republic he cherished, keeps America safe, free, and prosperous.

1
Chapter

How We Got Here

Blame Machiavelli.

The sixteenth-century Florentine writer, schemer, sycophant, patriot, politician, diplomat, civil servant, and scholar largely inspired the American prejudice against contractors in combat. It is not really his fault, but because he gets the blame, his writings remain the logical place to begin an explanation of the dramatic shifts in the roles of the public and private sectors in war and the West's enduring suspicion of both.

Understanding why Americans proved so quickly wary of the role played by contractors in combat in Iraq and Afghanistan begins on a sun-drenched Florentine palazzo centuries ago with a man whose name is both revered and reviled today.

Niccolló Machiavelli (1469–1527) had much in common with President Dwight Eisenhower's hero George Washington and, indeed, with many of the intellectuals in the Western world who thought about how to govern civil society during the years between the medieval period and the advent of the modern world. They were both ancients and moderns. On one hand, they drew heavily from the recovered writings of the classical Roman and Greek eras (whose texts offered idealized visions of republican virtue, rhetoric, and logic), adapting these classical ideas to modernity. On the other hand, they looked forward to a new shining city on the hill, adding their own contributions, anticipating the Age of Enlightenment, when scholars authored new frameworks for rational thought, advanced scientific methods, and placed ardent faith in human progress.

Of the many contributors to this era of Western political thought (running from the fall of Rome to the Industrial Revolution), Machiavelli often gets star billing. His fame and infamy persists to this day. In a magisterial work, *The Machiavellian Moment,* historian John Pocock argues that the Florentine is *the scholar,* the intellectual who links classical theories about government with the Atlantic republican tradition that inspired the British parliamentary system, the American experiment, and the French Revolution.[1] Machiavelli changed everything—particularly how Americans think about the role of the private sector in public wars.

THE ART OF WAR

Machiavelli's enduring reputation builds largely on two works. By far the most celebrated and condemned is *The Prince,* a guidebook for rulers that is credited with virtually inventing modern tough, realist politics that puts the quest of gaining and keeping power above everything else. The reputation of this book alone garnered Machiavelli a place as a world historical figure, earning him both credit for creating the modern state and vilification for fostering ideas that led to genocidal totalitarianism. *The Discourses on Livy,* by contrast, is a study of politics in the Roman Republic that exalts freedom, patriotism, and civic virtue, extolling the value of placing the welfare of the people above service for self.

Historians and philosophers have built careers trying to reconcile the apparently incompatible ruthless realpolitik of *The Prince* with the admirable, ardent republicanism of *The Discourses.* Today contemporary scholars agree that Machiavelli's seemingly disparate writings were parts of a whole. "Whatever the disparities," writes philosopher Isaiah Berlin,

> the central strain which runs through both is one and the same. The vision . . . of the strong, united, effective, morally regenerated, splendid and victorious *patria* [state], whether it is saved by the *virtù* of one man or many—remains central and constant.[2]

Machiavelli was most interested in how to make the state a success.

The author of *The Prince* also wrote *Arte della Guerra* (*The Art of War*), another canonical text that profoundly influenced political thought on both sides of the Atlantic. Today, the treatise is read by hardly anyone except academics. Yet, of all of Machiavelli's works, this book has had perhaps the most significant impact on shaping Western perceptions on how states should fight and how they should think about contractors.

Machiavelli authored *The Art of War* as a survival guide for his city. He worried about the fate of his beloved homeland in a dog-eat-dog world. The urban centers of early modern Italy, such as Florence, were wealthy mini-empires constantly at war with one another, scheming with Europe's great powers. The *cittadini,* Machiavelli's fellow men of substance and business in Florence, ruled over the *contado,* the territory surrounding the walls of the city. They employed *condottieri,* contractors who provided military forces for pay. Machiavelli proposed an alternative way to secure the city. As a government official, he implemented a plan to forgo dependence on the *condottieri* by harnessing the *contadini* (the farmers and townspeople of the *contado*) for military service. He formed them into legions and readied them for battle. Machiavelli failed spectacularly. The army he helped organize was driven from the field, precipitating the collapse of the city's republican rule and Machiavelli's exile from government. The Florentine penned *The Art of War* to defend and revive his vision for fighting and winning the city's battles.

Written as a dialogue between a noted *condottiero* (contractor) and a member of the *cittadini, The Art of War* is set in the garden of a well-known estate on the outskirts of Florence, a famed center for scholars of humanism (an important intellectual movement that fostered republican ideas). Everything about *The Art of War,* even the staging of its dialogue in a place near the city wall within sight of the disastrous battlefield that cost him his political career, was designed to speak directly to the *cittadini* of Florence.

Although he did not write *The Art of War* for the ages, Machiavelli did believe he was showing how to adapt timeless military principles to practical applications by authoring a guide for fighting and winning battles. That, however, is not his legacy in the Western world. Today, he is valued for political prescriptions about warfare—prescriptions he never provided—that nevertheless tell us what to think about contracting for combat.

MACHIAVELLI REMEMBERED

Not many scholars believe that *The Art of War* made much of a contribution to the way modern wars are fought, but in its time the book made quite an impression. Machiavelli was obsessed with classical Rome, as were many sixteenth-century humanist scholars. His prescriptions for battle called for modeling close-quarter combat on the organization and tactics of the Roman Army—reviving classical notions of disciplined, large-scale formations. These proposals must have had some utility for the military commanders of emerging nation-states, when armies still fought in massed ranks. By the end of the century, there were over twenty Italian editions of *The Art of War*, as well as numerous translations in four other languages—including English. Machiavelli was widely studied by leaders interested in military affairs for the next two hundred years. Thomas Jefferson owned a copy of *The Art of War*.[3] Despite being widely read, the Florentine's influence on purely military matters was not enduring, and for good reason.

Patterning all his recommendations for organizing military force on the lessons of antiquity, Machiavelli greatly undervalued the impact of technology. He dismissed the importance of gunpowder, though it eventually transformed the nature of warfare. In fact, he argued against using cannons. "Many very hardy armies have been beaten by their sight having been obstructed either by dust or the sun," he wrote, "and there's nothing that obstructs the view more than the smoke that artillery fire makes. . . . I would not fire it."[4] Such bad calls and persistence in mimicking classical warfare caused *The Art of War* to be largely ignored by modern military professionals. Today, a student of battle would be hard-pressed to find a copy of the book at any of the U.S. war college bookstores.

Although *The Art of War* had little long-term impact on making war, it had a remarkably profound, persistent influence on thinking about the politics of war, because Machiavelli described the essential nature of virtuous warfare for a republic. Above all, Pocock and other scholars credit him with extolling the value of citizen-soldiers over mercenaries, an early version of Eisenhower's dire warning against the military–industrial complex.

As modern interpreters of Machiavellian ideas argue, the Florentine's rationale went something like this: Militaries based on financial gain would eventually lead to corruption, because they would put their own interests above those of society, thus undermining the stability of the state, which would in turn cause the downfall of the state. The reliance of Italian city-states on the *condottieri*, bands of professional soldiers for hire, troubled Machiavelli. They could prove wildly undependable. He knew this first-hand. When Florence sent him to negotiate fees for invading Pisa, he observed one group of *condottieri* first refuse to advance and subsequently mutiny.[5] It is not hard to find reasons in plenty in *The Art of War*, *The Prince*, and *The Discourses* to condemn the *condottieri*.

Reading any English translation of Machiavelli's works, it is difficult to escape the conclusion that contracting military services was anything but an inevitable threat to the republic. Machiavelli, scholars contend, believed that only a militia— one comprised of citizens of the state who performed military service as part of their civic duty—could be depended on to protect the state without endangering it. This message has become virtually a maxim of Anglo-American political tradition.

It is a relatively easy matter to connect the dots and show how the Machiavellian mantra has become part of the American way of war. Peter Whitehorne, a soldier and contemporary of Shakespeare, completed the first English translation of *The Art of War* in 1560, arguably the first important military book translated from the Italian Renaissance writers. New editions followed in 1573 and 1588. Henry Neville, a notable republican polemicist, penned a new translation in 1680. Ellis Farneworth, a poverty-stricken rector, produced another new edition in 1763. To make ends meet, Farneworth hawked his book on street corners, one of the few works he produced that made any money—proof enough of enduring interest in the book over two hundred years after its first printing. All these editions repeat the lesson that military contractors and their primogenitors—soldiers who fight for pay rather than in service to their nation—are as great a danger as is any enemy.

The Machiavellian message became engrained in the Anglo-American ideology of civil-military relations, particularly after the experiences of the English Civil Wars (1642–1651) and the Interregnum (1653–1659). England's mid-century political upheavals became an object lesson for Americans. At the end of a bitter, violent civil war between crown and parliament, King Charles lost his head for, among other crimes, raising a standing army—including contracting with foreign mercenaries—and waging war on his own people. Dissatisfied with the government that replaced the king, Oliver Cromwell ruled as virtual dictator backed by an army of his own. The experiences of both the Civil War and military

dictatorship left the British deeply mistrustful of the toxic mix of politics and professional armies for hire.

By the time Parliament restored the crown in 1660, the anti–standing army
tradition had become firmly rooted in British political thought. After the king
took back the scepter of power, it was wholly natural that the firebrand Henry
Neville, who equated kingship with tyranny and published a number of antiauthoritarian tracts, chose to bring out a fresh translation of *The Art of War* as well
as other writings by Machiavelli that fed republican sympathies.

The anti–standing army idea crossed the Atlantic along with many British
political traditions. Washington invoked the principle in rebuking the alleged
Newburgh Conspiracy, an effort by a cabal of officers to forestall disbanding the
Continental Army after the American Revolution (1783).[6] Washington wrote that
any honest republican would express the "utmost horror & detestation of the man
who wishes, under any specious pretences, to overturn the liberties of our country, & who wickedly attempts to open the flood gates of civil discord, & deluge our
rising empire in blood."[7] The suggestion that the army would put its interest above
the directions of the Continental Congress infuriated the future commander-in-
chief. Putting hard cash before hard-won freedoms was the beginning of the end
of a free society. Such sentiments became an entrenched element of American
civil-military lore.

Little wonder that Machiavelli continues to be read and admired in the English-
speaking world. Allen Gilbert published a modern translation in 1965. Little wonder
also that Eisenhower's farewell address and warning against the military–industrial
complex mimicked Washington's words and the logic of *The Art of War*.

LOST IN TRANSLATION

There was only one problem with *The Art of War*'s damnation of military
contractors and pay-as-you-go armies: The book never argued against any use of
military contractors. Machiavelli didn't actually have a problem with the idea of
contractors on the battlefield.

As historian Paul Rahe explains, all English translations of *The Art of War* are
"misleading in the extreme" by

> persistently referring to mercenaries as "professional soldiers" and per-
> sistently rendering as "citizen army" Machiavelli's term *ordinanza*—a
> word that means "ordinance" or "that which has been ordained" and
> came to be used in Florence for shorthand both for the decree establish-
> ing Machiavelli's militia and for the infantry of the *contadini* that for a
> brief span of time he conjured into existence.[8]

In short, it was the English translators who made the pejorative term "mercenary"
synonymous with any soldiers who fought for pay and elevated the laudable term
"militia" as the only legitimate form of a citizen military.

The translation choices were understandable: English writers were predisposed to be skeptical of armies-for-pay. Still, all those word choices were wrong, as the most recent English version by Christopher Lynch makes clear. And worse, they completely confused scholars' interpretations of Machiavelli's prescriptions for military service. Earlier translations associate *any* soldiers that worked for pay as "mercenaries," or undesirable, and *only* militias as suitable military forces. In short, the wording suggests that forces that fought for pay could never be counted on. That, however, was not exactly what Machiavelli intended to say. As Rahe concludes, his "sole concern was the establishment of an infantry that would be both loyal and resolute."[9] In other words, Machiavelli's highest priority was to ensure that *whatever* forces employed on the battlefield remained resolved to serve the state.

In addition, the armies-for-hire were far less a danger than the translations, or the book itself, imply. The dominant role of the *condottieri* in Italian warfare was already in decline when Machiavelli penned *The Art of War*.[10] They were not the most serious obstacle to the stability of the Italian territories. The real problem was foreign powers fighting for influence and suzerainty over the small but wealthy kingdoms of Italy. The "mercenary" issue was more Machiavelli's scapegoat than a serious threat to the state.

The translators got it wrong. They mangled the Machiavellian message. Machiavelli never intended to advocate a permanent prejudice against professional militaries (though that is exactly what happened). He did, however, consistently insist in *The Art of War* and his other works that disciplined, dependable military service was the key to preserving the republic.

THREE AGES OF WAR

The actual changes in the nature of war across Western Europe over the course of millennia did not coincide at all with the mistaken Machiavellian legacy. In fact, they turn interpretations of Machiavelli on their head. The practice of armed conflict witnessed three world-historical shifts in the relationship between the private and public sectors of war. The first is the medieval age of contract combat. The second is the era of state-dominated warfare. The third is the age of private sector/public wars. Contractors played a prominent role in these transformations—and their impact has been largely positive.

AN ERA OF CONTRACT COMBAT

In Machiavelli's age, promoting an outright ban on paid contractors would have been nonsensical. War could not be waged without the private sector. States were still in an embryonic stage and rulers had limited capacity to harness the power of people for battle. In the Middle Ages, warfare was primarily a private-sector activity. The public role in mounting military operations was actually quite modest. This was an age of private wars.

It is wrong to think of medieval kings, queens, emperors, and empresses as the equivalents of the heads of a modern state. Some commanded little beyond the parapets of their castle or the walls of the capital. The reign of England's famed Henry VIII (1491–1547), a near contemporary of Machiavelli, offers a case in point. The rolls of Henry's parliaments are replete with bills assented to by the king, creating the impression that the rule of law controlled the countryside. In practice, however, the parliament would often pass similar laws over and over again—because the measures were often ignored, sometimes even by the king. Henry changed parliament, government, and church as often as his wife (he had six), all in an effort to rule an unruly kingdom.

Henry was not unique. In fact, he was better off than most. None had an easy time of it. Crowns never sat easy on royal heads, and in some cases (for example, that of England's ill-fated Charles II), heads became separated from shoulders. Sovereigns did not, by and large, control the instruments of government—including taxation, local administration and courts, and, most notably, large national armies and armories. They had to make deals, compromise, threaten, bribe, and plead to get things done. The public sector reigned, but it rarely ruled.

The private sector was nowhere more ascendant than in the practice of war. When rulers wanted to take up arms, the first task was to rent, borrow, buy, cajole, or connive for the troops, supplies, and administrative and logistical support to mount a campaign. Everything from cannonballs to horses and fodder had to be rounded up before kings could march off to battle. Most frequently the crown would turn to the local nobility, who controlled the land, wealth, and tenants of the land. In exchange for more land, honor, power, and a share of the booty, noblemen would help raise and lead forces in the field. They provided the crown with, among other things, the men-at-arms (well-equipped, heavily armored, trained combatants with a stable of their own support personnel) who formed the centerpiece of medieval armies. This was primarily a contractual relationship, negotiated beforehand. Feudal ties may have been bounded by tradition, obligation, and parchment, but in the end kings and lords cut deals to go to war.

European crowns might turn to other sources of support as well. They could float a loan from the great merchant banking houses, the most notable of which were the Bardi and the Peruzzi, the largest business concerns in the fourteenth-century Western world—"[a]n ancestral form of the modern multinational corporation," as historian Edwin Hunt writes.[11] In turn, crowns could use these funds to hire contract armies such as those provided by the *condottieri* or the German *Landsknechte*. Henry VIII (for example) was as anxious to contract combatants as anyone.[12] He and his fellow monarchs had plenty of choices. Switzerland, Scotland, and the German states, in particular, were well known for exporting private armies.

Despite Machiavelli's reservations, armies-for-hire often proved quite popular, offering the market a competitive alternative to reliance on feudal lords or, often as not, a supplement for filling out the ranks. John Hawkwood, a legendary *condottiero,* gave such worthy service to the city of Florence that he was not only given a magnificent public funeral, but plans were made for a monument in his honor next to the cathedral, and his portrait was hung on the cathedral wall.[13] For the right price, men like Bardi, Peruzzi, and Hawkwood would support any military venture a ruler might have in mind. By the late Middle Ages, the business of war was becoming largely just that.

The English word "mercenary" (denoting "soldiers who fought for profit and not in the cause of their native land or lord"[14]) appears to have come into common usage in the fourteenth century, almost two hundred years after armies-for-hire widely emerged as a practical alternative to feudal levies.[15] The original, pejorative use of the term did not come from contemporaries of Machiavelli, but from the nobility of an earlier age who saw armies-for-hire as a growing threat to their privileged status quo.

As the feudal system unraveled, the slur "mercenary" remained. Mercenary was a common insult used for disparaging troops in the enemy's service. Then, for Machiavelli's translators and those of their ilk, the term became a republican synonym of threats to liberty. Sir Walter Raleigh, for example, wrote in his *History of the World* (1614), "The extreme danger of such soldiers is well observed by Machiavel who sheweth that they are more terrible to those whom they serve, than to those against whom they serve. They are seditious, unfaithful, disobedient, devourers, and destroyers of all places and countries whereinto they are drawn."[16] That was a particularly damning indictment, especially for someone who had both hired military contractors and served as one. Raleigh, however, in a long and tumultuous career, felt ill-used by the crown. His *History of the World* was payback. The work became, according to historian Robert Lacey, "the backbone of antiauthoritarian thought through the years leading up to and following the [English] Civil War."[17] In the end, contractors put real private-sector power in the hands of kings who could afford it, provoking jealousy in those who could not.

In fact, monarchs across Europe were inclined to employ "mercenaries." They recognized, of course, that armies-for-hire could be as much a threat to their sovereignty as the feudal nobility. Thus, they developed an expanding system of administrative checks—including musters, laws, inspections, and accounts—all to make sure paid armies did not get out of hand.[18]

As the scope of private-sector activities expanded, successful sovereigns had to be more inventive in how they harnessed the dogs of war. Regimes required an administrative staff and system as complex as the task of mounting major military campaigns had formerly been. In addition to fighting soldiers, the men needed to support the field army—such as artillerists, wagon-drivers, carpenters, wheelwrights, fletchers, coopers, and victuallers—had to be contracted as well. By the thirteenth century, for example, English kings had rigorous measures in place, concludes historian Dave Bachrach:

> Royal officers routinely produced, transferred, and stored huge quantities of documents necessary to assure the continued allocation of men, money, and resources that made it possible to purchase nails, iron fittings, lead, and hides; to cut down and dress trees; to transport tools and workers; to pay carpenters, bargemen, carters, wagoneers, sailors, and guards, and to build storage sheds.[19]

Outsourcing was a fact of life for medieval sovereigns. The hallmark of a successful medieval ruler proved to be the capacity to effectively tap into Europe's nascent private sector.

The one "public" force that rulers could count on—a levy of farmers and townspeople for militia service—usually proved the least dependable. Often ill-armed, ill-trained, ill-supplied, and ill-disciplined, they looked less like the courageous citizen-soldiers described in *The Art of War* and more like the sad sacks portrayed in Shakespeare's historical plays. Historian Brian Downing labeled Henry VIII's army "little more than a rapidly put together collection of freebooters and dregs."[20] Discipline was a constant challenge, as evidenced by the expansive code of Tudor martial law. Men caught trying to establish their own brothels, for example, were imprisoned, and their "common women" branded on the cheek.[21] Mutiny, desertion, stealing, insubordination, and fighting were also common problems.

It would be inaccurate to dismiss the militias as wholly worthless, for they did not always fail. English levies helped turn back the Scots at the decisive battle of Flodden Field in 1513. When Henry VIII's daughter Elizabeth the Great ordered a national muster in 1587 to prepare for repelling the invasion of the Spanish Armada, the lord lieutenant reported that the kingdom could field an impressive force of 130,000 men.

Still, few sovereigns would have done as the interpreters of *The Art of* War suggested, putting their faith wholly in a militia, if they could help it. Elizabeth's citizen army, raised to repel the Spanish was an act of desperation, and it was never tested, because a storm wiped out the Spanish fleet. Elizabeth was lucky—only about a third of the militia was trained. There was such a shortage of arms that the cost of weapons skyrocketed.[22] Militias had their place, but they were not enough to secure a kingdom against a determined professional army or to take the fight into enemy territory.

THE AGE OF PUBLIC WARS

In the end, the expansion of the private sector helped states take over the business of violence, turning wars from a largely private enterprise into an essentially public activity. In this transformation, contractors, in fact, did far more than militias to help attain Machiavelli's goal of giving the state the monopoly over the art of war.

The expansion of the private sector and, in particular, the emergence of armies-for-hire allowed rulers to break their dependence on the feudal lords who had a vested interest in undermining the authority of a strong, centralized state. It should come as little surprise, then, that the English crown introduced new forms of taxation in the twelfth and thirteenth centuries even as it increased its use of contract armies. English kings looked to cut out the middleman, directly tapping into the wealth of the state and solidifying sovereignty's hold over the instruments of statecraft and soldiering. Historians still debate whether gaining control of armies allowed sovereigns to master the tools of statehood—such as taxation, public financing, and constitutional rule—or whether the opposite happened.[23] Either way, the upshot of this development was that the state increasingly gained the capacity to produce and maintain the instruments of war on its own.

But transformation took time. The famed British military historian Sir Charles Oman credits France's Charles VII (1403–1461) with establishing the first real standing army, the *Compagnies d'Ordonnance,* a professional force organized, managed, and paid by the king.[24] Still, it required over two centuries for the preponderance of European rulers to follow this example and break from their dependence on local elites, contract killers, and Italian bankers. Armies-for-hire played a significant role on the battlefield well into the sixteenth century.

The shift of military action from the private to the public sphere was most pronounced in maritime affairs. Commercial dockyards were not sufficient to build state-of-the-art warships. In practice, only construction or repair of the smallest combat craft could be contracted out to private yards.[25] Public financing, administration, and government shipyards came to dominate construction. Meanwhile, professional navies with staffs, officers, and government-employed seamen managed naval activities. In truth, the crown's monopoly on naval operations served to spur the development of commercial and industrial activities related to shipbuilding, a reflection of the growing prowess of the public sector in a world long dominated by private interests.

Although the public role in war-making eventually became dominant, it never became an exclusive monopoly. After kingdoms harnessed the power of the private sector to build public war-making institutions, contract armies still had their place. In addition, some jobs—such as teamsters to drive wagons and deliver supplies—remained contracted activities for a long time.

However, even with the lingering presence of contractors in combat, the public sector increasingly came to manage, oversee, and prescribe private contributions to war. Americans, for example, are generally familiar with the British practice of hiring Hessian troops to combat the colonial rebellion that broke out in 1776. These troops were not wholly private commercial enterprises. They were raised and commanded by a state sovereign—Frederick II, the Landgrave of Hesse–Cassel. He wasn't the only one. Five other German princes contracted their armies out for British service in the Americas and elsewhere; and although London proved Germany's best customer, German troops were rented out to other nations as well. It was the perfect feedback cycle: money translated into military power. Military power allowed the state to raise more money, which translated right back into political power. Thus, public and private pursuits became almost indistinguishable.

Likewise, at sea, conventional naval forces were still supplemented with private raiders, commissioned to attack enemy commerce (a practice that dated back centuries). Among the most famous were the "Sea Dogs," Sir Walter Raleigh and Francis Drake, who gained fame and fortune plundering Spanish ships and settlements for Elizabeth. Yet, even here, governments increasingly set the rules by which these raiders could operate, overseeing their activities. Privateers required a letter of marque issued by a legitimate government or else were considered little more than pirates.[26] In the end, privateers wound up strengthening, rather than undermining, sovereignty at sea.

On land and at sea, states in the Western world increasingly set the rules of war and conducted the preponderance of wartime activities themselves. Contractors remained on the battlefield, but they were largely subordinated to the state. This change not only marked the second great age of the Western way of war but also presaged the rise of the modern nation-state. In many ways this transformation also marked the dividing line between the medieval and the modern world.

ALBION'S SEED

If much of the story so far has focused on British examples to show the transformation from wars dominated by the private sector to warfare managed by public institutions, that has been with good reason. Britain was the archetypal example of a nation who came to power by harnessing the second age of war better than most. Britain was also the font for much of America's political ideology, particularly concerning armies and commerce. Even the American interpretation of Machiavelli came largely through a British filter. In many ways America grew from Albion's seed.

Chief among the components of American ideology was not only an inherited deep skepticism of standing armies but also misgivings of big business—a double distrust that made the colonials particularly wary of contractors in combat. American attitudes toward corporations drew, in part, from negative comments made by Adam Smith. This is truly ironic, for the eighteenth-century British scholar—one of the guiding lights of the Enlightenment (the European intellectual movement that gave birth to the liberal, secular ideas of the modern West)—is considered the father of free-market thinking, which fostered the growth of big business.

The author of *An Inquiry into the Nature and Causes of the Wealth of Nations* (1776), however, displayed a deep hostility not only to authoritarian rule, but to traditional businessmen as well. "The capricious ambition of kings and ministers," Smith wrote,

> has not, during the present and the preceding century, been more fatal to the repose of Europe, than the impertinent jealousy of merchants and manufacturers. The violence and injustice of the rulers of mankind is an ancient evil, for which, I am afraid, the nature of human affairs can scarce admit of a remedy: but the mean rapacity, the monopolizing spirit, of merchants and manufacturers, who neither are, nor ought to be, the rulers of mankind, though it cannot, perhaps, be corrected, may very easily be prevented from disturbing the tranquillity of anybody but themselves.[27]

According to *Wealth of Nations,* corporations could be as big a threat to freedom as could corporate warriors.

To be fair, Adam Smith had nothing against merchants and tradesmen as individuals operating in a free economy. When markets operated freely, they maximized the public good. Smith's vindictive was aimed at the seventeenth-century practice of "mercantilism," a collusion of government and corporate interests that distorted markets by creating monopolies. "In no way did he envisage," writes historian D.C. Coleman, "least of all approve of, a community in which the ownership of fixed industrial capital and the exercise of political power might be coterminous."[28] The merger of political and commercial interests could be calamitous for a free society.

Wealth of Nations is widely associated with the principle of laissez-faire. Smith was, however, not advocating "lazy-fare," where no one had to be concerned about governments and big business running amok, crushing the transparency, choice, and freedoms of a free market.

Adam Smith's ideas were of great effect. In the twenty-five years following the outbreak of the American Revolution, fourteen English editions of *The Wealth of Nations* were published. Thanks to Smith, Americans have always been cautious of the power of corporations. Eisenhower's fear of the military–industrial complex traces its lineage as much to *The Wealth of Nations* as to *The Art of War.*

THROUGH THE PUBLIC AGE

The ghost of Machiavelli and the invisible hand of Adam Smith overshadowed Americans' ways of thinking and acting about contractors in combat through the centuries that followed. But although Americans always had lingering doubts about contract warriors, they never stopped employing them or relying on the private sector to do what Adam Smith argued the private sector did best: unleash the creativity and productivity of individuals to generate the best goods and services that were most needed and wanted.

Even as the public sphere came to fully dominate public wars, military contractors continued to be a tool of the state. Despite their hatred of Hessians, the colonists had no problems employing contractors in combat. Notable "American" heroes—Friedrich Wilhelm Augustus von Steuben, the Marquis de Lafayette, and Tadeusz Kościuszko, who helped organize, train, and lead the Continental Army—were foreign officers in paid service: that is, mercenaries.

Contractors continued to play a role in American life from the earliest days of the Republic. When Meriwether Lewis—of Lewis and Clark Expedition fame (the great 1804–1806 exploration across the Great Plains to the Pacific Ocean)—as the first governor of the Louisiana Territory, asked for money, weapons, and supplies to raise a militia on the frontier, he got the cold shoulder from Washington. When he wanted to get anything done, he wound up contracting with a private company for military services.[29] It was the beginning of a long tradition.

Military contracting was an enduring feature of military operations. In some cases, success would have not been possible without their support. During the

Spanish–American War (1898), for example, the American army would never have reached Cuba without chartering vessels of every size and description to supplement the meager Navy fleet available to transport the invading force. The United States would never have succeeded in its campaign to drive Spanish colonial influence out of the Caribbean and the Philippines without support from the private sector.

Controversy was also a pervasive part of contracting in combat. During the American Civil War (1861–1865), Washington outsourced strategic intelligence. In 1861, General George B. McClellan, commander of all the Northern armies hired a private detective company run by Allan Pinkerton to gather information about Southern forces. The two had met before the war, when McClellan was an executive with Illinois Central Railroad for whom Pinkerton's company provided security guards. McClellan paid Pinkerton to spy on the South and got poor returns for his money (not much better than what the Bush administration received in intelligence assessments on weapons of mass destruction during the lead-up to the Iraq War). Pinkerton's agents offered wildly inflated estimates of Confederate forces, contributing to McClellan's overly cautious approach to the war, which eventually cost him his command.

McClellan's use of contractors was hardly the only controversy of the war. In the North, Congress was so enraged over reports of fraud by companies supplying the military that it established a special committee to investigate corruption.

The North's misfortunes did not hurt Pinkerton's business or that of his competitors. Pinkerton used his war profits to build a national agency. He had lots of company: seventy-four competitors in New York City and twenty-nine in Chicago and Philadelphia. These agencies exploded over the course of the nineteenth century, serving as virtual private armies for big business, investigating, surveilling, intimidating, and arresting criminals, labor organizers, provocateurs, anarchists, and innocents.[30]

Concern over intelligence companies and the "proto–military–industrial complex" culminated in the Anti-Pinkerton Act. Passed in the wake of the bloody suppression of a strike at a steel mill in Homestead, Pennsylvania (1892), Congress prohibited the government from hiring Pinkerton or other private police companies to break strikes.[31]

American ideology expected Congress and the American polity in general to be habitually skeptical of any mingling of politics, profits, and public interest; and the more money at stake, the more likely the suspicion. Complaints about contractors, particularly in wartime, also proved a common feature of American politics, and with good reason: wars had a tendency to make people in the private sector rich. Civil War profits helped fuel the rise of some of the giants of the American industrial age, including Carnegie, McCormick, Morgan, and Schwab. World War I turned DuPont from a modest chemical company into a global concern, with profits increasing thirteenfold in two years. In the first six months of World War II alone, Washington ordered $100 billion worth of goods and services. This spending filled the coffers of companies large and small. Every war helped make the rich richer and created a new rash of rich.

Throughout the age of public war, political factions habitually reacted to complaints about collusion between government's national security–related activities and the private sector. Eisenhower's concern about the military–industrial complex was neither the first nor the last expression of distrust by a politician. During World War I, the Senate launched a number of investigations into a $640 million aviation appropriation that promised to fill the skies over Europe's trenches with American planes, but which produced almost none. In the years between the World Wars, the House Military Affairs Committee believed the Army to be ripe with corruption. One complaint resulted in the investigation of an officer in charge of parachute development who tried to steer business to a firm in which he had a financial stake.[32] In 1933, the House McCormack–Dickstein Committee investigated the so-called "Business Plot," an alleged conspiracy of several wealthy businessmen who planned to overthrow President Franklin Roosevelt. Senator Nye's "merchant of death" hearings added more fuel to the fire, as did the Special Committee of the Senate to Investigate the National Defense Program (the Truman Committee) during World War II.

Thus, concerns about Kellogg, Brown, and Root (KBR), the largest government contractor during the U.S. occupation of Iraq, are nothing new. The Kellogg Company—one of the forerunners of the current engineering, construction, and services firm—has been one of the Pentagon's biggest services contractors since World War II. Among its wartime activities, Kellogg worked on the Manhattan Project, which produced the first atomic bombs. Brown & Root built naval stations and ships. During the Vietnam War, the company had the preponderance of construction projects in the country—and a public relations problem as well. Antiwar demonstrators called the company "burn and loot." A report by the Congressional General Accounting Office charged Brown & Root with unaccountability of funds. Congressional critics cited the company for fraud and corruption.

In the lead-up to the Vietnam War, Brown & Root's chief proponent in Washington was a Democratic senator, the vice president, and finally the President: Lyndon B. Johnson. A young Republican congressman from Illinois, Donald Rumsfeld (who later served as Secretary of Defense during the Iraqi and Afghan Wars), accused the administration of cronyism. In the years that followed Vietnam, the company's relationship with the Pentagon remained the same—only the politics changed sides. The Army's chief logistical support during the Bosnian War (1995) and the occupation that followed came from a "sole-source" contract with KBR. This was under the administration of a Democratic president, William J. Clinton, though KBR's parent company was chaired by a political ally of Rumsfeld's, a former Republican congressman and secretary of defense: Dick Cheney. Interestingly, during operations in Bosnia and Kosovo (1999), there were remarkably few complaints about KBR's operations. Cheney left Halliburton in 2000.

The history of complaints about contractors and government oversight of suspect practices have waxed and waned. They have included rooting out legitimate instances of fraud, waste, corruption, and abuse. These efforts also contained their share of political opportunism. The Nye "merchant of death" hearings, for example, were little more than blatant propaganda: an attempt by isolationist factions in the Senate to keep the United States out of the impending war in Europe. Nye, in fact, tried every charge of corporate collusion he could think of to keep the United States out of the war. He even promoted hearings lambasting Hollywood for making pro-war movies such as *Sergeant York*.

The history of contractors in combat has certainly been a mixed bag. Responsible governance and irresponsible fear-mongering both found their place in the debate. As a result, at the apex of the second great age of war, the American perception of the private sector's place in public warfare evolved in a schizophrenic manner. Many misperceive how the public's interests in combat are really secured; in turn, they have carried that baggage into the twenty-first century and are ill-prepared to think about war in the postmodern world as well. Thus, before looking at the third age of war, it is worth unpacking some of the intellectual baggage Americans carried through the twentieth century.

THE PUBLIC IN PUBLIC WARS

Political posturing or real oversight aside, in the end contractors in combat never rose to become a serious threat to the Republic. Throughout American history the practices of democratic governance and enduring commitments to transparency and free markets did much to keep contractors in combat from usurping the public monopoly on warfare. At the same time, however, the traditions of civic responsibility in military service have flourished to the point that they have overshadowed in the public's eye the importance of other checks and balances of good governance in keeping the private sector in its place.

From the beginning, writes historian Ricardo Herrara, in a survey of soldier attitudes from the founding of the Republic to the American Civil War, soldiers and civilians, thought they understood the problem—and the solution:

> A standing army was needed to defend the nation in a world full of potential threats. But an ideologically unsound army could just as surely become the instrument of internal oppression. . . . Political indoctrination would give some form of assurance that the regulars [i.e., the standing army] would remain loyal to the nation, and therefore would not attempt to subvert the people's rights. These concerns were not manifestly present in the ranks of the militia and volunteers who conceived themselves to be true guarantors of the republic's liberty.[33]

Perhaps the best example of this thinking was President Thomas Jefferson's decision to establish a military academy at West Point to ensure an Army officer corps committed to republican virtues.[34] In short, the Founding Fathers' answer was to ensure that warfare remained a public activity and that the activities of war remained governed by the precepts epitomized by the legacy of *The Art of War* and *The Wealth of Nations*.

In crafting rules to keep the public's military in check, the Machiavellian spirit appeared nowhere more enduring than in America's commitment to maintaining militias. When the representatives at the Constitutional Convention authored the documents that gave birth to the Republic, they believed (having read their Machiavelli and a plethora of English and American political tracts, pamphlets, books, and broadsides) that few institutions were more important to liberty than a well-regulated militia. Democratic traditions held that large standing armies could easily become instruments of tyranny. Better to rely, the consensus held, on citizen-soldiers: militia volunteers who would take up arms in time of crisis. The signers of the Constitution were so committed to the idea that they reaffirmed the right of individual states to raise and maintain their own home guards. Enshrined in the Constitution, the citizen militia became part of the bedrock of American governance.

Like other constitutional principles, America's citizen militia remains a living institution that has grown and adapted to suit the needs of the nation. One of the nation's first laws, the Militia Act of 1792, required all free white males between the ages of 18 and 45 to arm themselves and attend local musters. This law was never seriously enforced, and over the course of the century, militias were mostly local, volunteer, military organizations that varied widely in scope and character.

While the militia never evolved as Congress intended, citizen service nevertheless emerged as an ingrained element of American culture. During the Civil War, volunteer units (within the Union forces) dwarfed the numbers of the regular Army. The concept of the citizen-soldier, however, only became formalized in the wake of the Spanish–American War. By the outbreak of World War I, the American militia system was much more regularized, evolving into today's National Guard. The Guard not only performs state support but can be activated for federal service as well. Today, tens of thousands of men and women in the Army and Air National Guard are serving in Iraq, Afghanistan, and elsewhere around the world. In addition, the military has Reserves, the distinction being that, when called to active duty, these forces serve only in a federal role, unlike the National Guard. Reserve forces have no relationships with the states in which they reside. Altogether, the Reserve components represent today about 47 percent of the nation's available military. They include the Army, Navy, Marine Corps, Air Force Reserves, and the Army and Air National Guards, totaling over 1,200,000 men and women.

THE HOME GUARD

Many Americans, particularly because of the many deployments to Iraq and Afghanistan, know a good deal about the National Guard. The Guard, however, is not the only "authorized" militia in the United States. Less well known is the other guard: militias organized and governed independently by individual states.[35] These are also allowed under the militia clause of the Constitution. These state defense forces are guided by state laws and constitutions.

State defense forces (also called militias and home guards) first came to prominence during World War I, when the vast majority of National Guard troops were federalized and shipped overseas. States found that they needed a well-regulated militia to perform many of the tasks left undone when their Guard units departed for federal service. A few states—mostly in the north, such as Massachusetts and Connecticut—organized formal "home guards" made up of local volunteers. About 100,000 armed state militia personnel guarded ports, bridges, and railroads and secured the coastlines and land frontiers.

Likewise, many states turned to their home guards during World War II. About 200,000 state guardsmen replaced the mobilized National Guard. California, for example, was so concerned with the threat of a Japanese sneak attack that it spent $40 million on its guard during the course of the war. After Pearl Harbor, the California State Guard expanded to 20,000 volunteers. During the Cold War, many states relied on their home guards to support civil defense missions.

State defense force programs were revived in 1980 during the Cold War under the premise that personnel would have to replace the National Guard on the home front if troops were mobilized to fight in Europe. The total number of volunteers across the nation peaked at about 20,000. As the Cold War wound down, however, interest in the state forces lapsed. As a result, home guards throughout the United States represented an admixture of loosely organized and poorly run volunteer organizations, social clubs, and units that served mostly ceremonial functions. Some faculty of state military colleges—such as Norwich, the Virginia Military Institute, and Texas A&M—wear the uniform of their state defense force. A few states have truly effective volunteer organizations. Maryland and Texas defense forces, for example, assisted in the response to Hurricanes Katrina and Rita. Currently, twenty-three states maintain state defense forces of some kind, for a nationwide total of about 14,000 personnel.

Taken altogether, the National Guard, Reserves, and state defense forces have kept the tradition of citizen-solders firmly rooted in the American polity. Machiavelli would be proud.

THE REGULARS

Americans never thought, however, that militias alone would be enough. From the outset, the founding fathers understood that the Republic would need a standing army. In turn, they added checks and balances in the Constitution to keep the regulars under control. The president serves as the commander-in-chief of all military forces. Congress promotes officers, allocates budgets, and drafts laws overseeing the military roles and missions, organization, and procedures. These constitutional dictates demonstrated that public leaders intended to maintain overall management of the public's instruments of war.

The public sphere of the armed forces grew commensurate with the expansion of the United States from a backwater colony to a global power. From the beginning, the Republic maintained a standing military: the regulars. The United States started with a small Army, Navy, and Marine Corps. The Marine Corps was disestablished and then reauthorized. Over the course of the century, the Coast Guard was added, and after World War II, an independent Air Force. Today, there are about 1.5 million regulars in uniform.

SEVEN DAYS IN MAY

Despite the heated rhetoric surrounding the threat of standing armies to democracy, throughout history Americans have been remarkably sanguine about maintaining permanent military forces. Even American popular culture is largely devoid of cautionary tales in which the military threatens the sanctity of the Republic. One rare exception was *Seven Days in May*, a political potboiler penned in 1962 by Fletcher Knebel and Charles W. Bailey. Hollywood knew it had a hot prospect on its hands. The book ran forty-nine weeks on *The New York Times* best-seller list. The highly respected director John Frankenheimer turned the novel into a film two years later (in the same year that Kubrick released *Dr. Strangelove*).

The plot details how the chairman of the Joint Chiefs of Staff (a dashing Burt Lancaster) and a cabal of senior officers and politicians plan a coup d'état against the president (an idealistic but slightly befuddled Frederic March) for caving in and negotiating nuclear arms reduction with the Soviet Union. The conspiracy is foiled by a colonel on the Pentagon staff (an equally dashing Kirk Douglas playing Marine Corps Colonel Martin "Jiggs" Casey). Burt Lancaster's character quietly resigns, and Americans never learn how close they came to coming under a "Cold War Cromwell."

Even *Seven Days in May*, however, is not so much an indictment of the standing military. After all, it was a virtuous military officer who understood the obligation of soldiers to remain subservient to the state that saved the day. The anxiety expressed in the book and the film reflects more American uneasiness over the spiraling arms race and fear about nuclear war than it reflects concerns about military coups.

Frankenheimer's film received strong reviews and two Oscar nominations, and it also enjoyed considerable commercial success. It did not reflect a groundswell of concern over command of the military. Indeed, most of the top-grossing films of 1964 were comedies like *Tom Jones* and *It's a Mad, Mad, Mad, Mad World*, which raked in far more money than *Seven Days in May* or *Dr. Strangelove*. The truth is: standing armies have never been much of a serious concern either in Hollywood, Washington, or elsewhere in America.

THE ALL-VOLUNTEER FORCE

Although the Founding Fathers acknowledged the necessity of a regular army, they also followed the Machiavellian prescription against having a mercenary military. In the U.S. tradition, the standing military would constitute the

minimum needed to address security. These forces were to be supplemented by
the citizenry in times of national crisis. The government retained two options for
filling the ranks of its standing forces: volunteers and conscripts. In U.S. history,
conscription was never considered the preferred means to reinforce the professional army. In fact, in the eighteenth and nineteenth centuries, drafts were
thought appropriate only under the direst circumstances. Peacetime conscription
was considered an instrument of militarism and authoritarianism. Reliance on
the colonial, and later the state, militias (and their descendants, the Reserves and
National Guard) was the preferred method of supplementing manpower.[36]

Even at the outbreak of the Cold War, Congress rejected mandatory universal military training and service for all young American males in favor of what was
thought to be a temporary lesser evil: a mix of active (regulars) and reserve forces
supplemented by a two-year draft to fill out the ranks of the active forces. The
United States maintained its unprecedented "peacetime draft" until the Vietnam
War. In 1968, in the wake of the North Vietnamese Tet Offensive, President
Richard Nixon made an election-year promise to end the draft. Because popular
support for the war was declining, Nixon reasoned that such a promise would
remove one target of antiwar protestors and congressional opposition.[37]

Shortly after taking office, Secretary Melvin Laird recommended that Nixon
appoint a commission to determine the most practical means for abolishing the
draft while ensuring that the United States could still meet its defense commitments. The commission—established by Nixon on March 27, 1969, and chaired
by Eisenhower's former Secretary of Defense, Thomas S. Gates, Jr.—concluded
that an "all-volunteer force" could serve as a practical alternative to conscription.
Delivered on February 6, 1970, the Gates report served as the basis for subsequent
reforms.[38] In 1973, Nixon ended the draft, and the military remains to this day
staffed by volunteers.

At the time of its creation, there were those who complained that ending the
draft amounted to ignoring the Machiavellian caution against professional
armies. Creating an all-volunteer force, some argued, would yield an essentially
mercenary military that could be employed without regard to public opinion.
(Ironically, the same argument is used now both to demand that Washington
employ only the professional military and to warn against hiring contractors for
combat.)

It was Milton Friedman, the Nobel laureate, free-market economist, who
made the compelling case for a volunteer military to the Gates Commission,
shilling ideas he first outlined in *Capitalism and Freedom,* a 1963 book arguing for
volunteerism over conscription. Parroting in some respects the rationale first
expounded in Smith's *Wealth of Nations* (in a section titled "on Defence"),
Friedman based his point on economic efficiency: paying soldiers a competitive
wage would result in being able to recruit and retain enough citizens to provide
public security for their fellow citizens.

Friedman was right. The all-volunteer forces continue to recruit and train
adequate numbers over twenty-five years after it was started, even during the

six years of constant conflict since the September 11, 2001, terrorist attacks on New York and Washington.[39]

SOLDIERS AND POLITICS

Because standing forces and militias were maintained throughout most of U.S. history, there is a presumption that these instruments of the public sphere have played a prominent role in fulfilling the Machiavellian mandate of either preventing the armed forces from being used as a political instrument to subvert the freedoms of the Republic, or keeping commercialism in the military from threatening the sanctity of the state. Nothing could be farther from the truth.

Throughout U.S. history the military has occasionally been used as a tool for political oppression. There was enormous controversy, for example, in the post–Civil War period as to the role the army played in the reconstruction of the South. That debate culminated in the deployment of troops to polling booths during the 1896 presidential election. Congress responded by pushing through the Posse Comitatus Act of 1878, which generally prohibits the armed services from engaging in law enforcement activities inside the United States—such as investigating, arresting, or incarcerating individuals—except as authorized by federal law. The intent of the law was not to prevent the military from engaging in politics but to stop political leaders from using the military for political purposes.

Controversy did not end with the passage of the Posse Comitatus Act, however. Over the next fifty years, the military was frequently called out to quell violence during the bitter labor disputes at the turn of the century. And, in a highly controversial action, army troops were used to clear out a shantytown of "bonus marchers"—World War I veterans who had gathered to protest in Washington during the summer of 1932.[40] Every generation of Americans has witnessed charges that the military was being ill used by its political masters.

Furthermore, the Posse Comitatus Act has never been a serious obstacle to using federal forces to support domestic operations. For example, federal forces helped to end miners' riots in Idaho in 1899; protected James Meredith, the University of Mississippi's first black student, in 1961; assisted in controlling the 1992 Los Angeles riots; and helped to reestablish order in the aftermath of Hurricane Katrina. In fact, federal forces have been used to enforce laws over 175 times in the past two hundred years under the authority of laws such as the Insurrection Act.

Furthermore, the Posse Comitatus Act does not apply to National Guard forces unless they are mobilized as federal troops. The National Guard enjoys a unique legal status: when not on active duty, National Guard units remain on call to support the governors of their respective states. In that status, the Guard plays the primary role in augmenting state and local law enforcement under state control. This created a topsy-turvy situation in 1963, when Governor George Wallace ordered the Alabama National Guard to block the desegregation of Tuskegee High School, upon which President John F. Kennedy federalized the Guard and ordered them to escort black children to the school. Posse Comitatus notwithstanding, both governor and president had no compunction about using the military to enforce their political will.

THE ABRAMS DOCTRINE

In the end, neither particular laws nor militias or small standing armies kept people from playing politics with the military. Yet, the myth that they do some-how persists, and the ghost of Machiavelli lives on. Perhaps the most pervasive modern form of the myth is the "Abrams Doctrine."

The Abrams Doctrine is widely interpreted as an expression of Army Chief of Staff General Creighton Abrams's (1972–1974) determination to maintain a clear linkage between the employment of the Army and the engagement of public sup-port for military operations. According to the doctrine, Abrams established this bond by creating a force structure that integrated the National Guard and the regu-lar Army so closely as to make them inextricable, ensuring that after Vietnam pres-idents would never again send the Army to war without the Reserves or without the commitment of the American polity. The Abrams Doctrine, in effect, considered that requiring mobilization of the National Guard before entering a major military conflict would serve as an extraconstitutional constraint on presidential power.

People in and out of the military talk about the doctrine as if its existence were a matter of fact. John Groves, an Army National Guard general, wrote, in a paper published by the Association of the United States Army just before 9/11, that "following Vietnam, the implementation of the Abrams Doctrine began."[41] That is an assertion lacking much evidence to back it up. There is virtually no evi-dence that Abrams intended to father a doctrine. Nor can a credible argument be made that the way the military was organized could actually serve as a check on the president's constitutional power as commander-in-chief. Finally, as the Iraq conflict demonstrates, a massive employment of National Guard forces cannot keep a president from fighting an unpopular war or make a war more popular.[42]

It should come as no surprise that the myth of the Abrams Doctrine became so widely accepted. It appealed to the traditional American ideology that a smaller standing army and larger militia were inherently more virtuous. In all likelihood, however, Abrams's attempt to reorganize the Army was less an effort to resurrect the spirit of Machiavelli than a practical solution to trying to hold on to enough force-structure in the post–Vietnam military draw-down so that the Pentagon had enough divisions to send to Europe in case of war with the Soviets. He was more concerned about protecting the Republic from the Russians than about tin-kering with constitutional principles.

THE SOLDIER AND THE STATE

Indeed, Abrams would never have proposed a military solution that dictated how presidents could act. To do so would have completely contradicted all American military officers' deep-seated belief in Machiavelli's dogma that the soldier should be the servant of the state. Abrams hailed from a generation of brother officers whose beliefs regarding civil–military relations were described by Samuel Huntington in his seminal work, *The Soldier and the State* (1957). Abrams's generation deeply believed that civil dominance over the military was maintained, as historian Eliot Cohen summarized, by "carving off for it a sphere of action independent of politics."[43] In many ways, Abrams, intellectually, was the real-life embodiment of Kirk Douglas's fictional Colonel Jiggs Casey in *Seven Days in May* (though Douglas was definitely a lot better-looking than the craggy, cigar-chomping Abrams).

For Abrams, and most military men, *The Soldier and the State* was a touchstone for their beliefs. Huntington's work drew heavily on the Machiavellian framework of civilian supremacy over the public sphere of war. In short, *The Soldier and the State* contended that soldiers were to stick firmly to military missions and to ignore the political implications of the general's decisions by not commenting, criticizing, or contributing to political choices.

Under the "normal" theory of civil control, described by Huntington, a sharp division is maintained between political decisions and military operations. The military sustained its belief in this paradigm after Vietnam. Officers saw Vietnam failures in classic "Huntingtonian" terms. "The nation went to war," wrote H. R. McMaster—a young Army officer who in 1997 penned a scathing critique of the Joint Chiefs of Staff—"without the benefit of effective military advice from . . . the nation's principal military advisors."[44] The prescription for addressing political intrusion into the military sphere also remained consistent. When political leaders transgressed into decisions that properly belonged to soldiers, the generals' options were to protest or resign, not to cross over into the realm of politics. Creating force structures intended to skew political decisions seems to be at odds with the military's traditional conception of professionalism. Abrams would never have done that.

Ironically, using Huntington to debunk the Abrams Doctrine only serves to reveal the presence of the ubiquitous Machiavellian spirit in another form. Huntington's notions of civil–military relations have largely proven, under decades of rigorous academic scrutiny, to be mostly myth as well (though Abrams and the officer corps accepted them as a matter of faith).[45] As historian Elliot Cohen demonstrates in *Supreme Command: Soldier, Statesman, and Leadership in Wartime* (2002), neatly cleaving the responsibilities for command in war between political tasks and military missions is impossible. Political leaders cannot divorce themselves from their responsibilities as commanders-in-chief; nor can senior military commanders ignore the fact that their decisions will impact on politics. In reality, they share the burden of leadership in wartime. Yet the Machiavellian mantra, the Huntingtonian framework persists. *The Soldier and the State* is still in print and is widely read in military schools from West Point to the senior war colleges.

The persistence of the Huntington myth has important implications for the debate over contractors in combat. Huntington wrote during the "professionalism" craze of the 1950s, when political scientists were trying to codify the unique attributes of individual institutions. *The Soldier and the State* characterizes the specialty of the military profession in terms of the armed forces' role as "managers of violence." This characterization reflects the nature of an age when the public sphere dominated warfare. But, in the end, Huntington's definition was proven terribly wrong. To argue that soldiers have a virtual monopoly on the conduct of war is more caricature than characterization. Not only the views of politicians but also the conduct of contractors legitimately have import on the battlefield. Ignoring their role in war-making creates a deeply flawed view of military professionalism.

Today, many of the objections against contractors in combat simply mimic the lessons of *Soldier and the State,* arguing that military activities can only be conducted by the military. Such a conception of the armed forces simply does not square with the reality of American military history. Indeed, the culmination of over two hundred years of wars and American politics reveals that although the public sector dominated the conduct of warfare, the private sector still had a place. And although the influence of myths, from Machiavelli to Huntington, still persists, they are not in the end the principal means by which the power of war-making remained under the power of the state. Rather, it was the nature of modern democratic governance in general that maintained the state's dominance over the dogs of war. That truism is more than likely to remain unchanged in the future.

THE THIRD AGE

It would be a mistake, however, to say that the current era is just more of the same. Indeed, the world is entering a new age in warfare and rebalancing the role of the public and private spheres. The private sector dominated the age of war from the fall of Rome to the early Modern Era (Age I), and the public sector rose to prominence from then on (Age II), today the private and public worlds are more than ever equal partners in what they bring to the face of war (Age III).

The evolving character of the private sector in the twenty-first century is dramatically affecting the nature of conflict. The private sector is running amok, creating a level of globalization not seen since the end of the nineteenth century. Free markets are enjoying an explosion of freedom perhaps unmatched in history. The speed of this growth is breathtaking. In 1983, the World Trade Organization estimated total global exports at about $1.8 trillion; in 2005, the number was $10.2 trillion. Increasingly, this wealth, power, and capacity is in private hands. Privatization of government-controlled assets, particularly in industries related to defense and security, is a well-established global trend, bucked by only a few notable exceptions such as China and Russia. A global marketplace has an unprecedented capacity to provide global military services.

The global free market has become a reality, and commensurate with this economic condition is the emergence of an unprecedented capacity for the private sector to expand, innovate, and adapt to market needs—including an ability to provide what once were considered military services offered solely by national powers. The trend for militaries to increasingly outsource logistical and support functions is well established. Added to that, however, is the emerging use of private sector companies to provide traditional combat services, ranging from training soldiers to patrolling streets.

It is difficult to argue that the rise of the private sector is a bad thing. Private sector military capabilities, in the aggregate, have not been detrimental to the cause of peace and prosperity. According to a comprehensive multiyear study by the Human Security Report Project (based at the University of British Columbia) in the last few decades, while globalization has run rampant, the world has become not only a more prosperous place, but a safer one as well. Their report shows evidence of a major global decline in armed conflicts, genocides, human rights abuse, and military coups. Armed conflicts alone have dropped by 40 percent since 1992.[46]

Reliance on private sector assets in war is also probably irreversible. Unlike the public sector, the private sector is bred for efficiency: Left to its own devices, it will always find the means to provide services faster, cheaper, and more effectively than will governments. In addition, as governments lose their monopolies over the technologies and means used to generate combat power, their capacity to retain military prowess as a public activity will also be lost.

As long as free markets proliferate, the reemergence of the private sphere of war is inevitable. Nations that seek to resist this trend and limit the participation of the private sector will be left behind because they will lack the capacity to keep up with states that can harness the power of the marketplace.

On the other hand, there is good reason for liberal, developed states not to fear the reemergence of a prominent role for the private sector in war. There is little likelihood that the private sector's place in war will foster the rise of a new "Middle Ages" as sovereigns lose their capacity to manage violence. "Capitalism," as political commentator and editor of *Newsweek International* Fareed Zakaria cogently argues, is not "something that exists in opposition to the state. . . . [A] legitimate, well-functioning state can create the rules and laws that make capitalism work."[47] Unlike medieval kings, modern nations can use the instruments of good governance to control the role of the private sector in military competition.

The United States is a good example of how modern, liberal states enable and harness the commercial capabilities of warfare that may remain partially, or even entirely, in the private sphere. The means available for moderating interaction between the public and the private sphere includes the following:

- A well-established judicial system
- An activist legislative branch with its own investigative instruments (such as the Government Accountability Office)
- The "60 Minutes" factor—an independent press
- Public interest group proliferation, which provides a wealth of independent oversight and analysis
- An enabled citizenry with ready access to a vast amount of public information[48]

These assets offer unprecedented means of balancing the public and private spheres—not just for constraining government conduct but also for limiting the excesses of the commercial sector. In fact, these capabilities might suggest that in the long term, liberal, free-market democracies will prove far more effective at mastering the capacity of the private sector in the twenty-first century than have authoritarian states with managed economies.

That said, however, the role of the private sector in war raises innumerable legal, ethical, and practical issues that must be dealt with. Marrying to the private sector's capacity for innovation and rapid response to changing demands the government's need to be responsible and accountable for the conduct of operations is not an easy task, and one that will require militaries to think differently about how best to integrate the private sector into public wars. Nor can generals do this thinking in isolation. Modern military operations involve several agencies and require the support of many elements of executive power. The judicial and legislative branches of government have important roles to play as well. Indeed, many of the most important instruments for constraining the role of the private sector in war lie in their hands.

THE PRIVATE SECTOR IN PUBLIC WARS

The world is in transition. Much of the current anxiety over contractors in combat comes from the fact that the future arrived so quickly and unexpectedly— almost in the blink of an eye. In Vietnam, for every one hundred soldiers one contractor was employed. During the Gulf War (1991), one contractor was on the battlefield for every fifty soldiers. During Operation Iraqi Freedom, contractors made up one out of every ten personnel. Only six years later, one contractor supported government operations in Iraq for about every 1.5 soldiers.

Anxiety is high also because many misunderstand both the role contractors have played in combat and the key mechanisms states have used to keep them under control. Contractors have been ubiquitous on the battlefield since the Middle Ages. States have always faced the challenge of ensuring that the pursuit for profit never overshadows the goals of statecraft. States usually achieve that end; this shows that sovereign states and free markets (as Adam Smith had predicted) can flourish well side by side. What has kept contractors in line in the past, and what will likely serve to safeguard sovereignty in the future, is the practice of good governance.

Finally, the most troubling concerns expressed—that contractors in combat threaten the military institutions and traditions that serve to keep warfare a public practice and prevent the undermining of republican principles—turn out, on a more accurate reading of the historical record, to be matters of no concern after all. The Machiavellian mantra about mercenaries and militias is more a myth than a model for determining how to balance the public and private sectors in modern war. The legacy of Machiavelli—which includes Eisenhower's military–industrial complex and Huntington's concept of military professionalism—has served more to obfuscate than to enrich our understanding of what needs to be done, feeding fears and acting as fodder for fostering political agendas. They have contributed little to keeping America safe and prosperous: this task has been carried out by public and private sectors committed to the value of freedom.

In the end, the debate over public and private roles in war is secondary. These change and will continue to do so. More critical is examining the legitimacy and capacity of institutions for overseeing combat. Government can outsource many things, but it cannot outsource responsibility. That is the real lesson of history.

PRESENT IMPERFECT

The past is prologue, but it cannot solve the problems of today or forestall the rise of new challenges in the future. Fixing problems is the task of sound public policy-making. The past only serves to inform the process of right decision today. Crafting sound public policy for contractors in combat takes more than a good history lesson. It also requires understanding of what is being done today, why the present is imperfect, and what can be done to make things better. That is the subject of the rest of *Private Sector, Public Wars*.

2
Chapter

Where We Are

The future is not what it used to be.

At the end of the Cold War, Francis Fukuyama penned a popular, but ultimately wrongheaded, book entitled *The End of History and the Last Man* (1992). His argument (a kinder, gentler version of the case made by the nineteenth-century German philosopher Friedrich Hegel, who wrote quixotically about the future of the modern state) was that with the end of the Cold War, the evolution of civil society had come to an end. The liberal nation-state had triumphed. Everything left was simply details. But Fukuyama was wrong; the future did not turn out not to be just more of the same.

Although the nation-state is certainly alive and well, the post-Cold War world has proved as unpredictable, uncertain, and ambiguous as the past. There also proved to be plenty of new nutty ideas trying knock sovereign states off the top of the pedestal. That is part of the reason why getting contractors in combat right is so important. The future can still be a very dangerous place. The state still needs all the help it can get.

There was a military parallel to *The End of History*. In *Certain Victory*, a team led by historian, combat veteran, and Army Brigadier General Robert H. Scales presented the Army's official history of America's first war with Saddam Hussein. Published in 1993, the book read like a "victory" lap, heralding the rebuilding of the Army after the Vietnam War. It described a crushing lightening campaign called Desert Storm that rolled up the entire Iraqi military, apparently effortlessly, in less than a week of ground combat. Military history had come to an end. All the Pentagon would need to do in the future was repeat this approach—better, faster, and more lethally. Everything else was simply details. As experiences in Iraq and Afghanistan subsequently demonstrated, this idea was wrongheaded as well—particularly in regard to the role of the private sector in public wars.

The private sector played a part in the Gulf War, though clearly a supporting role. Apparently, to many observers (the authors of *Certain Victory* included), that role was completely consistent with the apex of an age that was long from over, an age in which the public sector dominated public wars. In *Certain Victory*, the private sector rates only the briefest of mentions—and even that is little more than an occasion for patriotic flag-waving. The Army, according to the book, was critically short of tires for its heavy trucks, and the company that produced them only cranked out forty tires a month. The dealer sent out a nationwide call to its distributors, the Army needed as many tires as it could get as fast as it could get them. Ken Oliver, a tire-dealer in Waco, Texas had seventy-four tires on hand. When he received the alert, he rented a truck, loaded the tires, and drove all night to Tinker Air Force Base in Oklahoma, handing his payload over to the military. Then he drove back home and called the company, reporting that "he figured the troops needed those tires as quickly as possible and did not want to wait."[1] The only other reference to contractors in the book mentions a company that got a contract for 4,000 on-site latrines.

Among the many changes in warfare that *Certain Victory* did not anticipate was the resurgence of the private sector in war. That was unfortunate.

In fairness to Scales and his study team, they were certainly far from the only ones to miss the impending transformation of the public and private sectors in war. Anthony Cordesman, the venerable Washington-defense analyst at the Center for Strategic and International Studies, produced a volume on the lessons of the Gulf War that ran to over a thousand pages. None of the chapters focus on the private sector. The word "contractor" did not even rate a mention in the index.[2] Likewise, in proceedings of a major conference on the war featuring four prominent U.S. military commanders in the conflict, the word "contractor" was never mentioned.[3] Examples do not stop there. The list of scholarship that neglects contractors in combat during the Gulf War is pretty long.

The inattention paid by serious defense intellectuals to the place of the private sector reflects how poorly Americans understood contractors' purpose on the battlefield before the onset of combat in Iraq and Afghanistan. Ensuring that the contractors in combat remain a cutting-edge capability for public wars requires knowing how contractors are employed and the state of the institutions that oversee them. For knowing "where we are," Desert Storm is probably the logical place to start.

INTO THE STORM

Certain Victory certainly missed the signs of the rise of a new age when the public and private sectors would share more equitable places on the battlefield. The signs, however, were certainly present.

Saddam Hussein's decision to overrun the neighboring nation of Kuwait using a dispute about oil-drilling rights along the countries' joint border as pretext caught the United States flat-footed. On August 2, 1990, 120,000 Iraqi troops and 2,000 tanks poured into the small Gulf state. Washington decided it could not do nothing—and that presented a real challenge. In the midst of downsizing the military after the collapse of the Soviet empire, virtually the last thing the Pentagon expected was to engage in a major ground war in the Middle East.

War came nonetheless.

First, Washington put troops on the ground in Saudi Arabia—Operation Desert Shield. Then the Joint Chiefs advised that nothing less than a full scale invasion would do—and that would require sending a much bigger land, sea, and air armada.

Fortunately for the United States, the Army had barely begun to bring forces back from Western Europe after the fall of the Berlin Wall. In addition, the services had literally just completed a long-delayed post-Vietnam cycle of modernization that introduced a vast array of new military capabilities, including precision-guided bombs and missiles, stealth aircraft, new attack helicopters, modern tanks, and the global positioning system (GPS) devices that could guide bombs to their targets and lead troops across the trackless desert.

Not only were the armed forces well equipped, they were spectacularly well trained. Since Vietnam, the Army, Marines, and Air Force had developed realistic "force on force" training where combat units conducted simulated wars against well-trained surrogate enemies (called Opposing Forces or OPFOR). Video, laser, and computer tracking were used to provide realistic feedback on the outcome of the battles. In 1987, the Army started its Battle Command Training Program to test how higher-level staffs managed unit combat, using computer "wars" to force them to make realistic battle decisions. The result of this training revolution created a peacetime army with almost wartime experience, even though the ranks of the U.S. military contained few combat veterans and the military had not fought a large-scale ground war in almost twenty years. As a result of training and equipment innovations, at the start of Operation Desert Storm, America's public sector, backed by a coalition of allies, had one of the most imposing armies in history.[4]

Despite the virtues of the twentieth-century post–Cold War military, the Gulf War could not have been fought without contract support, although the short nature of the conflict and the abbreviated U.S. role in restoring Kuwait left much of what they accomplished unnoticed. It was reported that only ten U.S. contractors accompanied the military into Iraq or Kuwait during the war. Nevertheless, for the military, reliance on the private sector was virtually unprecedented in modern memory.

For starters, the military had to mobilize the largest contractor support force it had seen since the end of the Vietnam War. In-theater, the Americans had almost 4,000 contractor personnel from ninety-eight companies, supporting mainly maintenance, supply, and transportation operations.[5] Outside the theater, the military was virtually dependent on private companies to feed the dogs of war. The Defense Logistics Agency, which is responsible for buying most of the military's goods and services, let over 550,000 contracts worth about $760 billion. Twenty-two thousand rail cars moved the goods to hundreds of privately owned ships, and more than half of the troops flew into theater on commercial airlines. All this effort went into what proved to be a 100-hour war.

OUTSOURCING THE PENTAGON

The massive use of contract support in such a short campaign should have served as a wake-up call about the changing nature of war. It did not. In fact, the shifting nature of public and private warfare went largely—albeit not completely—unnoticed. This obliviousness contributed to another one of the many myths surrounding contractors in combat: the U.S. military in Iraq and Afghanistan is said to be so dependent on the private sector because of the significant downsizing of the military after the end of the Cold War.

Desert Storm gave plenty of evidence to suggest that the Pentagon would have been dependent on large-scale contractor support in any protracted conflict after the end of the Vietnam War. The Pentagon had actually considered contracting in combat during Vietnam a big success. The military employed over thirty-five private firms that shouldered the burden for most of the defense construction efforts in Vietnam. That allowed the Pentagon to maximize the number of combat troops deployed to the theater instead of sending over more engineers, support, and transportation. One lesson the military took from Vietnam was to outsource wherever possible, letting the private sector do what the private sector does best and saving military manpower for combat roles.

In the years following Vietnam, the military became "hollow," lacking sufficient funds to pay for current operations, to modernize, and maintain a trained and ready force. If the Cold War had gone hot, the military would have had no choice but to fill the gap in its capabilities large amounts of contractor support.[6]

After the armed services had substantially rebuilt much of their capability during the years of Ronald Reagan's presidency (1981–1989), the Defense Department continued to place more emphasis on contractors. Even after the Reagan-era renaissance in military readiness, numerically the Pentagon still had more missions than it had military.

The rationale for contracting for contingency operations (unanticipated missions like the Gulf War) was simple: it was cheaper. Every asset the military kept on hand required funds for upkeep (including maintenance), salaries, and benefits. Contracting, on the other hand, saved money. By some estimates it was about 20 percent cheaper to have contractors do things such as drive trucks, clean washrooms, escort convoys, or stand guard than to have soldiers do them. One government study concluded that the military could save up to $30 billion a year by contracting.[7]

In 1985, the Army established its first post–Cold War program for large-scale standing contracts to provide services in case of wartime. The initiative was called Logistics Civil Augmentation Program (LOGCAP). Such contracts could in the end be worth billions to the private sector.

The move toward contracting services was a national trend, unrelated to the initiative of either political party or singular individuals. It would, for example, be hard to argue that Dick Cheney colluded with his future company to establish the potentially lucrative arrangements. The LOGCAP was established years before he became Secretary of Defense; and while he was Secretary of Defense during the Gulf War LOGCAP was not used. The Army decided it was not ready for prime time.

LESSONS LEARNED AND UNLEARNED

The Pentagon went to war without LOGCAP. It could not, however, fight the Gulf War without contractors. Largely unprepared for undertaking massive contracts during wartime, the military did what it always does when it goes to battle—the best it could. Although the private sector helped win the public war, there were innumerable bumps along the way. Many of the lessons learned from Desert Storm sound an awful lot like the litany of complaints about contractors in combat in Iraq and Afghanistan.

When military forces deployed, they were ready to do many things well, but managing contractors was not necessarily one of them. Field commanders had little "visibility" on contractors (knowing who they were, where they were, and what they were doing); they had insufficient personnel to oversee the management of contracts and inadequate means to communicate, coordinate, and integrate contractors into operational plans. On more than one occasion, the result was that contracts were issued with poorly defined statements of the work to be done or with ill-explained contractual requirements; in some cases, there was no clear statement of requirements at all.

Contractor shortfalls manifested themselves in four problem areas—performance, reliability, accountability, and discipline. These, in turn, led to complaints from the military, government auditors, Congressional overseers, and the media. In the end, however, contractors usually got paid. Government's failure to do its job right was not contractors' fault. This would prove to be one part of the "friction of war" that the Pentagon would never figure out how to completely eliminate. Complaints about contractors would prove endemic in the wars of the post–Cold War world.

Contracts, such as those let to support operations in Iraq, actually evolved from trying to learn some of the lessons of the Gulf War. The Pentagon was determined never to fight an unplanned war again without at least some capacity to let contracts in a systematic manner. At first, the Army allowed military commands to independently contract for services. In 1992, the Department of the Army, under the auspices of a democratic president, issued its first worldwide LOGCAP contract that put all prospective operations under the umbrella of a single overall prime contractor. The winner was Brown & Root Services (forerunner to KBR). In turn, the Air Force and Navy developed similar contractual programs.

Under LOGCAP, the prime contractor would be issued a task order including the kinds and amount of support that would be needed. This list might cover everything from building and managing mess halls and barracks to delivering supplies of fresh water and fuel. In turn, it was the responsibility of the LOGCAP contractor to determine how to best muster all the resources required when the military announced the launch of a contingency operation. The company might choose to provide the services itself or to recruit other firms to perform the tasks for it.

It is understandable why companies like Brown & Root, and only a handful of other major corporations with international reach and deep experience in large-scale engineering and service jobs, would bid for and get the Pentagon's business. The demands of the contract were fairly daunting. Initially, LOGCAP called for contractors to be prepared to establish support facilities for 20,000 troops in up to five base camps almost anywhere in the world. The contractor had to have an advance team on the ground in seventy-two hours and the first base camp up and running in sixteen days. The company had to be prepared to support the camps for six months and to expand operations to handle 50,000 soldiers for a year. The Pentagon was expecting a lot. Contractors would have to be able to go from zero to building the equivalent of small cities with no notice.

Considering how quickly companies might have to respond and ramp up what support they might have to provide for military deployments, and how lethargic and time-consuming the process for announcing, competing, awarding, negotiating, and signing contacts with the government can be, setting up contracts before the bullets started flying just made sense. Additionally, for the military, because there would always be a flood of unexpected activities and a fair amount of uncertainty involved in running off to any unexpected battlefields, knowing where and how basic support items and services would be delivered would allow more time to focus on the tricky life and death decisions of putting troops into harm's way. At least, that was the idea.

As it turned out, the military did not have to wait very long to test whether LOGCAP would stand up to the test.

THE LIFEBLOOD OF WAR

LOGCAP actually worked. In December 1992, the U.S. Army sent troops into Somalia. American soldiers spearheaded a UN operation intended to stem a nationwide famine in the small African country that had become a poster child for the term "failed state." The impoverished, lawless, and violent region proved one of the most inhospitable places on earth to set up shop. Brown & Root provided services for 22,000 American and other UN troops. The initial U.S. effort proved a spectacular success. The insertion of military troops, which provided a cordon of security for humanitarian relief efforts, helped break the back of the crisis. Later, however, American forces became embroiled in an extended UN mission to bring political stability. After a bloody confrontation with a local warlord, President Clinton ordered the precipitous withdrawal of American forces. Although that particular mission failed, it was, nevertheless, a well supplied failure.

The U.S. military also employed LOGCAP during the 1994 peacekeeping mission in Haiti. Like Somalia, Haiti was a challenging environment for contractors.

The country was a basket case, corrupt and impoverished. Washington threatened an invasion in order to restore the ousted, democratically elected president. The military junta ruling the desperately poor Caribbean nation disintegrated virtually overnight. The country lacked for virtually everything. Despite the desperate conditions, the American intervention was judged a winner.

Encouraged by the performance of LOGCAP, the Army called on it for contractor support in Bosnia in 1995 (under a NATO mandate to separate warring factions in the aftermath of a bloody civil war) and then again in a 1999 NATO operation in neighboring Kosovo. Not surprisingly, contractors made money. Brown & Root received $2.5 billion in support operations contracts in the Balkans between 1995 and 2003. In 1997, Brown & Root lost the contract renewal for LOGCAP to DynCorp, though the military, again under a Democratic administration, continued to contract support operations in the Balkans to the company under a separate deal that one observer called, "the mother of all service contracts."[8] The Pentagon was satisfied; LOGCAP was a proven system to support U.S. combat capabilities.

LOGCAP proved so important to the Pentagon because, as has so often been said, "logistics are the lifeblood of war." Supplying war, providing soldiers food, fuel and fodder, has, more often than not, been the primary factor determining when, where, and how militaries fight. This is particularly true for the American military. For every soldier on the battlefield, there are dozens providing everything from fresh water to Internet connections, all of which are essential to keeping combatants combat ready. Having a dependable source of support is an important part of military readiness. It was for that reason that once LOGCAP established itself, the Pentagon became a consistent consumer of these kinds of services.

Contractors and combatants were not the only ones who benefited by military deployments. During these operations, many of the employees were third-party or host-country (that is, of the state where the military and contractors were deployed) nationals. According to one industry survey, companies reported that over half of their staffs were host-country nationals.[9] In Bosnia, for example, many KBR employees went on to become subcontractors, starting their own small trucking, construction, and services companies. One of the by-products of contractors in combat is promoting economic activity in the countries, which helps kindle the postwar revival of private business. During one period, KBR was largest single employer in Kosovo. Many of the cottage companies that sprang up in Bosnia went on to operate as subcontractors for KBR operations in Iraq. In addition, many nongovernmental agencies (such as the Red Cross) relied on the same contractors when making their humanitarian operations more efficient and effective.

Although LOGCAP succeeded, it did not resolve every problem with contractors in combat. In the Balkans, for example, where the battlefield was in the middle of Western Europe, keeping account of employees proved to be nightmare. Some decided to drive to work in rental cars or live outside of base camp or even the country, and commanders had not the slightest idea where their workforce lived or how they would get to their jobs when they were needed—something of great concern if fighting broke out.[10]

The Pentagon ended its first decade after the Cold War with chinks still in its contracting armor. There were other problems as well. The military had contracted in big wars, such as Desert Storm, and in long wars, including its operations in Bosnia and Kosovo. It had not, however, let contracts for big and long wars. The services had no clue whether their capabilities to manage the private sector in expansive, persistent conflicts were up to the task. When they learned the answer, they were less than happy.

LAW AND WAR

The one problem with contracting in combat that is most cited was not in fact the most problematic. Although there were many contracting challenges, establishing a legal basis for operations was not one of them. There was much discussion about the legal status of contractors and accountability issues before and after Desert Storm, but these did not represent an insurmountable obstacle. Though lawyers, academics, and activists found many gaps and issues to debate, in the end there was no serious legal impediment to employing contractors in combat. The notion that contractors largely operate in some kind of shadowland outside the rule of law is largely another myth. The law of war was well established long before the first time America went after Saddam.

Since the early days of the Republic, America has fought its public wars under what is generally referred to as the law of land warfare, or the law of armed conflict. The two principle sources of this law today are (1) the Constitution and U.S. laws and (2) treaties or conventions signed by the United States and ratified by the U.S. Senate, which, according to the Constitution, also have the force of law. Additionally, in some cases, the United States relies on "custom" that includes unwritten or customary laws and practices firmly established by common international practices, widely recognized, and well defined. This is sometimes called "common law," part of a legal tradition inherited from Great Britain. All these laws have something to say about contractors in combat.

In particular, there are a number of treaties that pertain to the laws of land warfare. Perhaps the most well known and important are the Geneva Conventions. The conventions are four treaties negotiated and signed in Geneva, Switzerland in 1949 that set international standards for humanitarian concerns in wartime.

The conventions divide the armed forces of "belligerent parties" into combatants and noncombatants. To qualify as a legitimate combatant requires (1) coming under the command of a "responsible person," like a corps of commissioned officers in an established military, (2) wearing a distinctive "sign" or uniform that clearly identifies an individual as combatant, (3) carrying arms openly, and (4) complying with the laws of war. Any individual who engages in combat and does not follow these rules is not a lawful combatant.

Civilians or other protected persons (those who in the course of conflicts who comes into the hands of a warring party of which they are not members, such as residents of a town captured during an invasion) are considered noncombatants. The Geneva Conventions were specifically written to protect civilians in time of war. All civilians are entitled to humane treatment. On the other hand, if civilians engage in activities such as espionage, assassination, sabotage, outlawry, or combat, they forfeit many of their protections under the treaties.

For the purposes of the law of land warfare, contractors are, by and large, considered noncombatants. If contractors happen to perform tasks that support a warring party, anything from working in a munitions plant to washing dishes in a base camp, they could, however, be considered active participants in hostilities. That may make them subject to attack—and those attacks could be perfectly legal. For example, a belligerent might attack an enemy convoy carrying military supplies with civilian guards and drivers. If a lawful combatant harmed civilians in the course of the attack, such an incident would probably be considered an act of war and not a war crime. If the contract employees were captured by the enemy they would, under the Geneva Conventions, have to be treated like civilians.

Contractors in combat can even be armed without being considered combatants. Contractors can carry weapons for self-defense (such as small arms like pistols and shotguns), protecting themselves and others. On the other hand, to maintain their status as noncombatants they cannot carry "offensive" weapons (such as cannons, rocket launchers, or large-caliber weapons) or participate in overtly offensive actions (like attacking an enemy base camp). In short, there is nothing in the Geneva Conventions that impinges on employing contractors on the battlefield or endangers their civilian status, so long as they comply with the protocols of the treaties. In turn, the armed forces had no prohibition against hiring contractors for wartime service.

The United States military defined contractors in combat as "civilians authorized to accompany the force in the field." U.S. military contractors are identified by being issued a DD Form 489 (Geneva Conventions Identity Card for Persons who Accompany the Armed Forces). Under certain circumstances, the Defense Department authorizes contractors in combat to be armed. Pentagon regulations permit contractor personnel to use deadly force against enemy armed forces in self-defense. Private security contractors can also use deadly force when necessary to execute their security mission, such as protecting embassy personnel, consistent with the tasks given in their contract. These tasks cannot include inherently governmental military functions, like conducting preemptive attacks.

When it comes to determining what laws govern the performance of military contractors the answer was "it depends." Before 2007, civilians could only fall under the Uniform Code of Military Justice—UCMJ (the U.S. legal system applicable to all American military personnel no matter where they are in the world) if Congress officially declared a war—something not done since the outbreak of World War II.

If contractors committed crimes, they could be subject either to U.S. civilian criminal laws or the laws of the country in which they are serving. The determination over which country has authority in criminal cases is often determined by the Status of Forces Agreement (SOFA) that the United States enters into with the host country. If there is no SOFA agreement the host country can prosecute contractors for crimes under its own laws. That, of course, can cause problems, as in the cases of Bosnia, Somalia, and Haiti, where there were, in effect, no functioning legal systems with police, courts, lawyers, and prisons. Relying on the host nation also proved problematic when a country's legal system was corrupt or lacked transparency and a reputation for respecting human rights.

Congress further strengthened the legal authority over contractors in combat in 2000, when it passed the Military Extraterritorial Jurisdiction Act. Under the act, if a civilian accompanying U.S. military forces commits a federal crime he or she can be prosecuted in U.S. Federal Court. The effects of the Congressional act had practical limitations. The law might work well in an established theater, such as Germany or Japan, where U.S. forces have been stationed alongside other forces for decades, their host nations countries at peace and enjoying well-established civil societies with strong legal systems. In other parts of the world, exercising the long arm of American law proved to be a bit more difficult.

When contractors broke the law, punishing them required sending law enforcement into a combat zone to collect evidence and make arrests, then getting the accused and the evidence transported thousands of miles back to a U.S. federal court. That was easier said than done—tracking down criminal civilian acts in combat could be expensive, manpower intensive, and intensely dangerous. In Bosnia, for example, in a particularly infamous case, DynCorp employees were accused of crimes ranging from child prostitution to human trafficking and assault. The company did fire some individuals accused of criminal acts—but that was the extent of their authority. In an expanding controversy, two company whistle-blowers were also let go and later sued for damages. One won in a British court. The other settled out of court. Reported evidence in the case included a video tape of a DynCorp employee committing rape. However, even though military criminal investigators collected evidence of the crimes no U.S. criminal case was ever brought.[11] Prosecutions in a Bosnian court went nowhere. Arguably, this case, and others, demonstrated that justice had at times been ill-served in battle. Clearly, there was room for improvement.

The Fiscal Year 2007 Defense Authorization Act amended the UCMJ to give the court authority over civilians during "a contingency operation," including those "in which members of the armed forces are or may become involved in military actions, operations, or hostilities against an enemy of the United States or against an opposing military force" (US Code, Title 10, sec. 101 (a) (13)). This would include activities in Iraq and Afghanistan.

It remains to be seen how the military defines the limits of the UCMJ jurisdiction granted by the change in the law. In some respects, granting such potentially broad authority to the military may create as many problems as it solves, potentially complicating the relationship between commanders, contracting officers, civilians, and contractors.[12] The change was slipped into the law without much thoughtful debate. It remains to be seen whether merely expanding military legal authority over contractors is in any way a "silver bullet" or whether what is required is a more expansive kit of legal tools and resources allowing the government to use traditional law enforcement and legal systems or military justice based on the operational demands of a particular mission.

CUSTOMER SATISFACTION

There were other challenges as well that the law was ill-served to tackle. Crimes aside, the military and other government contractors had limited legal authority to govern the activities of contractors in combat. The military does not "command" contractors, though it can "manage" them. Where the military issues orders through a chain of command that runs from the president through generals down to officers, sergeants, and individual squad leaders commanding handfuls of soldiers, commanders have to coordinate for contract support through a contracting officer or their representative (a person in uniform or a civilian who has the legal authority to enter into, administer, or terminate a contract). In turn, contractors direct their employees.

What the armed forces could demand from contractors in combat was largely defined by the contract. If individual contractors or companies do not commit crimes, the military has limited capacity to address concerns in performance, reliability, accountability, or discipline. The usual answer is to have the contract modified or terminated. This might include changing terms in the contract, demanding that contractors counsel or discipline their personnel or even provide different employees to perform the work.

It becomes more problematic when contractors work for non-military employers, such as other federal agencies (for example, the State Department), nongovernmental organizations (e.g. the Red Cross), or another country (such as another NATO nation). In these cases, the U.S. military has no different authority over the contractor than over any other civilian on the battlefield.

Although it is clear that the military deployed contractors into combat with an expansive legal framework to build on, there were still problems. The major issue with contractors in combat resulted from the same practice that made the military so formidable in Desert Storm to begin with. A great part of the armed forces resurgence in the 1980s stemmed from the training revolution that superbly prepared soldiers for conventional combat (wars where similarly equipped forces fought each other in, for example, tank-on-tank battles). The Pentagon's training philosophy was called "train as you fight" and included mock wars in the air and on the ground using the same equipment and tactics employed in combat. Nothing in these exercises included contractors in combat, or (for that matter) the presence of any civilians on the battlefield. At the same time, military doctrinal manuals scarcely mentioned the subject. Students in courses from

ROTC (Reserve Officers Training Corps) at civilian universities or the military academies, like West Point, or staff or senior service war colleges would be hard pressed to remember a class on contractors. It was as if the art and science of war was a wholly public practice without any place for the private sector.

In the wake of military experiences from Desert Storm to Kosovo, the military developed additional guidelines and doctrines governing contract activities. From 1998 to 2003, the services churned out various regulations, field manuals, and joint (applicable to all American armed forces) publications (some of them written under contracts to the U.S. Army by other contractors). By the time the American forces entered Afghanistan, the military publications covering contractors amounted to a hefty library. Among other guidance, these writings helped codify the employment of LOGCAP operations.

Because the military did write some rules for contractors in combat, it would not be fair to say that the Pentagon had completely neglected its responsibilities. Still, there was a downside. It took over a decade for the military to craft its guidelines, and even then the effort was incomplete. The Army had issued the most guidance. The Joint Staff, in contrast, produced one chapter in one manual (*Joint Publication 4.0*). The Defense Department had produced nothing. It was October 2005 before the department issued a comprehensive policy guide, *Defense Department Instruction 3020.41: Contractor Personnel Authorized to Accompany the U.S. Armed Forces.* Even that, however, was incomplete. Military doctrine and regulations had little to say about how to handle contractors that the Pentagon did not employ but who worked for NGOs, other federal agencies, or governments instead. In Iraq and Afghanistan, there were plenty of those on the battlefield. To make matters worse, the doctrine was rarely fully tested. Even up to the eve of the Iraq war, soldiers continued to run their phony wars at the Army's training centers in the deserts, swamps, and forests without a contractor in sight.

It has only been in the last few years that the Army has even added civilians to the training battlefield, including people to play townsfolk, rioters, insurgents, and others in civilian clothes that soldiers encounter every day in a combat zone. Even then, the military never came close to addressing how it would field a substantial workforce of contracting officers and representatives to oversee large-scale contracts and harmonize their efforts with military commands.

"RIGHT-SIZING" THE MILITARY

The military's inattention to the importance of contractors in combat is inexcusable. The military failed to iron out the kinks in the rule of land warfare, establish training and doctrine for programs like LOGCAP, or build the capacity to manage large-scale contract activities after the end of the Cold War. Military leaders in the Pentagon might have argued, no doubt, that as the post–Cold War armed forces shrank, fewer people were available to do more—least of all to worry about contractor in future combat. That excuse, however, is cold comfort.

It is apparent that the Pentagon became complacent about contractors. As the military got smaller with virtually every deployment, its dependence on the commercial services grew—not only because the military had fewer forces, but also because the private sector repeatedly proved, again and again, it could make up the difference. The military might have wistfully hoped that if it just ignored the necessity for contractors, one day everything might change and the armed forces return to a time when they alone brought the preponderance of power to the battlefield. But, as one former Army Chief of Staff famously proclaimed, "hope is not a method." As the military downsized, it should have spent more time thinking about how it would harness the private sector for public wars.

The Pentagon's biggest problem was that the future just came too fast. The post-Vietnam expansion of the armed forces peaked in 1987. Almost immediately after the Berlin Wall began to fall, so did the ranks of the military. The post–Cold War peace dividend affected all the services. Not only did the numbers drop, but organizations shrank, bases closed, equipment was retired, and civilian employees were let go. Deciding how small the Pentagon's post–Cold War military should become became the dominating defense issue from the fall of the Wall until 9/11.

Cuts began in 1988, even before Warsaw Pact collapsed, with a process Congress established called Base Realignment and Closure—BRAC. Because no members of Congress would willingly stand by and watch the Pentagon shut a major defense installation in their district or state (and then hope to get reelected), they authorized the Defense Department to establish an independent panel to make the selections. In turn, the Pentagon would present the list to Congress, who could only vote up or down the whole list of recommendations. Altogether the Department of Defense held five rounds of BRAC, spanning democratic and republican administrations. The last was in 2005. Together, the BRAC decisions closed dozens of military bases.

Abandoning bases was only part of military downsizing. Military ranks were thinned as well. The first major force reductions, in fact, came at the Pentagon's insistence. As Chairman of the Joint Chiefs of Staff (who serves as the senior military advisor to the President and Secretary of Defense), General Colin Powell developed a concept called the Base Force (1989–1992). Recognizing that post–Cold War budgets would never sustain the existing number of troops and units, he developed a plan that envisioned a 25 percent reduction in the size of the military by 1995. The Base Force would have 1.6 million troops on active duty instead of 2.1 million. The reserves, including the National Guard would be cut from 1.5 million to 898,000. America's military would also have fewer Army divisions, fewer air wings, fewer ships, and a smaller Marine Corps. President George Bush announced the decision to the nation in a speech on August 2, 1990. The story should have made front page headlines. It didn't. The news was overshadowed by reports of Iraq's invasion of Kuwait. A follow-up press conference with Powell and Secretary of Defense Cheney to explain the rationale for the cuts and the new post–Soviet threat military strategy that would justify the size of the military was cancelled. For the immediate future, planning wars overshadowed planning for the new world order.[13] The hiatus in downsizing, however, did not last long.

By the time the Pentagon got back to determining how low the force structure could go, a new administration was in the White House, and a new Secretary of Defense at the Pentagon. Powell was still the Chairman of the Joint Chiefs, and although his views still carried considerable weight, he no longer called the shots. In one of his first initiatives as Secretary of Defense, Les Aspin undertook what he called the Bottoms-Up Review or BUR, a complete rethinking how big the military needed to be. Not surprisingly, the answer was—smaller, in part because of pressure to reduce defense spending in order to reduce the size of the federal debt. Released in 1993 after the Base Force reductions had already been implemented (two years ahead of schedule), the BUR proposed to cut the Pentagon from Cold War levels by a third.[14]

Shrinking the military was not over yet. A 1996 congressionally mandated report called the Quadrennial Defense Review (QDR) sliced even more from the top. The QDR envisioned reducing the total active force to 1.36 million by 2005 and the reserves to 835,000. The trend for long-term defense spending continued to look bleak, and the Pentagon was faced with some stark choices. Modernizing the military had virtually stopped a decade earlier, and the armed forces were growing increasingly desperate to buy new equipment to replace aging ships, vehicles, and planes. The best (though Faustian) bargain they could think of was to trade off more forces to free up at least some money for modernization. Not everyone was happy with the deal. Although the service chiefs signed on to the QDR, leaders in the reserve component had not. The Army National Guard in particular nearly staged a revolt protesting the cuts.

The private sector was at odds over the military's decision. The shadow of Eisenhower's old military industrial complex was not pleased at all. The post–Cold War world was not turning out to be a cash cow for the corporate sector. Even cutting more troops resulted in, at best, only an anemic plan to buy new equipment. The fact that nobody in Congress or the administration cared much about military woes reflected how little muscle defense industries really carried in Washington. Nor were these companies much excited by the increasing reliance that a smaller force would put on private sector service providers. The traditional, large defense companies only accounted for a modicum of the market share that garnered the contract services business.

Additionally, although service companies could potentially make billions from contracts in wartime, they themselves also had only limited clout. Their profits were still a fraction of those made by traditional defense firms. In turn, the defense industries were far from being the most deep-pocketed or influential companies lobbying in Washington. Ike would have been bemused at how low the military industrial complex had sunk. The private sector was more a bystander than a force in the management of the freefall of the military ranks. Indeed, defense companies spent most of their lobbying efforts aiming at each other, squabbling over the few major defense contracts that were up for grabs.

THE CHANGING TIDE

Cutting the military, particularly ground troops, proved to be a bipartisan sport. There were rumblings that the Republican Secretary of Defense Donald Rumsfeld in the incoming administration envisioned even further reductions. Then history intervened. The release of the 2001 QDR was preempted by 9/11, and the Pentagon decided to forestall talk of further cuts until the war on terror had sorted itself out.

As missions mounted and troops were sent to American airports, Afghanistan, Iraq, and then the Mexican border, it soon became apparent that the active army, which had shrunk to under 500,000, was too small to sustain multiple combat deployments. Even heavy reliance on Army National Guard and Reserves did not alleviate the strain of sending troops for multiple missions overseas and at home. From 2001 to 2006, about 683,000 soldiers (active and reserve) served in Iraq or Afghanistan. One hundred sixty-four thousand of those deployed at least twice.

Instead of cutting land forces, Washington grudgingly started to think about increasing them. In January 2004, the Defense Department reluctantly (and temporarily) added 30,000 soldiers to the active force. In 2005, Congress raised the Army end-strength by 20,000 and the Marine Corps by 6,000 with additional increases of 10,000 soldiers and 1,000 Marines for 2006. By the time the 2006 QDR came around, the Army was mired in wars in Iraq and Afghanistan, and further reductions were out of the question. Notably, however, the QDR did not call for a substantial increase in ground forces and explicitly stated that reliance on contractors was part of the military's "total force."[15]

DOLLARS AND DOUGHBOYS

Although the cutting of the ranks of the ground troops had stopped, it was readily apparent why both Democrats and Republicans had been so intent on thinning the ranks, so reluctant to grow the military even after 9/11, and ready, at some point, to start cutting them again. The reason is simple. Paying for troops has become the most expensive part of running the military.

From 1994 to 2004, the cost of paying for men and women in the military dropped from 28.4 percent of the defense budget to 24.6 percent. To make those savings, however, the military cut the force by about 800,000, not much of a payback for cutting almost a quarter of the force. Although the size of the military decreased, the cost of military benefits, including everything from pay to health care, climbed steeply. In fact, today a typical soldier's salary accounts for about only half the cost of keeping him or her in uniform. The rest goes to paying for healthcare, housing, schools, and other benefits provided to military personnel and their families, and these costs are skyrocketing. If the Army ever adds all the additional troops authorized by Congress after 9/11, it will find the price tag to be pretty hefty. It is estimated that the cost for every 10,000 active duty soldiers added is a whopping $1.2 billion per year. Ground troops cost a lot.

The expense of military manpower is not the only pressure humbling the size of the force. Overall spending by the federal government does not bode well for defense budgets. Clinton troop cuts helped balance the federal budget, but as a fiscal challenge, deficits in the federal budget pale in comparison to a looming fiscal crisis that casts a very long shadow across the Potomac River from the Hill to the parking lots of the Pentagon.

Thirty years ago military spending accounted for half of federal spending. Entitlement programs, like Social Security, consumed only about a fifth of Washington's budget. By 2006, programs like Social Security, Medicare, and Medicaid took up half the budget, and the Pentagon only about a fifth. And unless the government undertakes serious reform of entitlement spending, the balance is only likely to get worse. By 2030, the big three entitlements (Social Security, Medicare, and Medicaid) will absorb roughly 84 percent of all federal revenues. The Comptroller, General David M. Walker calculates that federal spending could consume roughly 40 percent of gross domestic product (GDP) by 2040. Most of that will go to shelling out entitlement checks. There may not be much left to pay for defense.

The importance of this evolution in fiscal policy cannot be understated. For most of America's history, the federal government's chief budgetary function was funding defense. The two-thirds decline in defense spending since 1962 has substantially altered the makeup and structure of the U.S. national defense. Government in the developed world has expanded substantially during the past century. The United States stands at the apex of this trend.

One of the best measures of the burden that the federal government as a whole imposes on the national economy through its spending policies is the percentage of GDP taken up by government outlays. During America's first 140 years, Washington rarely consumed more than a few percentage points of the GDP. In accordance with the Constitution, Washington focused on defense and certain public goods (like negotiating with foreign countries) while leaving most other functions to the states, communities, and individuals. That changed in the twentieth century. Between 1962 and 2000, defense spending plummeted from 9.5 percent of the GDP to only three. Nearly all funding shifted from defense spending went into mandatory spending (mostly entitlement programs). By 2000, entitlement spending accounted for a massive 12 percent of the GDP.

By 2007, spending on defense and homeland security in the United States stands at about 4.5 percent of the GDP, the highest level of investment since the end of the Cold War. However, this represents, on average, about half what the nation spent during the face-off with the Soviets. And, unlike the Cold War period, post–Cold War defense spending is faced with unprecedented competition for federal dollars because of mandatory government spending on entitlement programs.

Mandatory outlays for programs such as Social Security, Medicare, and Medicaid are consuming, and will continue to consume, ever larger percentages of federal spending and the GDP. As a result, they will apply increasing pressure, crowding out the resources available to field more ground troops—and that will likely change how future wars are fought.

Nor is the United States unique in facing this dilemma. European nations, which already spend, on average, less than 2 percent of their GDPs on defense and much more of their national budgets on social services and entitlements, face similar predicaments. As potential economic and military powerhouses like China and India move from the ranks of the developing to the developed, they will also confront the same kinds of challenges. In fact, India and China may encounter even more pressure to rein in defense spending if their much larger populations demand similar levels of social services.[16]

SHUTTING OUT THE DRAFT

Clearly, the upward-spiraling manpower costs and downward-spiraling size of the military have fueled the Pentagon's reliance on contractors. There are few prospects these trends will change dramatically. There are few practical alternatives.

One solution that has been proposed of late has not even a prayer of adoption. There have been persistent calls to reinstate Vietnam-era conscription to avoid reliance on contractors, a solution that is both ill-considered and unlikely. Peacetime drafts are not only antithetical to the volunteer traditions of the U.S. military but are increasingly seen by modern militaries as impractical. With a trend toward fielding forces armed with more technology and more sophisticated skills, short-service conscription is viewed as inadequate, not allowing sufficient time to train forces and requiring excessive costs to frequently retrain new recruits. Additionally, as militaries become smaller in developed nations, conscription will be acknowledged more and more as socially divisive because it will be difficult to equitably draw on the available eligible pool of recruits.

Conscription makes sense only in moments of extreme national peril such as the Civil War and World War II. During World War II, for example, virtually all able-bodied men of draft age (about 12 million) were needed to defend the Republic. In short, the draft was fair because virtually everybody who could serve had to serve. But those moments are rare. Imposing a draft at any other time creates not shared sacrifice or an efficient source of soldiers, but a lottery for the unlucky. In all likelihood, in the future military drafts will be viewed as inefficient and ineffective means for mobilizing manpower in developed, liberal democracies.

THE WAR OF HABITS

The final reason the size of ground forces is unlikely to change dramatically has to do with the manner in which America traditionally funds its military. Although analytical efforts such as the Base Force, BUR, and QDR quantified post–Cold War threats in order to justify the size of the armed forces, in truth, their conclusions did little more than rubber-stamp what the administration and Congress were willing to spend. These were hardly aberrations. Rather, they reflected how Americans traditionally funded defense.

Over the course of American history, the American people funded the military more out of habit than in response to specific dangers. That is why for most of the nation's past until the Cold War, the nation spent, on average, only a percent or two of total national spending on defense, regardless of national concerns (except in times of war). Likewise, except in the presence of wartime needs such as those surrounding Korea and Vietnam, the United States maintained its Cold War spending at about 7.5 percent. Reagan's ability to ramp up defense expenditures to the degree he did was a remarkable achievement rarely matched in presidential leadership. In his first three years in office, Reagan pushed through double-digit increases in defense spending, an almost unprecedented act. Even Franklin Roosevelt had meager success significantly spinning up defense spending, despite the impending outbreak of World War II. Americans have a habit of wanting to spend on defense about what they spent the year before.

Now that the United States is in a new strategic era, it will undoubtedly seek to find its new level of "normal" defense appropriations. Without question, the answer will be more than the 1 or 2 percent the nation spent before it was a global power. On the other hand, it is hard to imagine that any administration could convince Americans to fund the military to the level that was required to stand off against the Soviet Union. At the end of the Clinton years, defense budgets as a level of total U.S. expenditures dropped to under 3 percent. As the strains of Iraq and Afghanistan have shown, that level of spending was clearly too little. There is no consensus on how much is enough. Discovering the "new normal" will be the next great American defense debate.

The Pentagon's budget in 2007 hovered at around 4 percent. Even that level of spending is somewhat inflated with supplemental spending to pay for the wars in Iraq and Afghanistan. Reasonable estimates suggest that the federal government will have to spend at least 4 percent of GDP in the decades ahead to prevent the military from becoming a "hollow" force as it did after Vietnam.[17] Even if future presidential administrations manage to maintain defense expenditures at 4 percent and Americans got into the habit of accepting bigger annual military budgets, the Pentagon's future peacetime armed forces will be roughly about the same size as— perhaps even a tad smaller than—they are now; and that will mean that the future military will likely have to rely heavily on contractors in combat as well.

SOLDIERS OF FORTUNE

Public armies' trending toward smaller sizes and the ever-increasing reliance on the private sector were not the only emerging trends of the era President George Bush coined the "new world order." There was another trend regarding contractors in combat—one that looked more like the "new world disorder."

This trend was actually the focus of Peter Singer's *Cooperate Warriors*. It started in London and Pretoria with a company curiously named—Executive Outcomes. Formed in 1989, the year the Soviet Union dissolved the Warsaw Pact (the military alliance formed to counter NATO), and incorporated in Britain and South Africa, the company marketed security and peacekeeping services, according to its official mission statement, to "create a climate for peace and stability for foreign investment." These services included heavily recruiting from the former South African military special forces who waged a decades-long, bitter struggle supporting the government's apartheid regime (that forced separation of the races in the country). The company fielded its own army, complete with armored vehicles, helicopter gunships, fighter planes, and commercial air transports.

Executive Outcomes played a major role in the Angolan Civil War. In 1992, when a cease-fire and national elections brokered by the United Nations broke down, the National Union for the Total Independence of Angola (UNITA) and the Popular Movement for the Liberation of Angola (MPLA) renewed their conflict. The company was hired to help recapture and safeguard the territory surrounding the country's oil fields and diamond mines against UNITA incursions. In 1993, MPLA offered the company a $40 million contract to train its ground forces. The initial contract called for the company to provide over 5,000 men. In turn, the MPLA scored major ground victories backed by training, planning, direction, and also ground and air support from Executive Outcomes, including sorties by Soviet-built helicopter gunships and jet fighter-bombers, all piloted by Executive Outcome employees. The military support provided MPLA a decisive edge. UNITA sued for peace.[18]

By the mid-1990s it was clear that Executive Outcomes' business was the business of war in Africa—and business was good. In 1995, the government of Sierra Leone hired the company to help prepare its forces to fight an insurgency led by the Revolutionary United Front (RUF). In the end, Executive Outcomes wound up virtually taking over operations, directing everything from intelligence gathering and civic actions to gaining popular support in the countryside to mounting combat operations. Company-led operations put the RUF on their heels. Executive Outcomes went on to become involved in an expanding network of commercial activities that sent contract warriors to hot spots in Sierra Leone, Burundi, and the Congo.

MANAGING MERCENARIES

Companies like Executive Outcomes were clearly different from the contractors the U.S. military defined as "civilians authorized to accompany the force in the field." Because they employed offensive weapons, including fighter-bombers and armored vehicles with heavy-machine guns, they were clearly "combatants." That, however, did not necessarily make them mercenaries in the accordance with the modern legal meaning of the term.

Mercenaries are defined and outlawed by international convention. The definitions of mercenary activities, however, are specifically crafted to allow states to employ contractors in combat—even as combatants. Mercenaries are defined in the 1977 Protocol 1 Addition to the Geneva Conventions. There are six parts to the definition of a mercenary. All have to be satisfied before a contractor could be declared neither a legitimate combatant nor a noncombatant. Further, the UN Convention Against the Recruitment, Use, Financing, and Training of Mercenaries adds a further twenty-one articles defining mercenary activities. The upshot of these requirements, however, is that any body considered a legitimate government can employ contractors in virtually all roles on the battlefield in full compliance with their treaty obligations as long as they act in accordance with their status as combatants or noncombatants under the Geneva Conventions. By international standards, arguably the activities of Executive Outcomes (excepting where employees of the company might have broken specific criminal laws or violated treaty conventions) were perfectly acceptable.[19]

Admittedly, some of the elements of the definition under international treaties to which the U.S. is a signatory are vague and could be difficult to prove. Nevertheless, they represent the broadly accepted modern definition of the Machiavellian curse. In fact, it is a definition that Machiavelli himself might have been largely happy with it. The internationally recognized definitions do little more than reaffirm the principle that managing the exercise of violence is the province of states. That is probably good enough. What the definitions do not do (which is something that Machiavelli did not do either) is seek to overly constrain how states exercise that responsibility—other than to emphasize that they ought to exercise their power responsibly.

DOGS OF WAR

Most Americans were indifferent to the explosion of activity by private military companies and the publication of Singer's book *Corporate Warriors*. They assumed such activities to be an endemic part of the African landscape. Additionally, they could hardly make the distinction between the criminal act of being a mercenary and the pejorative use of the term bandied about in popular culture. In large part, Hollywood shaped their notions of contract combatants.

Before the Iraq war, if an average American had been asked to describe a private military company, their description would probably sound much like the 1981 film *Dogs of War*. Opening to mixed reviews and complaints about promoting a racist depiction of African politics, but also to a strong box office take, John Irvin's shoot-'em-up film featured Christopher Walken and Tom Berenger, hired by a mineral company executive to overthrow an uncooperative leader of an African nation and install a puppet dictator. The film was based on the equally popular 1974 novel by Fredrick Forsyth.

If the film and the book seemed to ooze the gritty, greedy reality of postcolonial Africa, it was for good reason. Forsyth knew his subject well. As European nations relinquished their control over territories in the 1950s and 1960s, African politics were riddled with corrupt and incompetent governments, multi-national corporations trolling for good deals, nongovernmental organizations, international institutions ineffectually attempting to manage mayhem, and European powers continuing to meddle in the affairs of their former colonies. Forsyth was witness to this witch's brew as a journalist and then as a war correspondent covering the Nigerian Civil War in the summer of 1967. He quit the BBC in 1968 amidst allegations of biased reporting and faking stories.

Forsyth went from reporting the news to making news. His career as a novelist who mixed politics, intrigue, history, and action earned him a global following. The research for *Dogs of War*, which reportedly included supporting a fake *coup d'état* in Equatorial Guinea, created additional controversy as well as allegations that Forsyth really intended to bankroll a coup.

Today, the mercenary activities described by Forsyth would be considered clearly outlawed under the UN Convention. Additionally, the world he described was already vanishing, being overtaken even as *Dogs of War* hit the screen, and replaced by proxy wars of superpower competition that saw the Soviets and the West both fueling regional conflicts by funneling arms, training, and military assistance to their respective sides. In the wake of Vietnam, the Soviets perceived that American power was a spent force and sought out new areas to expand their global influence. Angola and other countries fueled their internal and regional wars with support from the Soviets, Cuba, and the Western bloc. South Africa's apartheid regime, which enforced racial separation in the country, increasingly turned the military on armed insurgents battling the government as well as on the regime's political enemies, as part of a combating anti-Communist crusade. Over the course of the late 1970s and early 1980s, Africa became the Cold War's new battleground. That era of African history ended abruptly in 1989 with the collapse of Soviet power. The white-controlled South African government fell not long after in 1994. It was into this vacuum that private military companies such as Executive Outcomes stepped in.

OUT OF AFRICA

Part of knowing where "we" are today in terms of contractors in combat requires understanding that the Wild West days of contractor combatants in the 1990s are largely over. Executive Outcomes' lucrative but brief and controversial success ended abruptly in 1999 after the South African government passed legislation that made it difficult for the company to continue to operate. With the ranks of Executive Outcomes filled with apartheid-era military personnel and controversy surrounding its activities in war-torn countries across the continent, it was perhaps to be expected that the firm would exist at cross-purposes to the fledgling post-apartheid democratic government.

Private military companies like Executive Outcomes did not entirely disappear. Rather, they went through a transformation, shifting from companies that actually performed high-profile combat services, like planning, leading, and fighting in offensive campaigns against warring parties, into private security companies with lower profiles that undertook operations like guarding humanitarian supply routes, protecting refugee camps, and safeguarding public and private infrastructures. Today, these companies advertise their services in terms of

providing support to peacekeeping, humanitarian assistance, "demining operations" (removing land mines emplaced by armies during a conflict), and public
safety and security (such as guarding oil fields and pipelines).

The private security companies made the argument that they offer an important contribution to stability in Africa. They could point to the fact that, in places
like Angola and Sierra Leone, companies like Executive Outcomes had actually
stopped the fighting and alleviated humanitarian catastrophes. In others cases,
they could argue that their companies could provide services more cheaply or
more effectively than governments or could offer assistance to countries and nongovernmental organizations when the international community was unwilling or
unable to help.

No one has made the case for private security companies more forcefully than
Doug Brooks, who represents the International Peace Operations Association
(IPOA), the trade group to which many of these companies belong. In the 1990s,
Brooks served as a fellow at the South African Institute of International Affairs.
His research into the troubles of Sierra Leone convinced him that privatized secu-
rity companies had had a beneficial affect on the conflict, particularly in stem-
ming the advance of an oncoming genocide.

Brooks founded IPOA in 2001. He not only emphasizes the industry's effort
to establish and adhere to self-established standards of professional conduct but
also helped establish training courses and instructional material, as well as a
process for registering and adjudicating complaints of abuses by IPOA members.
The youthful, sandy-haired, fast-talking Brooks is often called on to serve as the
industry foil for Singer, the author of *Corporate Warriors*, and other critics who
emphasized the difficulties in holding contractors legally accountable, the collusion between the companies and oil and mining interests, and the frequent lack of
transparency and probity over contractor operations. After the explosion of contractor activity in the wake of the Iraq war, it was fairly common to see Brooks
paired with Singer in the press or media interviews. Brooks often found himself
representing the industry in numerous Congressional hearings and before representatives of various UN commissions.

Debates between Brooks and other industry defenders and their detractors
have become fairly ritualized—resembling something akin to a stylized traditional Japanese kabuki dance. The steps are always the same. Although Brooks
emphasizes the importance of companies regulating themselves and governments
providing appropriate oversight, critics contend these measures are inadequate to
forestall abuses. Detractors also argue, among other things, that because, in many
cases, there was no clear accountability and auditing, it is difficult to argue that
private companies provide cheaper, better, and more effective services than conventional militaries. More often than not, the character of these debates has the
feel of two sides talking past each other. And, although the rhetoric is often heated
and facts disputed, neither side believes that private security companies should be
able to operate beyond the law. Furthermore, both acknowledge that it is unlikely
that these businesses will disappear any time soon.[20]

Even the government of South Africa proved unwilling to ban private military security companies entirely. The country's Regulation of Foreign Military Assistance Act (1997) "precludes any South African citizen from participating in an armed conflict, nationally or internationally, except as provided for in terms of the Constitution or national legislation." On the surface, the law appears to ban military companies outright. Indeed, individuals have been prosecuted for violating its prohibitions. In 2004, Carl Alberts, a veteran of the South African defense force, was arrested, tried, and fined for conducting mercenary activities in the Ivory Coast. Other countries have conducted enforcement as well. On March 7, 2004, Zimbabwe arrested seventy individuals (mostly South Africans) on suspicion of mercenary activity.

Nevertheless, the laws of South Africa and other countries in the region do not prohibit a wide range of activities. For example, there are, by some estimates, up to 2,500 South African citizens working for contractors in Iraq. Technically, their status is legal, because, as they contend, they are not parties to the conflict but are providing humanitarian assistance, something allowed under South African law.

AMERICAN ENTREPRENEURS

U.S. companies were not absent from the stampede of private companies offering private military services. One of the first and most successful and notable efforts was by a company called Military Professional Resources International—MPRI. Established by a small cadre of retired senior U.S. military offices in 1987, the company foresaw the age of outsourcing defense activities to the private sector. Their business strategy, however, differed significantly from companies like Executive Outcomes. Rather than providing combat forces at the point of the spear, MPRI offered support services that tutored high-level staffs on how to organize armies and prepared military units for battle. Services ranged from organizing training to teaching how to draft battle plans to writing manuals and doctrine.

In 1993 Carl Vuono joined the company as its new head. Vuono was a former Army Chief of Staff (1987–1991), a combat veteran of the Vietnam War who, from his office in the Pentagon, had helped shape the armed forces first downsizing initiatives and the rush to provide support for forces during the Gulf War. It would be easy to credit his service at the head of the Army Staff with opening doors for the fledgling company. Vuono, however, brought far more than that to MPRI. Few officers understood better the direction that the private sector and the public wars were headed. Perhaps even more importantly, few understood better how to train, prepare, and lead military forces. He had been at the center of the Army's post-Vietnam training transformation. As a result, few had a better feel for what services the Pentagon would be seeking from private companies in the post-Cold War world and how to deliver it.

In a little over a decade, MPRI grew to 3,000 employees in over forty countries. Today, it provides a diverse array of support to the Departments of Defense and Homeland Security including everything from running Reserve Officer Training Corps (ROTC) programs delivering classes at civilian universities to serving as a subcontractor providing logistical planning for LOGCAP. The company also offers services to a number of foreign militaries.

MPRI was an increasingly successful, but little known, corporate warrior until Yugoslavia collapsed. In the wake of World War II, Josip Broz Tito had led an army that not only drove the Nazis out of Yugoslavia but established a Communist state that incorporated the territories of the former Kingdom of Yugoslavia (a state itself created in the aftermath of war, when a number of South Slavic states amalgamated into the kingdom in 1918). Tito brooked no resistance to his rule and even snubbed his nose at Stalin on occasion. His empire barely outlasted him. Ethnic tensions began to pull at the Socialist Federal Republic of Yugoslavia almost as soon as Tito died in 1980. In 1990, the state began to come apart. Croatia, one of the former Yugoslav republics, seceded peacefully in 1991 but then became embroiled in an irredentist war with Serbia.

MPRI contracts with the republic's fledgling defense forces put the firm on the map. Singer, in turn, featured MPRI in his book. Although Singer's coverage of the company is unflattering, critical, and accusing, his account actually served to be more advertising than indictment—adding to the legend that a handful of contractors turned a rag-tag military into a fearsome fighting machine.

The story of the company's efforts has been well told, even if the actual facts remain in dispute. Washington looked to Croatia to balance Serbia's expansionist aims against the members of the old socialist federalist state. A UN peacekeeping mandate had failed to stem the spiral of violence, but it prevented aiding the warring parties. In came MPRI, which signed to service contracts with the ministry of defense to help "professionalize" the military and prepare the country for eventual qualification for NATO membership. Before the year was out, in August 1995, the Croats launched "Operation Storm," a major military offensive that put the Serbians to flight. "Although MPRI categorically denies involvement in Operation Storm or related training," Singer observes, "the dramatic overall improvement in Croat strategic and tactical skills over the same span is difficult to ignore."[21] Whatever the truth of the allegations of the role played by MPRI, its reputation made the company a hot commodity.

MPRI soon had plenty of work. A democratic administration had encouraged the Croatians to hire the company, and Washington had plenty more business for MPRI. The United States contracted with the company to help restructure the Bosnian armed forces. The State Department hired MPRI in 1996 to support the Clinton administration's Africa Crisis Response Initiative, a program to assist militaries in improving their defense forces for peacekeeping and other contingency mission. Not all MPRI operations were notable achievements. A contract to work with the Columbian military, for example, was cut short. Among other complaints was that some of the advisors provided by the company could not speak Spanish.[22] Nevertheless, the company's reputation was more noted for its successes than its failures. L-3 Communications, one of the largest defense service providers in the country, bought the company in 2000. In 2005, L-3 reported revenues for its government services activities (which included MPRI) of more than $2 billion.

GLOBAL COMPETITION

Other U.S. companies joined the ranks of MPRI as well. There are at least a dozen major American companies that perform significant private military services for the U.S. government, state and local law enforcement, and other countries. They are not alone. Although there is not one single comprehensive list, it is generally assumed that there are almost one hundred large-size companies in the global marketplace. If every small company were included, adding those that provide a range of guard and law enforcement services, the number would be well over 10,000. In addition to the United States, the United Kingdom and South Africa dominate the list of countries with companies offering privatized military services.

Despite the lack of a definitive list of companies worldwide providing military-type services, the trend is clear. The number is growing. A 2006 IPOA survey found that 40 percent of the companies responding to an industry-wide questionnaire were established after 2001.[23] The United States and Great Britain are by far the largest consumers of privatized military services. Although the United States is certainly in a league of its own in terms of the amount spent on contractors, in terms of the percentage of defense business conducted, Britain's use is significant, dwarfing that of other European nations.[24] America and Britain, however, are not the only ones who rely on contractors in combat. Other countries are turning to them as well, and not just in Africa. Southeastern Europe, for example, is a rapidly growing market.[25]

Countries are not the only consumers of private services. In addition, the private sector (including businesses and industrial concerns) is relying more and more on other parts of the private sector to protect itself. International institutions and the nongovernmental sector, including at least seven UN institutions, the Red Cross, and other humanitarian groups, also employ the services of privatized military companies.

Use of private support and security companies by NGOs is somewhat ironic, given that NGOs are often among the industry's harshest critics. Yet NGO security and sustainment are major issues. Contractors can represent a Hobson's choice. On one hand, NGOs usually try to maintain strict neutrality, staying clear of military forces and their contractors. On the other hand, without security and logistical support, NGOs can be left vulnerable to the dangers of the battlefield. Both represent real dangers. In Somalia, for example, militias attacked the staff of World Vision in retaliation for a U.S. military strike against a local warlord. What's more, unprotected humanitarian groups had up to 80 percent of their food supplies stolen.[26]

Many private organizations realize that if they are going to have maximum impact in the crisis situations and humanitarian catastrophes in which they often find themselves, turning to reputable and dependable private sector companies that can offer effective services may be their best option. Indeed, just as the number of private military companies has grown since the end of the Cold War, so has the number of NGOs. The *Yearbook of International Organization* lists some 25,000 NGOs. The future, more often than not, may find companies and care-givers working side by side with increasing frequency. There is plenty of evidence that that is happening already. In the 2007 IPOA industry survey, 70 percent of respondents stated that they had provided services to NGOs, a 20-percent increase over results reported in the 2006 survey.[27]

The only other clear trend is that the list of private military firms is at the same time expanding, consolidating, and changing. KBR, for example, is by far the largest military service provider in the United States. Its market share accounts for about 5 percent of major DOD contract awards; the industry average is less than 1 percent. On the other hand, although its 2006 revenues topped well over $9 billion[28], the company's operating margin came in at only 2.55 percent, much of it from the LOGCAP operations in Iraq and an amount likely to decline when U.S. forces draw down. To remain profitable, KBR will have to figure out how to replace that revenue. Thus even though the company is still the Defense Department's fastest growing contractor, Halliburton (its parent company) spun off KBR as an independent concern. In contrast, L-3 Communications' acquisition of MPRI reflected a growing trend of traditional major defense firms buying promising companies performing military contract services. Meanwhile, many of the fastest growing companies, such as DynCorp and the Olive Group, are incorporated overseas. DynCorp, for example, brought in almost $2 billion in 2006, tripling its business in five years with profit margins more than double that of KBR.[29]

Regardless of how the marketplace evolves, because privatized services can be performed in a perfectly legitimate manner under international law, the globalization of privatized services will likely increase. The forecasts for the global demand of private security services alone (including everything from guarding warehouses to protecting oil fields) range from $150 billion to well over $200 billion by 2010. That growth reflects healthy annual single-digit increases.

America, Britain, and South Africa have all considered draft legislation further restricting the licensing and activities of domestic private military security companies or increasing their vulnerability to criminal prosecution or suits by third parties claiming injuries or abuse. Such legislation, if ever approved, is unlikely to stem the growth of global business; companies in other countries will likely sprout up to take their place—and the United States will likely be one of their biggest customers.

PARSING PRIVATIZATION

The private sector's role in public war has grown so quickly, and is changing so rapidly, that it has become difficult to quantify. Singer divides the military industry into "providers" that field personnel carrying weapons who might either provide security or actually serve as combatants, "consultants" that offer expertise and training, and "supporters" that deliver services ranging from food and fuel to battlefield intelligence. IPOA, in contrast, lists five categories: private security services, training and security sector reform services, information analysis and consulting, logistics and operations support, explosive ordnance disposal and mine clearance, and development services that include humanitarian assistance. Both acknowledge that private military companies cannot always be strictly categorized. Many provide a spectrum of services, and the services offered may represent merely a small part of the company's business. Sometimes they serve as subcontractors for one another, and sometimes they compete. Sometimes they share business. It can be difficult to know the players, even when holding a scorecard.

The services provided by these companies are also changing. In many respects, what these firms supply the armed forces has application to law enforcement, public safety, homeland security, humanitarian relief, and many commercial activities only remotely related to military activities. Law-enforcement activities alone are breathtaking and include everything from running prisons to providing cyber-security experts for combating white-collar crime. MPRI, KBR, Wackenhut, and AGS, for example, all share a $1.6 billion contract supporting a police training company working with the UN to increase law enforcement capacity in the developing world. In short, the private sector place in the public world is so dynamic that it defies any static effort to define it. The only thing that can be said about it for sure is that it is getting bigger every day.

INTO IRAQ

Even before the first soldier headed for Iraq, the U.S. military was heavily dependent on the private sector. By some estimates, a little over half the Pentagon's budget goes to pay private contractors. In the five years running up to the war, the Pentagon let over 2 million contracts. Iraq, however, has seen contracting on steroids.

The expansive use of contractors in Iraq is without modern precedent. Through 2006, KBR was, without question, the largest private company operating in Iraq, thanks to its LOGCAP contract. But, it had lots of company. KBR had over 200 subcontractors. In addition, there are at least a dozen other major contractors in the country, with innumerable subcontractors. Contractor operations also extended beyond the border of Iraq, with supporting activities in Kuwait, Jordan, and other countries in the region. Much of the logistical base for operations in Iraq is in Kuwait. Training Iraqi police forces takes place in Jordan. Dubai is the major transshipment port for supplies shipped to Iraq.

The Defense Department let the vast majority of its contracts for operations in Iraq. The State Department, the U.S. Agency for International Development (USAID), and other federal agencies, however, also employ private sector assets. There is no precise count of the ranks of contractors toiling away for Uncle Sam. Part of the reason for that is that no uniform reporting procedure exists. In addition, the number is extremely dynamic—workers enter and leave the country, are hired and fired, and finish, abandon, and start jobs all the time.

One thing known for sure is that most of the contractors in combat are not Americans—less than 20 percent are.[30] According to one count in 2005, KBR had about 50,000 logistics contractors (including everything from cooks to carpenters), most of them third-party nationals (employees not from Iraq, the host country, or from any of the coalition powers, such as Britain or Australia), many of them Filipino. Between 40,000 and 70,000 contractors support various reconstruction activities, hailing from a dozen or more countries, and upwards of 150,000 Iraqis are employed by numerous companies and Iraq government entities; another 15,000 Iraqis act as security guards in oil fields.[31]

Contractors are targets as well as combat assets. Estimates of contractor casualties vary. According to one investigative report (derived largely from information provided by the Department of Labor), by 2007, in Iraq over 900 contractors died and some 12,000 were wounded.[32] About 240 of the total killed were security providers, such as the individuals murdered in the ambush at Fallujah. Most contractor deaths were related to convoy-activities. In 2007 the rate of contractor causalities paralleled fairly closely those military killed and wounded. On the one hand, that statistic appears rather alarming. On the other, because military forces are much more heavily armed and protected than most contractors, and because both are equally the targets of insurgents and terrorists, contractor losses do not seem out of proportion at all. In addition, considering the extraordinary level of violence in Iraq since 2005 compared to previous intense conflicts, the proportion of loss and injury due to enemy action is fairly modest.

What has garnered the most attention and the most gleeful reporting has been the employment of companies providing contract security services. A 2004 Congressional Research Service report identified about a dozen private security companies doing business in Iraq.[33] A report by the British American Security Information Council produced that same year listed over sixty.[34] In 2007, there were about 20,000 armed contract security employees in the country, a fraction of the total contractor force and about another 10,000 company employees. The cost of these services is estimated at under $2 billion per year, again a small percentage of the total spent on contractor support.

The Defense and State Departments are the primary consumers of contract security services. In addition, USAID hires its own security. The Pentagon does not provide comprehensive public information on its security contracts in Iraq. Still, open sources suggest that defense contracts account for about 80 percent of the armed contractors in Iraq. The State Department employs three prime security contractors—Blackwater, DynCorp, and Triple Canopy. These companies operate under the Worldwide Personal Protective Services umbrella contract. The services they perform include acting as bodyguards, safeguarding convoys, and providing static guards at buildings and other sites. They protect government employees, visiting dignitaries, and Iraqi officials. The total number of State Department contractors is under 1,500.[35] Although the State Department contractors represent the smallest portion of the workforce, they have been involved in many of the most controversial incidents. Indeed, much of the concern about contractor involvement in "deadly force" incidents, where contractors were either victims or alleged to have committed improper acts, concern an extremely tiny fraction of the employees serving under federal contracts in the country.

CONTRACTING COMBATANTS

Understanding the current state of contractor support does not tell the whole story. It is easy enough to explain why contractors are on the battlefield. It is *not* the result of party politics, of privileging parts of the private sector, or of Eisenhower's feared military–industrial complex. Contractors are in combat because they are an integral part of modern military power. Their presence is justified under law and proven to be effective in contingency operations from Desert Storm to Kosovo to Kabul. What is not clear is why, after over a decade of practice in the post–Cold War world and multiple years on the battlefront in Iraq and Afghanistan, problems persist. The answer to that question requires understanding how contracts are conceived, competed, and controlled in combat.

3
Chapter   How It Works

We live in a contract nation.

In a way, it is remarkable that Americans could get so worked up over military contracting. Few peoples in the world are more complacent about the central role contracts play in their lives. Americans believe (drawing on their Anglo-Saxon ideological heritage) that even government itself is a matter of contract. John Locke (a near contemporary of Charles II, the king who lost his head over the whole debate) remains the thinker who most influenced U.S. political ideas. Locke argued that the sovereignty of the state resides in the people. In his *Two Treatises of Government* (1689), he posited that although the citizenry always retains the right to govern itself, it contracts with the government, granting rulers the authority to provide for the protection and good order of the state in accordance with the rule of law.

Contracts created America. One of the primary justifications cited for the American Revolution was that George III, the king of Great Britain, had violated his contract with the colonies to reign justly. This position is well laid out in the American *Declaration of Independence* (1776), which provides a detailed list of the crown's violations of the contract (including, interestingly enough, "transporting large Armies of foreign Mercenaries to compleat the works of death, desolation, and tyranny, already begun with circumstances of Cruelty & Perfidy scarcely paralleled in the most barbarous ages, and totally unworthy the Head of a civilized nation"). Because the crown had abrogated the contract, the American people no longer owed any allegiance to the crown. Apparently, even sacred contracts were made to be broken.

Americans place great confidence in the value of contracts as a means to ensure that people do what they are paid to do. Contracting is so ubiquitous that we rarely reflect on how much confidence we put in the process. It was no coincidence that when Congressman Newt Gingrich galvanized the Republican conservative movement during the 1994 Congressional elections, he did it by proposing a "Contract with America." Gingrich understood that Americans have an instinctual trust in the promise of a contract.

Although Americans love contracts, they are not naïve. We know that contracts are not always worth the paper they are written on. Trouble happens. Americans are pragmatic. A signing ceremony does not mean that problems will not present themselves—troubles that range from simple misunderstandings to fraud, waste, and abuse. Contractual disputes are accepted as a matter of course—because we have faith that there is a system for resolving disputed contracts. America is perhaps the world's most litigious nation. Americans spend about 4 percent of their GDP—approximately what they spend on defense—on suing one another. When trouble happens, the rule of law serves as society's failsafe.

Contracts and the rule of law are nothing less than a cornerstone of American freedom. They allow us to make choices while being protected from malicious consequences. They are also part of what we depend on to keep us safe from the two threats Eisenhower warned us about—big business and big government. That said, it is remarkable how quickly charges are made that contracting in combat inevitably puts national security, sovereignty, and civil society at risk. Complaining about the concept of contracting is certainly understandable. It emanates from beliefs as deeply rooted as America's love affair with litigation—a national distrust of power and money. Sometimes the long shadow of the trinity—the legacies of Machiavelli, Adam Smith, and the military–industrial complex—get the better of us, feeding our fears and undermining our confidence in one of the fundamental principles of a free society.

A more sober (and, frankly, more all-American) approach would shift the debate away from a Manichean choice over whether the private sector in public wars is inherently good or evil. That debate has been over for centuries. Contracting is an integral part of a free society. A more useful and practical discussion would focus on the efficiency and effectiveness of government contracting. Starting a different discourse begins with understanding how Washington undertakes contracts—as well as why, all too often, it gets them wrong.

CONTRACTS 101

To say that "contracting is nothing new" could be the ultimate understatement. The American concept of contracting and contract law evolved from twelfth-century English common law. An over 800-year-old tradition of passing money and suing people lies behind what the U.S. government does today in order to buy goods and services in the public marketplace.[1]

A contract is a legally enforceable agreement. The agreement defines the conditions for an exchange of goods or services between two or more parties. In fundamental ways government contracting differs little from commercial contracting. It is the vehicle through which the government details the tasks that it wants a contractor to accomplish and specifies what will be provided to the contractor in return.[2] Once the pact is sealed, it is subject to review by law and is enforceable by civil or criminal penalties.

Contractors are persons or businesses who provide products or services for monetary compensation. A contractor furnishes supplies or services, or performs work, for a certain rate of pay based on the terms of a contract.

Contractors include subcontractors. A subcontractor is a contractor who signs an agreement to fulfill part or all of the obligations of another contractor's contract. The contract employees killed during the incident in Fallujah, for example, were not working for the U.S. military. Rather, they were guarding supplies as part of a subcontract to another subcontractor who was supporting the contractor who was supporting the Army's LOGCAP contract. The authority to subcontract government work, and the limitations and requirements for subcontracting, are often also spelled out in the contract. The government, however, has a contractual relationship with only the "prime." It is the responsibility of the prime contractor to manage the subcontractors.

Although the principles of government contracting are similar to practices in the commercial sector, they look nothing like the process of signing a car loan or obtaining a new credit card. Corporate lawyers, on the other hand, would find government contracting procedures vaguely familiar, though at times convoluted, capricious, complicated, and conspicuously absent of clarity. The explanation for all this is simple: to a degree unmatched in the private sector, government contracting is layered with congressional mandates, White House policies, and departmental regulatory requirements.

Calling government contracting "highly regulated" is far too kind. The many congressional, executive, and judicial strictures are intended to make the process fairer and more transparent, and to ensure that the government gets the best quality of service at the lowest price. Whether they always accomplish those noble objectives, however, is often fiercely argued.

The mother of all guidelines for government contracting is the Federal Acquisition Regulation—the FAR. The impetus for standardizing and simplifying government acquisition came from President Ronald Reagan, who followed through on an election-year pledge to eliminate 2 percent of the federal budget by cutting fraud, waste, and abuse in federal spending. What he wanted was a process that was simpler and that saved taxpayers money.[3] The FAR was one of the first steps he took. By implementing FAR and by encouraging a Republican-controlled Congress to enact further legislation, Reagan did far more to institute policies to keep the private sector in its place than has any other modern president. Many of the tools available today to control contractors in Iraq and Afghanistan trace their lineage to the Reagan era.

Created in 1984 to make government contracting policies uniform, the FAR instructs virtually every acquisition by every federal agency, governing every step of the process. The regulation is supposed to make procedures consistent across the federal bureaucracy, but after years in practice, it no longer works this way. Every department has added its own supplementary implementing guidelines. The Pentagon, for example, issues the Department of Defense Federal Acquisition

Regulation Supplement (DFARS). Although agency directives such as DFARS cannot conflict with FAR, they can create enough additions and changes to make the contracting process so different that it is almost unrecognizable between agencies.

Despite the many distinctions in contracting from department to department, to comply with FAR all must include dozens of "standard terms and conditions" dictated by the regulation—many of them nonnegotiable. Mandatory conditions include such requirements as ensuring a "drug-free" environment in the workplace and maintaining compliance with federal equal opportunity guidelines. These types of requirements rarely appear in commercial contracts. It is not unusual for the page counts of some government contracts to run into the hundreds.

Mandatory federal conditions also include imposing standards of ethical conduct on contractors. Contractors are barred from making false claims or statements to the government (such as overbilling or charging for services not provided), are required to establish procedures preventing conflicts of interest in dealings with federal employers, are prohibited from offering or accepting "kickbacks," and are prevented from using appropriated government money for lobbying.

Other commonalities exist in government contracting as well. Only federal contracting officers have the authority to enter into, administer, or terminate federal contracts. The specific scope of a federal contracting officer is described in a written permission to perform contracting duties, called a "warrant." Unlike in some commercial practices, in Washington, there can be no debate over who has authority to manage or amend a contract.

Procedures for competing government contracts also have many common features. Unlike the private sector, which has no universal standard for determining how or to whom a contract is awarded, federal agencies have to follow very specific rules. An agency desiring to let a contract has to issue a Request for Proposal—an RFP. The RFP represents an invitation to companies to bid for submitting a proposal to provide goods or services to the government that are specified in the RFP. RFPs are issued even if there is no competition and the contract is "sole-source." The proposals offered in response to RFP are intended to be the basis on which the government selects a contractor. Often, in addition to providing a proposed price for the contract, companies are asked for information that elaborates upon their suitability to fulfill the contract, including financial status and data on technical capabilities. FAR also establishes rules on how to evaluate competing proposals and how to award contracts.

TO OUTSOURCE OR NOT?

Washington also issues guidance about when it is appropriate to contract for services from the private sector. Some guidelines are found in the FAR, but it is mainly the "A-76" process that drives the decision. A Circular A-76 is issued by the Office of Management and Budget (OMB), the part of the executive office of the White House responsible for the administration's procurement, financial management, and regulatory policies. An OMB Circular A-76 describes how to decide what missions are inherently governmental and what tasks might be better performed by commercial enterprises.

The notion of establishing a process to encourage federal agencies to obtain commercial services from the private sector (the Commercial Activities or CA Program) was, not surprisingly, started in a Republican administration—under Dwight Eisenhower in 1955. That's right: the president who warned direly about collusion between government and business established the means by which to turn over the government's business to business. It was in 1966, however, under Democratic president Lyndon Johnson, that OMB issued its first circular. The A-76, which has been revised and updated on numerous occasions, has been employed by every administration since.

The A-76 process inaugurates a competition to determine whether the government or a contractor can provide better services. Some governmental activities and functions are defined by statutory restrictions that prohibit outsourcing. Contracting officers, for example, must be government officials. In other cases, the determination process is overseen by a Competitive Sourcing Official appointed for each agency. The process begins when an agency or component of the agency nominates a function to be potentially outsourced. Before anything is turned over to the private sector, however, a "public–private" competition has to be conducted.

A sourcing competition contains several mandatory steps and begins with the process of defining what is being competed for. The government must issue a Performance Work Statement (PWS) that describes the kind of work to be performed and the standards for its performance (for example, how many computer repairs a company might be required to perform, and how long repairs should take once they are requested). The competition involves comparing private companies' proposals to fulfill the PWS against what it would cost to have a government workforce perform the task—the "in-house" cost estimate (in Washington parlance this is called the search for the most efficient organization, or MEO). The private sector usually wins the competition if its commercial services are at least $10 million, or 10 percent, cheaper than the government's. When the results of an A-76 study suggest it is more advantageous for the government to buy services, the government lets a contract.

From its inception, the A-76 process has been controversial. Government workers complain that their jobs are being outsourced unfairly. The private sector counters that the government officials judging the A-76 competition are prejudiced in favor of the government workforce. These complaints are legion, and the debate over A-76 activities endures. Unions representing government workers do not like the process at all. Members of Congress periodically try to influence the outcome of A-76 studies—sometimes in favor of government workers and other times in favor of constituents.

Whether Washington actually saves money by competitive sourcing is also a subject of some debate. A dizzying array of issues affect the calculation of the costs and benefits of outsourcing or forcing government agencies to become more efficient (in order to keep from losing contracts to the private sector). Because commercial firms have to demonstrate the potential for significant savings in order to wrest work from the government, they may offer unrealistically low cost estimates. The long-term costs of buying services may prove significantly higher than the original estimate. Thus, cost comparisons based on a proposal might make an offer seem like a really good deal when it is less so in practice. In order to retain work, government agencies may pare back their workforces, promising to do more for less. This is often possible, because the A-76 may not necessarily force an agency to explain how it plans to meet the same performance level as a private company. The reasonability of bids can sometimes not be fully assessed. Sometimes, the government may save money on paper but find that it ultimately gets less for its money.

The results of decades of serious defense outsourcing are suggestive. In 1999 the Defense Department calculated that a sample of 286 studies done under A-76 in one year saved taxpayers $290 million. The General Accounting Office, however, concluded that it was "difficult to estimate savings as precisely as suggested by the Department's report."[4] In contrast, a RAND report in 2000, based on a survey of seven years of defense outsourcing efforts, found that bidders accurately projected personnel cost savings and achieved them over time. Likewise, a study by the Center for Naval Analyses (CNA) that looked at an even longer period (1978–1994) estimated annual savings at $1.5 billion.[5] In general, analysis suggests that overall the government is paying less for services than it might have if large-scale outsourcing via competitions had not taken place. However, it is not clear that the government saves money in every instance or that the value of what it receives always reflects the value of what it spends.

Perhaps the most difficult factor to measure involves the intangible costs and benefits of outsourcing. On one hand, when the government outsources an activity, it merely receives services or goods for a fee; the human capital developed during the course of the contract belongs to the company. Thus, if the Army hires a contractor to write a manual, the knowledge and skills accumulated during that project disappear when the work is completed. If a military officer had been tasked to do the work, that expertise would have remained available to the government throughout that officer's career, an asset that could undoubtedly benefit the government in myriad ways. On the other hand, the ability to contract commercial practices gives the government the flexibility to buy the latest skills and technologies from the private sector without having to invest in the costs of their development. Evaluating the way that these limitations and advantages affect the long-term capabilities of government is difficult to determine. Deciding the right course of action can be more art than science. How right a decision really is can only be discovered with time.

OUTSOURCING ON STEROIDS

Today, few government institutions place more emphasis on competitive sourcing than the Pentagon. Although interest in outsourcing has been around since the 1950s, there was significantly less emphasis on A-76 from the Reagan years in the mid-1980s to the Clinton years of the mid-1990s. Ironically,

Reagan, the great champion of the private sector, invested far more effort in making sure the private sector did not rip off Washington than he did in giving commercial companies government duties. In contrast, Clinton, scrambling to find means to save money and balance the federal budget, anxiously advocated the use of better, faster, cheaper commercial services to fulfill government functions. If contemporary critics are unhappy with the current state of military contracting, they should turn their attention to the Clinton presidency. It was during Clinton's years in the White House that the foundations for today's outsourcing practices and policies were laid.

In 1995, as part of a concerted campaign to reduce federal expenditures— and defense spending in particular—the administration turned to Congress. The Federal Activities Inventories Reform (FAIR) Act jump-started Washington's renewed intent to outsource. FAIR required agencies to inventory their workforce and list which activities were inherently commercial, and hence subject to public–private competition, and which were governmental, and therefore exempt from competition. The intent of the law was to offer greater transparency regarding the range of government business that could be undertaken by private businesses. When the White House went from the Democrats to the Republicans, the outsourcing effort hardly seemed to notice the change. In 2002, the inventories found that commercial positions already accounted for 26 percent of the workforce—and that there was room for more.[6]

No federal entities moved to implement FAIR more aggressively than did the military. The Department of Education had the highest percentage of commercial positions (62 percent), but in absolute numbers no one topped the Pentagon.[7] The scope of the Pentagon's effort to buy commercial services is daunting. The Army staff alone invested a small army of 100 to 150, including platoons of lawyers, in order to identify new outsourcing opportunities. The Department of Defense plans by September 2009 to submit at least half of its nearly 453,000 commercial positions for competitive sourcing under the A-76 process.[8]

The DoD's enthusiasm for A-76 continued even after 9/11 and the jumps in military spending that followed it. By law, during times of war and military mobilization, the Pentagon has the authority to suspend outsourcing, but as a matter of policy, the Pentagon elected not to do so. Instead, the Department of Defense directed that the armed forces press on in their efforts to outsource. Services wishing to cancel an A-76 study because of war demands are required to provide analysis justifying their actions and submit it for departmental approval.[9]

ABANDONED WARRIORS

No case intensified the debate over A-76 more than did a scandal over the care of soldiers, injured in Iraq and Afghanistan, at the Army's Walter Reed Medical Center in Washington, D.C. The troubles at Walter Reed demonstrated the dangers of a system out of control. In February 2007, *The Washington Post* unleashed a blitzkrieg of articles levying withering indictments of alleged patient neglect. The facts they assembled were troubling: seriously injured soldiers are evaluated by a physical evaluation board that judges whether they should remain in the Army. Until that decision is made, wounded soldiers are in limbo. The Defense Department says the process should take no more than 120 days, but at Walter Reed the average was 270. Some of the patients waiting for board review were warehoused in the now infamous "Building 18," occupying moldy, bug-infested rooms with leaky plumbing. The Army disputed the scope and severity of the problems at the medical center, but something was clearly amiss. The dominos fell quickly—one general was discharged, and another was forced to resign. The Secretary of the Army quit. A slew of government and congressional investigations and hearings followed.

Many described the conditions at Walter Reed as a "perfect storm," the confluence of (1) an unanticipated explosion of patients from casualties in Iraq and Afghanistan, (2) a BRAC decision to phase out Walter Reed that diminished the money available for upkeep, maintenance, and staff at medical facilities planned to be shut down, (3) military underfunding (even after the budget increases intended to pay for the war), and (4) pressure to outsource activities to the lowest bidder under A-76.

Of the four winds pushing the management policies of the medical center, A-76 was the one most under the Pentagon's control—but that was not saying much. The competitive sourcing process at Walter Reed had been long and contentious, filled with official protests, challenges, petitions, and congressional intervention that dragged on from 2000 through 9/11 and the invasions of Afghanistan and Iraq all the way into 2006. During that period, problems piled up: maintenance was deferred, skilled personnel left, and the costs of outsourcing climbed. The history of A-76 had seen no greater failure.[10]

Had the wars in Iraq and Afghanistan not proved so deadly and protracted, the budgets not been so small, the Walter Reed A-76 process not been so prolonged and problematic, or the Pentagon not refused to cancel the A-76 at the war's beginning, all the troubles at the medical center might have been manageable. But none of these things happened. Each course of action followed its own track until they culminated in a train wreck. Yet it is wrong to blame outsourcing, per se, for the outcome. Rather, the failure of government to effectively manage its own processes proved its undoing.

COUNTING CONTRACTS

The tragedy of Walter Reed makes it clear that much of the success of contracting rests on the capacity of government to make smart choices. But there are so many steps in federal contracting that Washington has more than enough opportunities to get it wrong.

One action that affects how much value the government gets for what it spends is picking the right kind of contract. The federal government awards sixteen kinds of contracts. The FAR lists eleven criteria (ranging from urgency of need to complexity of requirements) for determining which type of contract is most advantageous to the government.

By far the most prevalent type of agreement is a form of the fixed-price contract. A "firm" fixed-price contract, for example, means that the government simply gets what it pays for regardless of the costs incurred by the contractor. Other forms of fixed contracts allow for limited adjustments, such as price shifts based on costs of labor or materials. Because contractors receive set fees in these kinds of contracts, they have every incentive to keep costs down; the lower the costs, the higher their profits. In 2005, the federal government issued well over 1.5 million fixed contracts, valued at well over $180 billion. That number represented just under half of all the federal dollars spent on contracting.[11]

Fixed contracts appear to offer a clear manner for determining whether the government is getting a fair deal. It is a wonder that the government does not always use these kinds of instruments; even the FAR directs that the firm, fixed-price contract should usually be the contract of choice.

Fixed contracts work well when the prices of goods and services are clearly established by the marketplace and when competition and market experience offer fairly clear guides as to what reasonable expenses and profits should be. When the military lets a contract, say, to hire custodial staff at Fort Benning, Georgia, it can base its requirements on the going rates paid by commercial firms purchasing similar services.

But when conditions on the ground are less predictable, fixed-price contracting is more problematic. Contingency operations offer a clear example. Contractors may have little idea what the full costs of fulfilling the contract might be, in time and resources. Not knowing their costs, it is difficult for them to predict the profits they might be able to gain. Companies may be leery of competing for work that offers no clear chance of generating profit. When neither the government nor bidding companies can look to the marketplace for insight into what to reasonably expect in terms of operating costs and profit margins, they are forced to turn to alternative methods of pricing.

Other types of agreements are various versions of a "cost-plus" contract. In cost-plus contracting, companies can pass on operating expenses to the government. If costs grow, contractors' profits are unaffected. This arrangement might make companies more willing to undertake risky contracts where costs might spiral out of control. On the other hand, companies also have less incentive to keep operating expenses down. To counteract this problem, some contracts include "award fees" that reward companies for excellent performance. Thus, companies that save the government money instead of running up costs can generate additional profit. The trick is to get an effective awards process in place early that satisfies both the government and the contractor—something not always easy to achieve, particularly in war zones.

Managing cost-plus contracts in places like Iraq is no easy task. One Government Accountability Office report concluded that these agreements

> have developed into a useful tool for the military services to quickly
> obtain needed support for the troops deployed to troubled spots around

the world. Because of the nature of these contracts, however—that is, cost-plus, award fee contracts—[the contracts] require significant government oversight to make sure they are meeting the needs in the most economic and efficient way possible in each circumstance. While the military services are learning how to use these contracts well, in many cases they are still not achieving the most cost-effective performance and not adequately learning and applying the lessons of previous deployments.[12]

At best, the Congress's auditing watchdog found mixed results in the Pentagon's handling of contracts that amounted to anything more than a simple exchange of fee for service or commodities.

The state of the government's ability to manage cost-plus contracting is no trivial matter. Washington writes a lot of cost-plus contracts—their number more than doubled in the five years after 9/11 to $110 billion. They are used extensively in Iraq. The single largest cost-plus contract is LOGCAP. In 2005, it was worth over $5 billion to KBR, but that hardly meant that KBR made outrageous profits. On average, the company's profits for LOGCAP in Iraq were lower than those for the LOGCAP contracts it fulfilled in Bosnia. Nor was the KBR deal unprecedented. In 2005, the Defense Department handed out three cost-plus contracts for managed health care that totaled almost $6 billion.[13] Interestingly, although the KBR LOGCAP contract garnered many headlines and sparked salacious stories, the health-care contracts attracted scant attention from the national media.

COMPETITION 101

Another major factor influencing the effectiveness of contracting is the scope of the competition and negotiation with potential bidders. The FAR and the Competition in Contracting Act of 1984 (another Reagan-era initiative to ensure that taxpayers got good value for their dollars) require "full and open competition" for government contracts. There are, however, certain allowable exceptions to this rule. The FAR indicates seven circumstances in which the Defense Department may to certain degrees waive the requirement for full and open competition. If the Secretary of Defense finds that a process of open solicitations and bids might compromise national security, or if a national emergency exists, other alternatives can be used.[14] In some cases, the government can simply let sole-source contracts, which are not subject to competition at all.

The war on terror has created a hurricane of sole-source contracting. In the year before 9/11, according to one congressional report, the federal government issued $67.5 billion in sole-source contracts, but in 2005 the figure more than doubled to $145 billion. Sole-source and limited-competition contracts are used extensively in Iraq. Many reconstruction projects let in 2003, for example, were limited to a handful of companies bidding for cost-plus contracts worth billions.[15]

On the other hand, sole-source contracting is far less common than is commonly assumed. By and large, private security companies do not operate under sole-source contracts. Blackwater, one of the major security companies operating in Iraq (and certainly the most controversial) received only one such contract early during contingency operations, which was later replaced by a contract won in competitive bidding. In 2007, all Blackwater's Iraq contracts were won in open competition.

Although contracting security is not primarily a sole-source activity, other private-sector support activities *are* typically awarded in contracts with little or no competition. The suitability of these contracts remains a subject of concern. When the Government Accountability Office examined the issue of sole-source or limited-competition contracting in Iraq during 2003, it found a mixed bag of results. David Walker, the Comptroller General of the United States, reported that agencies, including the Defense and State Departments, "generally complied with applicable laws and regulations." But his investigators also found that contracting officers had included tasks and orders not within the scope of the contracts. In other words, they had added work for goods and services that either should have been obtained through a competitive bidding process or should have been separately justified as a sole-source or limited-competition contract.[16] Walker concluded that even though the military might have obtained what it needed when it needed it at a reasonable price, the issuance of these contracts could have been better managed.

CATCH-22

Even though dozens of laws and thousands of pages of federal regulations govern government contracting, Americans are quick to be suspicious of how Washington spends their money. This distrust of big government is thought to be primarily a preoccupation of the conservative right; no American leader captured the concern of conservatives better than Ronald Reagan, who famously said that "a government big enough to give you everything you want is also a government big enough to take everything you've got." Mistrust of government, however, is also a passion of the left. It should be no surprise that liberal voices are the first to shout in chorus about the "military–industrial complex." There is a reason that both sides of American politics claim they are really "Washington outsiders," come to town only to tame Washington's ways. They share a common culture: distrusting government is neither an exclusively conservative nor uniquely liberal impulse—it is simply American.

In part, Americans are cautious of government because of the contractual nature of republican governance. In a contractual relationship, it is incumbent on both sides to look after their independent interest and not to simply place their trust in the other party to hold up its end of the bargain. The adage "buyer beware" is as all-American as it gets. Certainly, of course, some generations express their uneasiness over whether Washington is fulfilling its part of the deal more deeply than do others. Eisenhower, who coined the phrase "military–industrial complex," came from a generation that embraced big government and big business. It was the age that William H. Whyte described in the title of his best-selling book as that of the *Organizational Man* (1956), a time when men spent their entire lives working for two employers—the U.S. government (largely as draftees into World War II) and a company such as General Motors or General Electric. That age came crashing down in the 1960s in the turmoil of the Vietnam War. It is no surprise that many of today's skeptics, dubious of government contracting, came of age in that era.

No author anticipated that America's postwar romance with big government was coming to end better than Joseph Heller. Heller, himself a World War II veteran who served as a bombardier in combat missions over Europe, wrote a bestselling novel that anticipated the angst of the 1960s generation—a novel that has a great deal to say about its waning trust in government to do the right thing. The book was called *Catch-22* (1961).

In *Catch-22*, the novel's anti-hero, Captain Yossarian, desperately wants to get out of combat duty but finds that military rules preclude that. As another character in the novel explains,

> There was only one catch and that was Catch-22, which specified that a concern for one's safety in the face of dangers that were real and immediate was the process of a rational mind. Orr [a hard-luck pilot in the squadron who was frequently shot down during combat missions] was crazy and could be grounded. All he had to do was ask; and as soon as he did, he would no longer be crazy and would have to fly more missions. Orr would be crazy to fly more missions and sane if he didn't, but if he was sane he had to fly them. If he flew them he was crazy and didn't have to; but if he didn't want to he was sane and had to. Yossarian was moved very deeply by the absolute simplicity of this clause of Catch-22 and let out a respectful whistle.
> "That's some catch, that Catch-22."

Americans found something authentic in the absurdity of Catch-22, which warned that the rules were not always in their interests. The book is still in print.

Hollywood embraced *Catch-22* as well. Its film version appeared in 1970 at the height of disillusion over the Vietnam War. Mike Nichols directed the movie, and Buck Henry wrote the screenplay; the movie featured a stellar cast led by Alan Arkin as Yossarian. Although the film retained its World War II motif, it was clearly an antiwar movie intended to evoke concerns about Vietnam. *Catch-22* was released to mixed reviews and a modest box-office take. It was as if by the time the movie was made Americans no longer needed anyone to convince them that government and the rules it wrote could not be trusted.

CONTRACTORS GONE WILD

Americans may have inherited a popular culture that encourages them to believe that the rules are part of the problem, but that does not necessarily mean that that concern is always justified. Contracting in combat is often a case in point.

It is clear that the routine practices of contracting were greatly stressed to meet the demands of the war on terror. It is not clear, however, that contracting the private sector to fight public wars is the root of the problem. Merely focusing on the scope and scale of sole-source and cost-plus contracts (as many critics of the Bush administration and the war in Iraq have done) suggests that Washington jettisoned traditional acquisition methods to dump as much cash as possible into the hands of a few privileged companies. This explanation makes for a compelling recasting of Eisenhower's military–industrial complex, but it is wrong. Operations in Iraq and Afghanistan are not a case of "contractors gone wild." What is ignored in narrow indictments that focus on the rapid growth of contracting in combat are the politics in Washington and the events on the battlefield that contributed to the rapid escalation of contract costs.

From the day Saddam's statue came crashing down, overwhelming pressure was put on the Pentagon to push for success as rapidly as possible. Many of the same critics who had castigated the administration for issuing sole-source contracts (employed as a shortcut in the contracting process) lambasted the administration for being too slow in spending billions of dollars on Iraqi reconstruction.

Sole-source and limited-competition contracting represented a legitimate effort to speed support to the field—not an end run around regulations. The FAR specifically provides for agreements to limit competition under certain circumstances. These contracting methods have been readily used by Democrat and Republican administrations and funded by Democrat- and Republican-controlled Congresses since the FAR was established. Indeed, these kinds of contracts were specifically intended for use in unforeseen contingencies such as the situations in Iraq and Afghanistan.

Nor is it apparent that the Bush administration is addicted to sole-source contracting. In 2006, the Pentagon reopened the competition for LOGCAP, awarding parts of the contracts to three firms: Fluor Intercontinental, DynCorp, and KBR. Two losing companies protested the decision, prompting further contraction negotiations.

Criticism of cost-plus contracting is equally incomprehensible. What has driven up the cost of cost-plus contracts in Iraq (faster by far than has any other factor) is the skyrocketing cost of implementing agreements—not of windfall profits for the private sector. The expense of providing security for operations has been particularly daunting. In 2004 spiraling violence (often targeted specifically against contractors and reconstruction efforts in order to frustrate U.S. efforts to rebuild Iraq's infrastructure, undermining stability) doubled the percentage of contracts that had to be let for security operations. Security averaged 20 percent of the whole price of any action.[17] The costs of some projects increased by a third or more. In one instance, USAID canceled two electrical power generation projects and diverted its $15 million of construction funds to pay for security for other projects. In turn, many contractors resorted to hiring private security to safeguard their employees, convoys, and work sites. In 2004 alone, according to the Government Accountability Office, agencies and companies operating in Iraq committed $766 million to buying security.[18] The costs of contracts rose dramatically in Iraq because the costs of war went up—not because the profit margins of contractors did.

What is remarkable is that goods and services continued to flow to the troops at all, given the escalating violence and uncertainty in the country through the summer of 2007. In fact, part of the military's success in getting its job done can be attributed to the use of cost-plus agreements. Cost-plus contracts allowed the government and its contractors to adjust to the situation on the ground.

At the outset of the occupation, few practical alternatives existed to the large-scale use of cost-plus contracting. It is not apparent how large firm, fixed-cost agreements would have served the government any better. As costs shot up, the government would likely have simply paid the same amount for less return. Companies might have been unwilling to provide services at all or would have demanded astronomical fees before accepting fixed-price agreements. Had services been performed by the military instead of by contractors, costs would have risen equally. As levels of security dropped, the military would have required more security as well, which would have required more troops and therefore driven up the cost of operations even more. Because it is generally accepted that, in many cases, contractor support costs less than using government resources, greater military involvement in operations in Afghanistan and Iraq would have likely been just as costly as hiring contractors—if not more so.

To escape the torrent of criticism over its contracting efforts in Iraq and Afghanistan the administration would have had to have acted blindingly fast and with devastating efficiency. There are many reasons why the U.S. government did not, but one of them is not the kinds of contracts Washington let—there were bigger problems.

MANAGING MAYHEM

A large part of due diligence in contracting is knowing when things are going wrong and understanding how to fix them. Competing and awarding contracts is only one small step in the process, albeit the part that gets the most press coverage and scrutiny. The real labor lies elsewhere. Negotiating, managing, and providing contract oversight is more often than not where the real battle for efficiency and effectiveness is won or lost.

In retrospect, it is easy to see that this is where the services lost most of their battles. The lack of foresight was truly shocking. On March 8, 2002—a year before the war in Iraq—the secretary of the Army, Thomas E. White, wrote to the undersecretary of defense in charge of acquisition to point out that a third of the service's budget went to pay contractors. Yet, with a much smaller military workforce, "Army planners and programmers lack visibility at the Departmental level into the labor and costs associated with the contract workforce and of the organizations and missions supported by them."[19] This, it seems, was clearly evident before the Pentagon went on its contracting binge.

Without any real capacity for overseeing how the public sector took the private sector to war, the Pentagon had to rely on the soldiers in the frontline trenches of the contracting campaign to manage the government's business—and those ranks were pretty thin.

CONTRACTOR COMMANDERS

The first line of defense in ensuring that government contracting serves the government well is formed of contracting officers. Contracting officers are part of the federal acquisition workforce, which is a large part of the problem. The number and size of government contracts has exploded, but the workforce to manage them has not. Like other components of the military, the defense acquisition workforce downsized with the end of the Cold War. From 1994 to 2005, the Defense Department acquisition workforce was cut in half. Of all the decisions made in the Pentagon, cutting the contractor force might have been the most problematic, because a smaller military might well have to rely in increasing measure on contract support. Too small an acquisition corps has proven to be as much a challenge for the military as has too few troops being available for combat duty.

In addition to being too small, the ranks of the contracting workforce face other challenges as well. Turnover is a problem. The Defense Department averages over an 11 percent turnover. Of all the services, the Army has the worst turbulence—14 percent. State Department turnover is 12 percent (all these numbers are higher than the federal workforce average of 9 percent). The ranks are aging, and increasingly large numbers are approaching retirement. In 2016 a whopping 65 percent of the Army workforce will be eligible to retire, the fourth highest level in the federal government. The DoD's average will be a little over 32 percent, and the State Department's rate will be 31 percent.[20]

Not only is the Army's acquisition army not much of an army, but it was also ill-prepared for the war in Iraq. According to the Government Accountability Office, U.S. Central Command (the military headquarters responsible for planning the invasion) did not even develop plans for LOGCAP until May 2003, two months after the toppling of Saddam's statue. Before the war, planning efforts overwhelmingly focused on—of all things—planning for the war. The Office of Reconstruction and Humanitarian Assistance (ORHA), a hastily assembled effort to manage nonwarfighting postconflict tasks, overwhelmingly focused on preventing a nationwide humanitarian crisis. Contractors were hardly consulted on what they might have to do in postwar Iraq.

All this was an inauspicious start for what would prove to be the largest contract effort of its kind in Army history. Units deployed by the military to support LOGCAP had no knowledge of how it worked. Likewise, many military commanders and staff officers had scant experience working with contractors or bringing them into planning efforts. The Defense Contract Monitoring Agency, which provides administrative and technical support for contracting officers, deployed too few staff too slowly. One agency representative was assigned twenty-seven locations to monitor—more than he could visit in a six-month tour.[21] The Army's contracting force was overwhelmed by the conditions in post-Saddam Iraq almost as quickly as the Army had overwhelmed Saddam.

It is difficult to argue anything but that, from the start, the federal agencies operating in Iraq lacked the capacity and expertise to manage all the goods and services they bought. When the Army sought to let a contract for restoring the Iraqi oil infrastructure, it paid KBR $1.9 million to help draft the agreement, after which KBR attempted to bid on the contract. The contracting officer wanted to exclude the company, arguing that it had an unfair advantage over the competition because it had written the contingency plan it was bidding on. After much dispute, KBR received a sole-source contract for the work. An inspector general later ruled that the pressing nature of the contingency made the award appropriate. Still, the situation should never have occurred to begin with, and would not have, had the military had an acquisition workforce with adequate capacity and technical expertise to manage its own affairs.[22]

Many of the mistakes made in employing LOGCAP on previous deployments were repeated—and on a larger scale. One of the most common was the tendency to use the LOGCAP contracts even when they were not the most cost-effective or appropriate means available. In some cases, government contractors were the force of choice because the military had done a poor job planning requirements for its own forces. Commanders simply found there to be no one else available to do the job. In other cases, contracting officers turned to contractors for convenience. Under the stress of deployments and pressing requirements, and with staff inadequate to undertake all the demands of conducting a full and open competition, it was often easier to use the contract at hand, even if it cost the government more. This problem was particularly acute during the early years of the occupation; it was not until near the end of 2003 that the Defense Department instructed Central Command to pay more attention to the economies of its contracting efforts.[23]

In many cases, the military wasted money by persisting in relying on cost-plus contracts even after the nature of the contingency was better understood. Money poured into renewed agreements could have been saved by restructuring Requests for Proposal (initial statements of work required of contractors), defining task orders more precisely in order to convert them into fixed-price contracts. But in the press to get things done, this failed to happen. It was not until years after the occupation had begun that a concerted effort was made to recompete contracts in a manner more advantageous to the government.[24]

Other agencies operating in Iraq did little better than the Pentagon. Little integrated planning was shared between the military command, the Coalition Provisional Authority, and USAID, all of whom issued their own contracts via their own contracting processes. In 2003, it was not unusual to see USAID overseeing a reconstruction project in an area where local commanders knew nothing about the agency's activities. USAID contract supervisors often feared to visit work sites in areas patrolled by the U.S. military out of safety concerns. The State Department had virtually no contracting role whatsoever in Iraq (other than hiring DynCorp to train Iraqi police) until 2004, when the Coalition Provisional Authority (CPA) was disestablished. At that point, when the State Department took over many of the CPA's duties, the workforce from Foggy Bottom was also thrust into the contracting morass. In addition, USAID and the State, Defense, Treasury, and Justice Departments, as well as the Department of Health and Human Services and the U.S. Corps of Engineers, also issued contracts for Iraqi reconstruction.

Each of the major agencies in-country suffered its own share of problems. It took USAID two years to build the contractor force it required. The military rushed to get numbers but as a result employed many who lacked adequate experience and who thus had to learn on the job. The State Department had more time to get ready for the challenges of contracting in combat but inherited a bewildering mass of tasks from the Coalition Provisional Authority, and afterward struggled to keep an experienced workforce in the field.[25]

To do the job right, the government needed contractors with skills and numbers beyond what it had available. Washington's contract army had much more to do than simply order goods and sign contracts. The Federal Acquisition Institute lists the plethora of competencies required, which include market analysis, strategic planning, workforce planning, contract management, negotiation, cost analysis, financial management, financial oversight, labor relation, and information technology management. All these talents were needed on the ground in Iraq and Afghanistan.

Had the U.S. government had the means to quickly tap into all of government workforce worldwide, it might have been able to deal with the crisis; but the Federal Acquisition Institute's 2007 survey of the acquisition workforce concluded that "contracting workforce technical competencies are generally appropriate for the positions held."[26] A big part of the problem, then, was simply finding the right people with the right skills—and getting them to the right places. No agency had a contingency plan for rapidly recruiting, preparing, deploying, and maintaining a large contract force in a combat zone. In Iraq and Afghanistan, contracting officers often found themselves underskilled and overworked.

ADJUDICATING AND OVERSEEING

But contracting officers are not alone in the campaign to control contractors in combat. Many elements of government are responsible for making the private sector serve the public good on the battlefield, and they look both to the interests of the government and to those of contractors.

Government and commercial contracts are similar in that both are legally binding instruments. The means of oversight and enforcement by Washington are unique. The Contracts Dispute Act (1978) and the FAR govern disputes between the government and its contractors. Contractors can, for example, avail themselves of procedures to protest the awarding of a contract if they believe the government has violated the rules of full and open competition.

Likewise, both government customers and their contractors have mechanisms by which to raise concerns when dissatisfied with how an agreement is implemented. Contractors and contracting officers are expected to informally resolve disagreements; but if that fails, contractors can issue claims against the government requiring contract officers to negotiate claim settlements or to issue written agency decisions. At that point, contractors can take the government to court—but unlike a business suing in a local civil court, contractors appear before an administrative law court, the Board of Contract Appeals. Further appeals are made to the U.S. Court of Federal Claims.

The federal government also audits federal contracts. By law, Washington has the authority to audit the costs incurred by contractors as well as their profits, progress, and performance during the period covered by the agreement and for up to three years after the conclusion of the contract. The government has many tools with which to take to task contractors that go wild. In Iraq, audits and investigations can be conducted by a contracting agency's Inspector General, by the Special Inspector General for Iraq (SIGIR), by the Army Audit Agency, by the Defense Contract Audit Agency, and by the Congressional Government Accountability Office. Senate and House committees have also launched their own investigations and hold uncounted hearings on government contracting during the war. All of these institutions have in fact been very busy. In the first four years after the invasion, the Government Accountability Office (formerly known as the General Accounting Office) alone issued sixty-eight reports and testimonies.

Of the many offices overseeing contracting in Iraq, SIGIR is among the most innovative. Inspectors General (IGs) are established by law and serve under the general supervision of an agency head. By statute, however, they are independent, though they report both to the agency head and to Congress. All federal departments have an IG, but none was in a good position to oversee efforts in Iraq. The project was too big in scope, and involved too many federal agencies, to be overseen by any single IG. In October 2004, Congress established the Special Inspector General for Iraq Reconstruction, or SIGIR (the successor to the Coalition Provisional Authority's office of Inspector General).

According to its October 2007 quarterly report to the Department of Defense and the Department of State, SIGIR, over the course of its operations, has overseen over $100 billion dollars in U.S. and international funds spent in the combat theater. The report describes the programs and initiatives funded and evaluates their effectiveness. As of 2007, the SIGIR reports were the product of 200 audits and investigations conducted by the Inspector General.

The government can also avail itself of a wide range of criminal investigation tools. Virtually all federal agencies have an internal law enforcement component; the defense services, for example, have criminal investigation divisions. The Department of Justice can also support efforts to uncover criminal activity on the part of contractors and government employees. Contractors failing to abide by ethical standards or other requirements in their contracts can face civil litigation or criminal prosecution, as can civilian employees of the U.S. government. Military personnel are subject to the Uniform Code of Military Justice and can in some cases also be tried in civilian courts.

Much as in the case of the other elements of contracting in combat, the principal difficulty in enforcing and auditing has been setting up the infrastructure needed to get the job done. Such federal agencies as the Defense and State Departments and USAID had a modicum of experience in monitoring operations in challenging environments that included Bosnia, Kosovo, Somalia, and Haiti, but nothing in those places had adequately prepared them for the tasks of the wars in Afghanistan and Iraq. At the outset of these wars, no comprehensive plan existed for overseeing an army of contractors.

All major efforts for overseeing contracting evolved ad hoc, and all struggled to find the resources for their operations before finding, deploying, and supporting qualified personnel. All were required to develop procedures for applying the rule of law on a chaotic and violent battlefield, and all had to develop ways to do their jobs without unduly impeding daily military missions to bring stability and security to Iraq. Every effort was largely begun from scratch. In many cases, the lessons of the new world disorder, learned earlier in Bosnia and elsewhere, had to be relearned.

JUSTICE FOR SOME

Plenty of evidence exists to suggest that although conditions in Iraq were disorganized and dangerous—particularly from 2004 to 2006—the presence of contractors did not make the country another Wild West.

Although many agencies have undertaken enforcement activities, SIGIR has the largest criminal fraud investigation effort ongoing in Iraq. On any given day, the Inspector General has 30 investigators, auditors, and inspectors on the ground in the country. By 2007, SIGIR had opened more than 300 cases, and 57 investigations were ongoing. Five individuals had been convicted and sentenced, and thirteen more were under arrest.[27] Accusations involved fraud, money laundering, and bribery, and individuals convicted included both civilians and U.S. military personnel. The Army barred fourteen contractors and companies from operating in Iraq, and by 2007 SIGIR had referred another twelve for debarment.

Not all the faultfinding in Iraq involves criminal offenses, however. Often inefficiency or slackness in performance is simply the result of lax oversight or poor quality control. In one case, Stuart Bowen, the head of SIGIR, reported that "auditors found a number of problems in KBR management of the provision of food, fuel, and shelter to the Embassy in the Green Zone [the secured U.S. compound in Baghdad]. As the problems were uncovered, management and KBR corrected them such that, by the time the audit was published on June 22 [2007], almost [all] of the problems were remediated."[28] By 2007, SIGIR reported that its audits had prevented over $70 million in waste.

INVESTIGATING INVESTIGATORS

Even the auditors and investigators in Iraq have not escaped attention. Getting adequate, trained investigators to the field is an enormous challenge. Finding all the information required to make an assessment can be problematic as well; and private contractors frequently complain that government investigators lack the expertise to oversee their operations, or that they come to the table with their own agendas.

SIGIR, which had enjoyed a reputation as an effective oversight agency, has also become the subject of serious controversy. In 2007, in response to lengthy anonymous complaints by former staff members, the FBI investigated numerous claims of wrongdoing. Whether the charges are legitimate or unfounded remains to be seen. Nevertheless, these allegations illustrate the challenge of providing effective oversight in the heat of battle. Even when done well, it is a contentious and controversial business.

What is remarkable, however, given the vast amount of money spent, the confusing and turbulent conditions in the country, and the weaknesses of the government's contracting workforce, is that the intense effort of SIGIR and other government investigators has only uncovered a modicum of criminal fraud. Compared to the abuses seen in past American wars, the challenges of Iraq do not seem out of proportion. Most of the problems documented by SIGIR and others amounted to cases of waste and abuse in which the government misused resources, failed to exercise responsible oversight, or poorly let contracts. In short, Washington could have done better. Figuring out how to do that is the real challenge of managing contractors in combat.

CUSTER'S LAST BATTLE

One of the most controversial and telling illustrations of the challenges of overseeing contractors in Iraq concerned Custer Battles, a private security company. It is hard to think of a more cautionary tale when attempting to understand the obstacles faced in enforcing the rule of law on the battlefield.

Scott Custer (a former soldier) and Mike Battles (a West Point graduate and former CIA employee) established Custer Battles one month after 9/11. Even before the war in Iraq, the company's business grew quickly, and its clients included NGOs and four different states (Maine, Nevada, New Hampshire, and Rhode Island). Four months after the war in Iraq began, Custer Battles competed for and won a contract (often erroneously reported in the press as a sole-source contract) from the Coalition Provisional Authority to guard the Baghdad International Airport (BIAP). The firm, fixed-price contract was in force for a year and paid $16.8 million. Custer Battles obtained other security contracts in the country at the same time.

The BIAP contract was not only lucrative but vital. Once the airport was reopened, it would be one of Iraq's lifelines to the rest of the world, something all too evident to Iraqi insurgents. For some time, the route from downtown Baghdad to the airport, or Route Irish, was one of the most dangerous drives in Iraq. It was nicknamed "IED Alley" after the improvised explosive devices, produced in covert bomb factories, that were hid or buried in the road or carried in vehicles. BIAP was in the heart of the battle for Baghdad.

Less than one year later, Custer Battles was at the center of a storm of controversy. The facts surrounding the deluge of legal disputes are still in dispute, but the case against Custer Battles explodes the myth that sole-source, cost-plus contracting is the root of all problems in Iraq. Although the company was awarded neither kind of contract, it still became the subject of extreme scrutiny.

In October 2004, a U.S. court unsealed a lawsuit by Robert Isakson and William Baldwin, two Custer Battles associates, that alleged massive overbilling on two separate contracts. Another case was brought against the company for its management of the airport security contract. In March 2006, a jury found against Custer Battles for thirty false claims, fining the company over $10 million, a verdict overturned in Federal District Court. In February 2007, the court also dismissed the airport security contract case, finding no evidence of fraud. Custer Battles filed countersuits against Isakson and Baldwin, claiming the two were "disgruntled employees" playing "litigation roulette" for personal profit. The civil trial was settled out of court.

The aborted case against Custer Battles was not the result of work by platoons of government contractors and auditors. The Department of Justice declined to join in either case. Rather, Isakson and Baldwin filed the claim against Custer Battles under the False Claims Act, a law passed in 1863 to help fight corruption during the Civil War. The act is intended to punish anyone who makes a "false claim" against the government in the act of fulfilling a government contract. In 1986, a Republican-controlled Congress (part of Reagan's effort to fight wasteful government spending), believing the federal government did not have enough resources to combat fraud, amended the act to make it easier to bring an action to court.

Under the law, individual citizens are permitted to sue contractors alleged to have defrauded the government. If the prosecution is successful, the parties bringing the suit are rewarded a portion of any fines levied by the verdict. If convicted of fraud, the defendant can be liable for up to three times the damages sustained by the government, as well as $5,000 to $10,000 in fines for each false claim made. From 1987 to 2005, the Justice Department received almost 8,869 cases, most involving either defense contractors or health-care fraud. [29] Since 1986, the government has recovered over $17 billion under the law.

Since the start of the war, dozens of false claims suits have been filed against contractors in Iraq. The Custer Battles case was the first to reach resolution and illustrates the limitations of the law as a useful instrument for managing contractors in combat. It is clear that the False Claims Act may have utility in fighting fraud in the United States, but it is hardly the best tool for managing contractors on the battlefield, where far more than money is at stake. Success or failure of contract operations can determine whether soldiers live or die. Oversight on the battlefield needs to be appropriate for conditions on the battlefield. The government, not individual citizens, should have the preponderance of responsibility for ensuring that work is done properly, and for determining whether its needs are being effectively met. Contracting, law enforcement, and auditing teams are needed, however, to do the job right.

BUYER BEWARE

Government contracting procedures are far from simple. The effort to make them fair, transparent, and cost-effective has created a web of requirements that has made contracting complicated and ill-suited to overcoming the fog of war and the friction of battle. But, to paraphrase Defense Secretary Donald Rumsfeld (who oversaw the invasions of Iraq and Afghanistan), "You go to war with the contract law you have—not the contract law you want." In the decade before 9/11, Washington did little to prepare for contracting in combat except to increase its dependence on contractors through initiatives like the A-76 process. What Washington did not do was build the workforce it needed to manage the contractor force it took into battle. Instead, it figured out on the job how to manage the parts of the private sector that it contracted for public wars.

4

Chapter

What It's Like

Contractors have no red badge of courage.

For Americans, war is a highly personal act. Americans interpret the experience of war in the first person. Personal battle narratives, real and imaginary, heavily influence the presence of armed conflict in the modern memory. Today, if asked to tell what the Civil War was like, the average adult would likely describe something akin to Stephen Crane's *The Red Badge of Courage* (1895). Although Crane was born after the war and never saw a battle in his life, his novel of how young Henry Fleming responds to the terror of combat became the universal Civil War experience read by American school children for generations.

For every generation, there is a literature that defines the nature of war. Even if people did not themselves read the books, they no doubt heard the songs or stories or saw plays, paintings, movies, comic books, magazines, advertising, fashion, comedy, drama, television (or now YouTube videos and computer games) that drew on the interpretations and inspiration birthed by those books. The defining literature of a generation has a great deal to say about the popular culture of the age. The distinction between American and British remembrances of the Great War offers a case in point.

Postwar British literature reflected the troubles of the First World War's veterans who came home from the front after years of sacrifice, death, and misery to find a crumbling empire abroad and disillusionment at home. British literature of the time featured the victim-hero, such as portrayed in Robert Graves's *Goodbye to All That* (1929). The British narrative told the story of the "lost generation" that spent years in battle, sacrificing everything to save nothing. Unlike the British Army, most Americans were at the front for less than a year and returned home to find the U.S. economy booming. Thus, American literature, with a few notable exceptions, recalled the war as a great adventure, the last hurrah of the young individualist—the story of brave, courageous and resourceful, natural-born soldiers. Many of the most popular books were personal war memoirs like *Woodfill of the Regulars: A True Story of Adventure from the Arctic to the Argonne* (1930). In the introduction, Lowell Thomas described the Medal of Honor recipient as an "American frontiersman, a real survivor of an earlier day, thrown into the infernal mechanism and modernistic terror of the greatest of all wars." America remembered Woodfill and all their doughboys for their pioneer spirit and all-American attitude.[1]

American war literature elevates the experience of the individual soldier to near mythic status. Because of this, Americans think of wars as being about great soldiers, like Woodfill, Sergeant Alvin York, or flying ace Eddie Rickenbacker in World War I, or great generals like George Patton, Douglas MacArthur, and Eisenhower in World War II, or about the loss of countless individuals like the thousands of names inscribed on the Vietnam War memorial in Washington.

Wars in modern American memory also tend to ignore that there is anyone else on the battlefield. In contrast to battle books about warriors, books documenting the trials of civilians in conflict are far less prevalent. It is not that no one writes about innocents in harm's way. They do. Some of these texts are canonical in American literature, like *Gone with the Wind* (1936). Such narratives rarely, however, appear in books about military history and, as a result, Americans rarely connect them with the story of combat.

And if the noncombatants are rarely memorable in America's war literature, the civilian combatant is hidden. No civilian's story is less well documented than the contractor in combat. Contractors (although they have been present in every American war) have been virtually invisible on the pages of history. Because of this, even though the conflicts in Iraq and Afghanistan have catapulted the place of the private sector combatants into front-page headlines and made them the subject of Senate hearings, Americans have only the vaguest notion of what life is like for contractors. They have even less idea of how civilian contractors affect the American way of war—or what that all means for the future of war.

Knowing who contractors are, what they do, and how they live in harm's way, occupying the same ground as soldiers wrapped in body armor, women shrouded in burqas, and diplomats clad in sweat-stained suits, is also a large part of understanding the private sector in public wars.

CURRICULUM VITAE

There has never been an age during which most combat contractors found employment by replying to post office box numbers from an advertisement in *Soldier of Fortune* magazine. Contract employees get their jobs pretty much like everyone else. They apply for them. Many subcontractors (who comprise the majority of contract employers in Iraq and Afghanistan) do their own recruiting, drawing from the citizens of their own country, the host country, and up to thirty other nations.

In the United States, most combat contractors find their jobs like most Americans—on the Web. On any given day, going to Monster.com, the world's largest Internet job search engine, and typing in the word "Iraq" generates hundreds of job offerings. IPOA has a Web site where for $40 a year, applicants can post their résumés, making them available to member companies. Jobs are also widely advertised on company Web sites. The KBR site lists work available in a dozen countries in almost 100 categories: everything from accounting to welding. Some companies also engage in their own recruiting efforts, usually well-publicized job fairs at downtown hotels and shopping malls, or during career days at colleges and universities.

Networking (having someone pass along a résumé or recommend an acquaintance, friend, colleague, or relative for a job) is something (as in many businesses) that happens as much in the combat contracting industry as in any other. "The best way to land a war-zone contracting job is to network," one study concluded, "to know a guy who knows a guy."[2] Most networking is pretty innocuous.

There are exceptions.

When Hamid Karzai emerged as the leader of the post-Taliban government in Iraq, one of the first contracts let was for his personal security detail. Craig Maxim, a retired Army veteran with plenty of connections in the special operations community (highly trained forces that conduct "special" missions such as combating terrorism and hostage rescue) proposed the idea of a private guard force for Karzai to the State Department. In turn, the department hired a team led by Maxim under an existing contract with DynCorp. Within three months Maxim had a 39-man Karzai protection detail on the ground in Kabul. Maxim and his crew quit a few months later in a dispute with DynCorp over "holiday pay."[3] Maxim soon found more work. He now holds a program manager position with a rival company—Triple Canopy. Maxim's team got the job not just because of what they knew, but who he knew (though they reportedly did their job very well). Such contracting arrangements were, however, the exception, not the rule. Cloak and dagger activities, such as those mounted in the early days of operations in Afghanistan, and such unconventional recruiting account for a small fraction of the contracting business.

Networking has actually proven more troubling in government employment than in contractor hiring practices. When the government needed to vastly expand its capacity to fill positions in the many agencies with staffs operating overseas, there was no bench to turn to (even if they could have deployed masses of their employees to Iraq and Afghanistan, doing so would have merely emptied out offices in the United States). Unlike the military, Washington had no civilian reserve, nor even a database of qualified or retired personnel that might have been quickly vetted and offered employment. Instead, what the administration did (which has been widely acknowledged) was turn to its friends, sending out a net call to conservative and republican groups for prospective staff. The result was, at best, a mixed bag, including (1) well-qualified persons; (2) what RAND analyst James Dobbins called "heroic amateurs" who had little professional qualifications but were sincere, smart, and hardworking; and, (3) individuals with little to recommend them other than a well-placed acquaintance.

Whether candidates find out about a position through networking or Net surfing, applying for work in Iraq or Afghanistan (whether for providing security or servicing trucks) starts as a pretty mundane process. As with most jobs, it starts with submitting résumés and then enduring rounds of interviews. The occupation of Iraq involves personnel in a diverse array of positions, and the arena is a competitive one. By and large, U.S. companies have had no difficulty recruiting for positions that range from jobs requiring a high school diploma and two years of experience to positions demanding advanced degrees and special expertise. Many have waiting lists for employment.

"SPECIAL" CONTRACTORS

A small percentage of the jobs filled by civilians who support the military in war zones require specialized security skills. The contractors seeking to fill them recruit either from pools of people with current or prior military or law enforcement experience. Robert Pelton, in his book *License to Kill*, reports that Triple Canopy, one of the major private security companies in Iraq, gets over a thousand résumés a month. Of that number, only about 150 will be worth looking at.[4] The only reason private security companies have to give a résumé a second glance is some indication of training or job experience related to security work. Particularly prized candidates are special operations veterans like Craige Maxim.

All of the branches of the U.S. military have Special Forces or Special Operations teams. In 2007, the ranks of special operations were almost 48,000 strong.[5] Special Operations and Special Forces are unique personnel in the military. Usually, soldiers in units that conduct special operations are only recruited from individuals who are already in the service and have exemplary records, excellent physical condition, an aptitude for functioning in dangerous, high-stress environments with little guidance, and excellent leadership potential including initiative, resourcefulness, determination, and dependability. Thus, the very selection process of qualifying for special operations makes these military personnel "special." In addition, Special Forces receive specialized training including language instruction, hand-to-hand combat, and many other individual skills, as well as schooling in tactics for all kinds of missions from civil affairs to combating or conducting guerrilla-style operations. Special Forces often use specialized weapons and equipment including specially outfitted boats and aircraft (like the AC-130 gunship, which carries up to five different types of side-mounted weapons and a host of sensors to find targets day and night).

One concern about the use of civilian contractors in combat is the fear that recruiting by the private sector will deplete the ranks of the special operations command. That fear is largely unfounded. U.S. Special Operations command, which supervises the use of Special Forces worldwide, concluded in 2007 that both recruiting (getting sufficient soldiers to qualify for and complete special operations training) and retention (getting soldiers to reenlist in the military after their term of service had been completed) had been adequate. The command found that overall, after six years of the war against terror and the explosion in the use of private security companies in Iraq and Afghanistan, the inventory of Special Forces is still "healthy."[6] In fact, the Pentagon plans to expand the size of Special Forces.

Some argue that the growth of private security companies has, in fact, helped recruiting and retention. Skilled veterans wanting to continue to put their skills to work either after they retire or after their term of military service has expired can usually find gainful employment with private security firms. The option of civilian employment based on skills learned in the military makes military jobs more, not less, attractive and aids the recruiting effort.

Another reason that the private companies do not deplete the ranks of the armed forces is that the demand for highly trained military personnel for similar private-sector work is more modest than is commonly assumed. In practice, only a very small portion of the global contractor force comes directly from the U.S. military. Triple Canopy, for example, reports that out of a typical batch of qualified applications only about 15 to 20 percent comes straight from the services.[7] Additionally, the demand for special operations experience, while strong, is not overwhelming. The entire armed security contractor force in Iraq, for example, is only about 10,000, and not all these jobs require special operations qualifications; many can be filled by individuals trained in law enforcement, public safety, or physical security (such as guarding facilities). State Department contracts, for example, require Protective Security Specialists to have a minimum of one year experience that could come from Special Forces but could also be gained from other military experience or by working in the Department of State Diplomatic Service Security, the Secret Service, any federal law enforcement agency (like the FBI), or civilian law enforcement.[8]

Whether drawing from the military or law enforcement, the qualifications for U.S. employees involved in armed security work are generally high; the quality of American military and law enforcement training is considered superior, and major companies can be fairly discriminating in hiring for the most difficult and dangerous work. In addition, these positions are normally filled by American, British, or South African personnel, among the most highly skilled in the world. Companies responding to the 2007 IPOA industry survey, for example, reported that a majority, albeit not all, of their armed employees were from the parent country, third-party and host-nation country personnel being less likely to serve in an armed role.[9]

In general, adding personnel with professional public experience in security increases the proficiency and dependability of private sector security firms. That's not to say that hiring military veterans preclude things from going wrong. For example, David A. Passaro, a former medic in the Army Special Forces, was implicated and convicted in crimes related to the death of a detainee in Afghanistan. On the other hand, military veterans are sought-after employees; indeed, government contracts often stipulate that service in the armed forces is a qualifying factor in determining whether employees hired to fulfill a contract are competent. These facts reflect that more often than not veterans prove to be exemplary employees—honest, dependable, and skilled.

Additionally, even if the private security companies do draw some military men (and women) into the private sector, that disadvantage to the government is more than outweighed by the advantage of the pressure they take off the Pentagon to raise more troops to do the work performed by private companies. Blackwater, for example, has only a few hundred armed employees in Iraq. It is estimated that to field Army units to do the contract security work performed by the company would require three brigades. Each brigade deploys with about five thousand. In addition, if the Army sent three brigades into battle, that would require at least some intermediate headquarters and support forces to manage them—perhaps another thousand troops. At the same time, because the Army sends units to Iraq for 12 to 15 months, to maintain that rotation, for each unit deployed at least one has to be preparing to replace it and another returning from Iraq, recovering from service in the country. That means the Army would have to retain a whopping 48,000 soldiers (the entire size of the military's Special Operations Command) to replace less than a thousand contractors on the ground.

On the surface, the comparison seems incomprehensible, but looking at what security contractors do and how they are organized in comparison to the military, the difference in force requirements actually makes pretty good sense. Unlike military units, contractor services are scaled precisely to the task order in the contract. Maxim's detail in Afghanistan offers a case in point. It grew to only forty people. That's the equivalent of less than one company of infantry foot soldiers. Maxim's operation replaced SEAL Team Six, a part of the Navy's special operations that cost far more to train, organize, equip, and maintain than what was required to babysit Karzai.

There is good reason why contractors can get away with a lot leaner look than an infantry company loaded for war. Military units, unlike contractors, are built to perform a range of tasks and sustain themselves during conventional conflicts. Therefore, they come with lots of capabilities, training, and costs that contractors do have to worry about. For example, of the companies that responded to the 2007 IPOA survey, half reported that they had headquarters staff with less than 25 people. The smallest was two. The largest was 250.[10] In contrast, military units have staffs overseeing everything they do from the battalion level (with a few dozen people in the commander's staff section) all the way to the Department of Defense. Adding up all those troops easily equals a number in the thousands. In short, a global military comes with a lot overhead that a contractor does not. That's how contractors are often able to provide the same services (as long as they are narrowly defined) with less.

WAR BY THE NUMBERS

Long before and after the invasion, the experts, including an authoritative study by RAND, an official government think tank, flatly concluded that U.S. troubles in Iraq could be traced to a lack of "boots" on the ground. The conventional wisdom was that an occupation without at least 300,000 troops was a forlorn hope. The country couldn't be pacified by anything less. RAND even produced equations, charts, and statistics to make their case. After the violence swelled in Iraq, anyone who swore that many hundreds of thousands of troops had to be used to subdue Iraq was declared a prophet. This particular criticism of American policy has been repeated so often that many accept it as a historical fact. Yet the testimony delivered to Congress during the September 2007 Congressional hearing reminds us that Petraeus tackled the problem with about half the "magic" number needed for victory and produced real results, under conditions far worse than those U.S. forces encountered after toppling Saddam. The argument that the military needed a lot more troops on the ground—much more than it needed contractors— is specious.[11]

That requires some explaining.

One maxim often imparted in military training is "that God was on the side with the biggest battalions," a reminder that quantity has a quality all its own. Perhaps it was that kind of thinking that inspired the boots-on-the-ground crowd in their unshakable belief that flooding Iraq with troops was not only the answer—but the only answer.

Although it is always nice to have more forces than the enemy, there is no rulebook or fixed set of guidelines (regardless of what some analysts at RAND might believe) that guarantees victory. Mathematical formulas cannot spit out what was required to win.

Military officers have another saying, quoting Napoleon (the great nineteenth-century French field commander and master tactician): "The mental to the physical is as three is to one," a reminder that there is more to winning wars than wielding big numbers. Napoleon, of course, loved big armies, but he also on many occasions fought—and won—while outnumbered.

Numbers alone don't tell the whole story. What often matters just as much, if not more, is how troops are trained, equipped, led, and employed. The genius for war, the ability to fight smart, is an incalculable combat edge. It's worth conjecturing how events in Iraq might have turned out had postwar operations been better managed. In short, it's interesting to muse what might have been if America had had a military in 2003 capable of doing the things that the Army in Iraq did under Petraeus in 2007, with skills learned in on-the-job training and honed by leaders in the field.

America's troubles in Iraq began not because it had too few boots on the ground and too many contractors in the foxholes, but because America began the occupation lacking the mix of civilian and military capabilities, political and combat leaders on the ground, and integrated planning and execution necessary to fight and win a peace against determined, resourceful adversaries.

Contractors are part of the solution, not the problem. Hiring fewer might have made the job even harder than it was.

GOING UP COUNTRY

Once hired, one fate that all contractors share in Afghanistan and Iraq, whether they have military experience or not, is that they are going in harm's way. It is difficult to imagine that any U.S. contractor headed to Iraq would not know that he (or she) is going into a very dangerous place (even after the decrease in violence in 2007).

If potential employees never watched CNN or read newspapers, all they would have to do was read the Department of State's travel advisory for Iraq to get a pretty clear picture of what they would likely face. In 2007, the advisory (available on www.state.gov) included such tips as:

- Remnants of the former Ba'ath regime, transnational terrorists, criminal elements and numerous insurgent groups remain active. Attacks against military and civilian targets throughout Iraq continue, including in the International (or "Green") Zone.
- Targets include convoys en route to venues, hotels, restaurants, police stations, checkpoints, foreign diplomatic missions, international organizations and other locations with expatriate personnel. These attacks have resulted in deaths and injuries of American citizens, including those doing humanitarian work. In addition, there have been planned and random killings, as well as extortions and kidnappings. Several U.S. citizens subsequently were murdered by terrorists.
- Civilian and military aircraft arriving at and departing from Baghdad International Airport for other major cities in Iraq have been subjected to small arms fire and missiles.
- All vehicular travel in Iraq is extremely dangerous. There have been numerous attacks on civilian vehicles, as well as military convoys.

The dangers of the desert are well documented.

One particular risk in Iraq turned out to be especially daunting for contractors. In 2004, as violence in the country escalated rapidly, the tactic of kidnapping contractors came into vogue. Hundreds of foreigners, including contractors, were abducted over the next two years. In April 2004, laundry manager Gary Teeley (a British citizen working for a Middle East company subcontracting work in Iraq) fell hostage in the southern Iraqi city of Nasiriya. A week later, he was rescued by Italian Special Forces when they stormed local militia headquarters. Others were not so lucky. Dozens were executed and their murders videotaped and distributed on DVDs and the Internet.

The fact that Iraqi forces were specifically targeting contract employees was a troubling development for the coalition forces. The problem became so acute that the State Department set up a Hostage Affairs Working Group in Iraq (later reorganized as the Hostage Affairs Office). The Hostage Affairs Working Group coordinated military, intelligence, law enforcement, and diplomatic efforts to break the back of the insurgent kidnapping rings and to organize efforts to secure the release of individuals that had been seized. After a while, the plague of kidnapping contractors abated, but the experience was a deadly reminder of the dangers the private sector can face when it fights public wars.

If employees do not know about the risks of kidnapping and other battlefield dangers when they first sign up, they will learn them before they depart for overseas. U.S. companies typically put employees through a predeployment orientation (that can last from a few hours to weeks). Although no industry standard exists, most include warnings on what contractors face as well as dealing with medical exams and administrative matters like pay and benefits. Depending on the nature of their work, some contractors may require special training and security clearances. Many of these are specified by the government. State Department contracts, for example, require Private Security Specialists to have 164 hours of instruction in eleven different areas from instructors certified by the Diplomatic Security Service.[12]

Contractors will also need passports and visas. U.S. passports have to be valid for at least six months, and most Americans also have to obtain visas from the Iraqi government through the embassy in Washington. Staying in Iraq for more than 10 days requires a residency stamp, which can be obtained at the main Residency Office in Baghdad near the National Theater or at the Karadat Mariam Police Station in the International Zone. Staying longer than two months requires an extension from the Residency Office.

With all the preliminary matters taken care of, with job contracts, visas, passports, and training and medical certifications in hand, employees are ready to go to work.

COMPENSATING CONTRACTORS

Nobody on the battlefield fights for free. Soldiers and civilians laboring for the Department of Defense, are paid by the federal government; contract employees, however, are paid by their contractors, who are in turn paid by the federal government. The compensation and benefits employees receive are largely determined by the marketplace, salary negotiations, and legal requirements stipulated in the government contract (which are usually established by the FAR).

Salaries are often mentioned as the most contentious and controversial issue regarding contractors in combat. Critics often decry that contractors are paid $1,000 each day, while the average soldier makes only about $40,000 per year. These comparisons are highly misleading in many ways.

The claim that contractors make $1,000 day is largely a myth. In Afghanistan, armed security professionals, who are among the most highly paid and conduct the most dangerous work, receive an average of $450 to $650 per day. Adding the administrative costs to what the individuals are paid (in other words, the total cost charged to the government) might drive the expense of the contractor per day closer to the $1,000 range—but that figure does not represent what the worker on the ground is putting in his (or her) pocket.

Nor are contractor salaries out of proportion to what military personnel receive in wages and benefits. Looking at what a contractor is paid per day does not provide a full picture of contractor compensation. Blackwater, for example, pays its security specialists by the day, not an annual salary, so the amount of money employees make is determined by how many days they work on the contract. In effect, each employee is like a mini-independent contractor. Paychecks are lump-sum payments. Employees are responsible for paying their own taxes, insurance, and benefits. The average compensation paid to a Blackwater professional over the course of a year is $57,250. While that is a higher figure than the take-home pay of the average soldier, sailor, or marine, simply comparing salaries does not tell the whole story.

The difference between civilian and military compensation has to include more than comparing base salaries. For example, if a soldier serves a single day in a combat zone, his or her entire pay for that month is tax-exempt. On the other hand, contractors must be out of the country for 330 full days over a consecutive 12-month period to qualify for any "Foreign Income Exclusion" tax exemptions (it does not matter whether earned income is paid by the U.S. or a foreign employer). Military personnel and their families also receive in-kind, cash, and deferred compensation—everything from vacation to combat pay (also hazardous duty or imminent danger pay) to privileges for shopping in the Post or Base Exchange (the military's grocery and shopping stores, where prices tend to be lower than those in civilian stores) to cost-of-living allowances (COLA), extra money for living in areas with high costs of living such as Washington, D.C., or San Francisco. Adding the cost of these benefits increases the value of military compensation at least half again over the base salary of a soldier. Additionally, military personnel, if they stay until retirement, can receive benefits, including retirement pay up to three-quarters of their base salary and medical care for life. Many contractors, on the other hand, receive no long-term benefits after leaving employment. Both soldiers and many contractors receive meals, housing, and medical care while they are deployed in theater. Accounting for all these factors makes the pay received by military personnel and security professionals comparable. At the same time, in comparison to many other contractors (who are host-nation or third-party nationals), military benefits often far exceed what the average contract employee receives. Pay for third-country nationals, for example, can average only about $65 to $122 per week.

In addition to salaries, the FAR requires U.S. contractors and any subcontractors they might employ to carry workers compensation insurance. The idea that contracts in combat need insurance coverage is far from new. The Defense Base Act (DBA) of 1941 extended workers compensation to American workers on overseas military bases. At the time, the U.S. military was feverishly trying to strengthen its defenses in the Pacific as the threat of war with Japan loomed. The act was passed none too soon. Contractors did indeed wind up in harm's way. In December, after the bombing of Pearl Harbor, the Japanese attacked the U.S. base at Wake Island, capturing 1,150 employees of Morrison-Knudsen Corporation, an engineering firm working for the U.S. government. (Such events prompted the only significant film during World War II that actually addressed contractors in combat, 1944's *The Fighting Seabees* with John Wayne. In the film, after the Japanese attack their construction site, Wayne and his fellow contractors are motivated to join the Navy to form combat construction battalions.) In real life, the Japanese captured the civilian construction employees and kept some on the island as workers. They executed the 98 survivors in 1943.[13] Clearly, from the war's first days it was obvious that contractors in combat needed some kind of disability and death coverage.

Since its inception, the DBA has been amended and its scope broadened so that it now covers just about everyone in Iraq and Afghanistan working on a prime contract. The law is applicable to all public works contracts by all federal agencies and operations involving national security abroad, including military or public works contracts with foreign governments. The insurance is mandatory for all government contracts. All nationalities, not just American citizens, are covered under the act.

Employers usually fulfill their responsibilities under the DBA by buying DBA insurance for employees. If injury or death occurs in the "danger zone," then a claim can be made even if the loss did not occur in the performance of duties under a government contract. Benefits can include disability compensation, medical treatment, death benefits, and vocational rehabilitation. The act requires notice of an injury (in writing) to the employer within 30 days. Benefit claims have to be filed within one year. The Department of Labor is responsible for monitoring claims and resolving disputes, with oversight from the federal courts.

The War Hazards Compensation Act (WHCA) of 1942 extended the benefits of the DBA to specifically cover "war hazards." The WHCA also provides coverage for war-risk hazards to employees not eligible for benefits under DBA. On average, only about 10 percent of losses incurred in Iraq are eligible for WHCA; in other cases employees receive benefits under the DBA.

Companies are forced to insure their workers for good reason. Many need it. In 2003, according to Labor Department statistics, there were over 800 claims, mostly from Iraq and Afghanistan in 2003, over 5,000 in 2006 and an estimated 14,000 claims in 2007. Not surprisingly the most claims came from the company with the most employees overseas. In 2004, for example, Halliburton (then the parent company of KBR) led the list with 346 claims—unsurprisingly, because it was the largest contractor in the country. No security company was in the top ten. Overall, the number of claims in relation to the size of the workforce and the dangerous nature of duties in Iraq do not seem unreasonable.

AIG, one of the major companies issuing DBA insurance (the other two are ACE-USA and CNA), claims it resolves 90 percent of its claims without dispute. Some companies offer DBA supplemental accident, life, and disability insurance, policies that offer additional benefits in the event of injury or death. Many employees also purchase additional medical and life insurance policies.

Despite the availability of insurance, the issue of disability claims for contractors remains a subject of controversy. Headlines periodically trumpet contentious cases. Perhaps the most well-known is the dispute over liability for the deaths of the four Blackwater employees in Fallujah. The company argues its liability is governed under the DBA. Members of the workers' families accused Blackwater officials of gross negligence and fraud. In this and other instances, claims can drag on for years. Facts about what happened, when, and where on the battlefield can be difficult to verify, and they complicate the challenge of resolving disputes. The Government Accountability Office found, for example, that sometimes it was difficult to gather information for claims by host-nation employees because of local laws or customs. Their investigation also concluded there was not sufficient information available on how federal agencies administered DBA to ensure that the program was being run in the most cost-effective manner.[14]

Even if all the issues raised by the Government Accountability Office are resolved, the challenges of contractor injury and compensation will likely grow in time—not because of inadequacies in insurance coverage, but because knowledge about the battlefield and what happens to humans in battle is changing. As the way we wage war changes, it has necessarily become the case that combat zones are increasingly dangerous places. The ability to understand the medical and environmental hazards of war has grown substantially over the last century.

Our knowledge of the evils of war is always developing. In World War I, soldiers were shot for cowardice for behavior that in World War II was recognized as combat exhaustion. The debilitating impact of post-traumatic stress disorder (PTSD) was not even widely recognized until after the Vietnam War; today, claims of PTSD are becoming increasingly prominent in injury claims. Similarly, although the military long acknowledged "shell shock"—the injurious affects of proximity to a massive explosion—medical science now recognizes that even repetitive small concussive effects cause memory loss, attention deficit, and other forms of neurological disorders.

In the future, advances in science will likely expand our understanding of battlefield hazards even further. Part of that understanding may translate into abilities to reduce the risks on the battlefield. Part of knowing more about dangers in danger zones no doubt will also expand the scope of what injuries are considered legitimate, and thus require compensation. Contractor practices, protective equipment, and other mitigation measures, as well as more applicable insurance benefits, and treatment and rehabilitation regimes will have to keep up with the expanding knowledge of risks on the battlefield. Otherwise, the risks and costs of contractors in combat may loom so large they outweigh the benefits of private-sector support for public wars.

LIFE ON THE EDGE

Even under the best of circumstances, contractors share the soldier's lot. Most contractors in Iraq and Afghanistan live and work in conditions not too different from that of the military. For the most part, life revolves around LOGCAP. KBR likely does their laundry (18.5 billion bundles in Iraq as of July 2006). Pretty much everybody eats the same spaghetti and steaks in a KBR-run mess hall—also called a dining facility or DFAC (as of mid-2006, 375 million meals were served across the country). Soldiers and civilians alike go to the same medical clinics and usually live under the same primitive conditions: a building with the bare-bones basics, or a crowded tent. They line up in front of the same KBR-serviced outhouses and showers.

In many other ways, the life of contractors in combat parallels very closely the soldier's daily grind in Iraq and Afghanistan. The memories of warriors in every war often sound the same—hours of boredom or drudgery shattered by moments of violence, heart-racing danger, and terror. Many contractors, particularly professional security personnel, might recall their experiences in combat in much the same way.

Contractors also tend to exhibit the same kinds of behaviors in the face of adversity that are demonstrated by military units. Where they are deployed as teams and work together, they develop bonds of trust and confidence in one another. They show pride in their professionalism, and satisfaction in doing a job well. They serve, sacrifice for, and care for one another. Where leadership is poor, workers' performance and attitude reflect that as well. Contractors have also exhibited signs of single-minded self-preservation and undertaken acts of unmatched bravery. There are documented cases, for example, of contractors refusing to deliver food or other supplies in dangerous areas, but also instances in which contractors risked their lives to protect, rescue, or care for other contractors, civilians, and military personnel.

On occasion, contractors have even received military distinction. Andrew Bendy, an employee of Aegis, received the Commander's Award for Civilian Service. According to news coverage of the award ceremony, if he had been in uniform, Bendy would have received a medal for bravery. "During an honest-to-God, extended mortar barrage," Bendy continually exposed himself, leaping across rooftops to maintain Army communications lines.[15] Contractors can be courageous, too.

ORDER 17

Another area in which soldiers and contractors in Iraq were treated equivalently was their treatment under host-nation law. The Coalition Provisional Authority Order 17 (June 2004) gave immunity to both against prosecution under Iraqi law. However, contractors were exempt "with respect to acts performed by them pursuant to the terms and conditions of a Contract or any sub-contract thereto." This immunity was actually much narrower than that granted to the military and government employees, who received exemption from Iraqi legal processes under any circumstances. Contractors are only exempt for actions that they are required to perform as part of fulfilling their contracts. Additionally, crimes, such as rape, murder, and theft, are not covered under Order 17.

At the time, the promulgation of Order 17 made sense. Iraq had no functioning legal system. The police had been infiltrated by insurgent groups. The responsible ministry was undependable.

Issuing Order 17, however, contributed to the belief that contractors were "above and beyond" the law. That's a myth as well. For example, the order also stipulated that nothing in the order relieved MNF [Multinational Force] Personnel from their responsibilities for "preventing acts of serious misconduct by Contractors." Contract employees could certainly be arrested and prosecuted for criminal acts unrelated to their contract duties. There were, in addition, other means for disciplining contractors who did not fulfill their contracts or punishing those who broke the law. Contracting officers could hold companies accountable to the standards of performance stipulated in their contracts.

A number of U.S. laws are also applicable to contractor behavior on the battlefield. The Arms Control Export Act of 1968, for example, regulates exporting security services and establishes licensing requirements. Contractors are also liable for prosecution under the Military Extraterritorial Jurisdiction Act, and a recent change in the law now makes them potentially subject to the Uniform Code of Military Justice as well.

The arrest and conviction of David Passaro offers, perhaps, the best evidence that contractors in combat are not above or beyond the law. In 2006, a jury in a federal court in Raleigh, North Carolina, found him guilty of two counts of assault with a dangerous weapon and two counts of assault resulting in serious injury. Passaro served as a contract employee with the CIA. The charges related to the treatment of Abdul Wali, a detainee who died in U.S. custody during interrogation at a remote military base in Afghanistan. Although the trial and conviction of Passaro offers no assurances about the claims that abuses at the hands of contractors are not adequately addressed, nor resolves how government oversight of the contractors in this case failed and allowed these illegal acts to happen, it does demonstrate that unlawful behavior by contract employees is not beyond the reach of justice.

RULES OF THE ROAD

As might be expected when employing contractors in security positions, there occasionally arise situations in which contract employees use deadly force in ways that either military personnel or civilians find inappropriate.

Specific rules govern the use of force on the battlefield for both military and civilians. Military "rules of engagement," often just called ROE, are approved by the senior military command, in this case the U.S. Central Command. They dictate when and how armed forces personnel can appropriately use their weapons. Generally, two sets of rules govern the conditions under which military troops can use weapons. One is called the "restrictive" use of force, though it is actually the more permissive set of rules used when the military is less constrained in how it employs its weapons. Restrictive force is more appropriate for conventional combat. The use of force should be proportional (in other words, it would not be right to bomb a city to dust to take out a sniper) and legitimate (it would, for example, be unacceptable to intentionally target civilians or shoot an incapacitated and wounded enemy). In large part, however, commanders scope the authority to use force to the nature of the mission.

The other set of ROE commonly employed only permit the use of weapons in self-defense. Under these conditions, troops are prohibited from using their arms to take offensive action. An ROE that limits the employment of weapons to protecting

U.S. forces and any personnel they are safeguarding is usually required in situations where the threats to military units are manageable and the risk of civilian casualties is high. American troops, for example, are periodically deployed within the United States to deal with civil disturbances and natural disasters. When they are armed, the ROE is usually highly restrictive, limiting troops to employing deadly force under situations similar to those that govern domestic law enforcement.

Unlike the armed forces, employees working under contracts or subcontracts with the U.S. government can only employ weapons in self-defense (this includes defending the lives of individuals contractors have been assigned to protect and preventing "life threatening offenses against civilians."). The terms of use and the types of weapons contractors can have are stipulated by the government. Contracts also require that armed employees be trained and certified in the laws of armed conflict and the rules for the use of force before performing services under the contract. Armed employees are usually required to be briefed on use-of-force rules before each mission they undertake. All these checks do not preclude contractors' use of excessive force but are practical measures similar in many ways to the kinds of restrictions and requirements placed on law enforcement officers in the United States.

Anecdotal evidence also suggests that the inappropriate use of force, while perhaps not endemic, is certainly not unheard of. Paul Christopher, a retired military veteran and a contractor in Iraq recalled:

> I have observed confusion over the roles of the military and the private sector. . . . I have also encountered numerous instances where the line between what is permitted and what is prohibited was not understood by the private contractors, and certainly not by the Iraqi civilians. While traveling "low profile" in light traffic along the highways in Baghdad, I have been physically forced off the road by personal security teams in SUVs. I have been subjected to intimidation with loaded weapons for no apparent reason. I have seen the lives of innocent Iraqis disrupted and their property destroyed without provocation.[16]

Such instances, Christopher complained, not only undermined the mission of bringing security and stability to Iraq, they undercut the utility of contractors as an adjunct to the military forces.

FOG OF WAR

Both the military and armed contractors have to report when they engage in hostile fire—and with good reason. Restoring peace and stability to Iraq and Afghanistan requires reducing the levels of violence that skyrocketed civilian casualties. That demands not only eliminating the danger of terrorist and insurgent attacks but also limiting casualties caused by "friendly fire," the unintentional injury or death of friendly troops and civilians caused by military action.

Friendly fire is a problem of war that is as old as war. As a subject of military history the topic has been little studied, though there is plenty of history to write about.[17] During Operation Cobra in Normandy, France (July 25, 1944), for example, Allied bombings reportedly killed 108 and wounded 472. In addition to these deaths, many civilian casualties—innocents caught in the bomb corridor—were uncounted and unreported.[18] It was one of the war's most notable disasters, though now the battle is hardly remembered. The absence of much scholarship on such issues reflects another of modern memory's blind spots.

The dangers of friendly fire remained almost a forgotten issue until Desert Storm. According to the Department of Defense, friendly fire accounted for over 17 percent of American combat deaths during the first Gulf War. Even though the total number of deaths (147) was remarkably small in comparison to the scale of engagement, the losses startled many and prompted the Pentagon to devote more time and energy to studying the problem.[19] The military made some progress in its next invasion of Iraq, including developing a system called "Blue Force Tracker," which provides combat units with the locations of other units to help preclude friendly fire. Additionally, the United States deployed more precision guided weapons, which enabled them to more accurately attack targets in areas populated with civilians. At the outset, however, the military did very little to develop weapons, tactics, or training to safeguard civilians in small-scale engagements on city streets and roadside checkpoints.

The number of civilian deaths in Iraq as a result of malicious or negligent acts by armed forces personnel or contractors remains a subject of unrelenting controversy. The military did not begin to keep comprehensive statistics before 2005. The data is not generally available. Precise information on the nature of casualties, the adequacy of reporting, and the resolution of investigations remains elusive.

In Iraq, when U.S. forces are responsible for the death of innocents, the U.S. pays. The Army administers restitution under the Foreign Claims Act. The act sets requirements to settle "claims of inhabitants of a foreign country, or a political subdivision thereof, against the United States for personal injury, death, or property damage caused by service members or civilian employees, or claims that arise incident to non-combat activities of the Armed Forces."[20] Documents obtained under the Freedom of Information Act by the ACLU in 2007 showed 479 claims made to Foreign Claims Commissions in Iraq to 2006, the vast majority of which dated from 2005. One hundred sixty-four resulted in cash payments to victims' families.

FACING THE FUTURE

Disputes over friendly fire and other concerns about contractor behavior in Iraq are unlikely to subside any time soon. On the one hand, activist groups like the ACLU decry alleged abuses and demand greater accountability.[21] On the other, both military personnel and contractors chafe under the second-guessing of decisions made in the heat of combat and increasing demands for more reporting and more detailed restrictions. Overly prescriptive supervision limits initiative and flexibility in dangerous situations, putting more, not fewer, lives at risk.

The link between escalating violence in Iraq and escalating complaints of the excessive use of force by contractors and military units seems fairly clear. That suggests, among other measures, that creating a safe and secure environment is the most essential and most effective way to address these concerns. Peace really is the answer. Indeed, as violence ratcheted down over the course of 2007 so did anecdotal evidence of, and complaints about, the inappropriate employment of force.

Nevertheless, complaints about contractor use of deadly force resurfaced in September 2007 when the Iraqi Minister of the Interior alleged that Blackwater employees escorting a convoy in downtown Baghdad engaged in a firefight. The ministry asserted that the Blackwater employees were responsible for a number of malicious deaths and injuries. The facts of the case were hotly contested. Even the veracity of the Iraqi ministry came into question, because it was well known that its offices had been infiltrated by insurgent groups and that the organization was wracked by sectarian divisions. It was thus unclear how much of the ministry's allegations represented sincere concerns and how much was about playing politics with contractors. The FBI launched an investigation, as did the Department of State, which oversaw the contract. After an internal review of its procedures, the State Department announced that additional oversight measures would be put in place, including having Diplomatic Security Service personnel accompany the contractors.

The reporting of deaths and adjudicating of claims cannot but help to remain controversial. The term "fog of war," ascribed to the famed nineteenth-century Prussian military philosopher Carl von Clausewitz (another product of the European Enlightenment), describes the uncertainties, ambiguities, unknowns, and confusion that always accompany battle. The fog of war makes no distinction as to the kinds of wars that are fought. The battles of Iraq, where soldiers fight terrorists and insurgents hunt contractors at the side of women headed to market and children on their way to school are no different—in fact, they could be worse. On such battlefields, responsibility and accountability in the use of force are simply more difficult matters—and always will be.

As with most battlefield challenges, the best means for clearing the fog of war is not more restrictions and regulations and rules. Here, the military can learn a lesson from the rebuilding of the hollow force of the 1970s. What makes a military perform best in battle is building a force that is trained, equipped, and prepared for battle—*before* the battle. Limiting the extent of civilian causalities by soldiers or contractors to the maximum extent possible (in keeping with the demands of fighting and winning an imperative to safeguard civilians as much as humanly possible) is an endless challenge that will be endlessly imperfect and that requires endless effort. Tragedy, mistakes, and abuse will always occur, but willful disregard of the laws of war is something that can never be tolerated.

FRACTURED BAND OF BROTHERS

Soldiers and contractors face many similar difficulties. Following the ROA on traffic-jammed streets, crowded marketplaces, and stretches of highway known for snipers and suicide bombers is only one of them.[22] That said, despite all the conditions and challenges they share in common, it is still not uncommon to find expressions of animosity between public warriors and private sector contractors.

There is no definitive study of soldier–contractor relations. Anecdotal stories, however, abound. Often complaints involve contract employees who do not work under military contracts. Rather, they are subcontractors or contractors answering to the State Department, USAID, or other agencies. Distrust of "the other guy's" contractors is understandable. Military commanders can influence their own contractors through the contracting officer or their representatives, who are either military personnel or Defense Department employees. In contrast, military commands have no formal means to supervise another agency's contractors.

Having distinct chains of command for different contractors is symptomatic of a deeper and fundamental flaw in the occupation of Iraq. From the outset, Washington fractured responsibility for overseeing operations. That decision had a crippling effect on the Americans' ability to keep up with their enemies in Iraq.

POSTCONFLICT

Postconflict operations include those minimum military activities that are required in the wake of war. After any campaign, the United States will have moral and legal obligations to restore order, provide a safe and secure environment for the population, and prevent a humanitarian crisis by ensuring that people are fed and preventing the spread of infectious disease. In short, the military's task is to provide a secure atmosphere for the reestablishment of civilian government, as well as domestic security and public safety regimens. In addition, maintaining a safe and secure environment in the postconflict phase is vital for securing the national interest that precipitated U.S. involvement, whether that task is disarming and demobilizing an enemy force, hunting down the remnants of a deposed regime, or restoring a legitimate border.

Postconflict operations are *not* the same as an "exit strategy," which implies that exiting the country is the focus of operations. Instead, achieving American national objectives must retain primacy during planning. Getting American troops out of the country may be an objective, but American troops are still stationed in Europe and Japan for reasons completely unrelated to the original objectives of World War II, the war that brought them there 60 years ago.

Postconflict operations are among the most difficult to plan and execute, even under the best of circumstances. Expectations that postconflict activities will be smooth, uncomplicated, frictionless, and nonviolent are unrealistic, as is the assumption that grievous policy errors or strategic misjudgments cause all difficulties. After all, the former enemy gets a vote, and how indigenous opposition forces or outside agitators choose to defy the occupation partially determines the course of events. For example, in postwar Germany, the poor organization and subsequent collapse of planned Nazi opposition made the Allies' task of reinstituting civil order significantly easier. The Office of Strategic Services estimated that the Allies would face a guerrilla army of about 40,000—an assessment that proved wildly inaccurate.

Additionally, it is often forgotten that there is a "fog of peace" that is as infamous as the "fog of war". This "fog of peace" undermines the notion that outcomes can be precisely predicted or that there is a prescribed rulebook for success that any military can follow.

By its nature, regime change is a multi-agency operation and usually involves a coalition of other countries as well. Despite the multiplicity of actors, a single agency or headquarters must command the operations. There is no other way to be ready for the fog of peace—particularly when the peace is a war. Splitting authority for operations in Iraq between military commanders and a civilian administrator was a mistake and complicated the problems of implementing the disease and unrest formula. In contrast, the post–World War II operations remained under a single command authority, and this decision contributed to their success. Unity of command allowed the occupying forces to learn more quickly from their mistakes and to adapt better to unforeseen circumstances. That did not happen in Iraq. Lack of centralized control over contractor was just part of the problem.

Too many bosses in Iraq created lots of opportunities for things to go wrong. How some contractors were treated was only one of them.

TROUBLE IN PARADISE

There was trouble in paradise. Ask David Phinney.

The story of rigged celebrations in *al-Firdos* square was not the first or the last scandalous story in Iraq. Some were more important than others. Seymour Hersh made a lot of headlines with his writings on Abu Ghraib, but by the time he published, the military had already started to address the appalling situation at the prison. There are other reporters who have written stories that have received far less attention but made more impact in changing how things are done in Iraq. David Phinney might be one of them. A journalist and broadcaster based in Washington, he has been doing investigative reporting on operations in Iraq for years. Phinney hit on at least one issue that proved to be a serious problem for contracting in combat. It is the story of how many contractors came to Iraq.

The companies performing the preponderance of the work in Iraq and Afghanistan are incorporated in a relatively few countries, including the United States and Britain. However, with the exception of security personnel, most contractor employees are not citizens of these countries. Most employees are from the home country or are recruited from other nations. In 2006, for example, the U.S. military reported that KBR had about 48,000 personnel employed under its contracts and subcontracts in Iraq, about 35,000 of whom were third-country nationals, who are more at risk of abuse and exploitation than are either American soldiers or contractors.

The IPOA code of conduct specifically addresses the treatment of host-country and third-party nationals. Among the relevant requirements, contractors must

- Ensure employees are fully informed regarding the level of risk associated with their employment, as well as the terms, conditions, and significance of their contracts.
- Use adequately trained and prepared personnel in all their operations in accordance with clearly defined company standards.
- Act responsibly and ethically toward all their employees, ensuring that employees are treated with respect and dignity.
- Pay differing wages to different nationalities based only on merit and national economic differential, not on racial, gender or ethnic grounds.
- Respect the age-minimum standard of 15 years of age as defined by the International Labor Organization Minimum Age Convention (1973).
- Not deny the right to terminate their employment. Furthermore, no signatory may retain the personal travel documents of its employees against their will.

These standards are reasonable and appropriate. Most of the principal U.S. contractors in Iraq and Afghanistan are members of IPOA and voluntarily bind themselves to comply with the association code of conduct.

Phinney's reporting, as well as a groundbreaking series in the *Chicago Tribune* in October 2005, revealed that there were a number of subcontractors in Iraq that were not following the code. In fact, they were trading in people.

When the U.S. military investigated the allegations, they discovered that many of them were true. Across the Middle East and South Asia, overseas brokers rounded up thousands of workers, many of them illiterate and impoverished. They promised them high-paying jobs but charged them exorbitant fees, sometimes stealing their money and stranding them. Other times they shipped them to Iraq, where they worked and lived in substandard conditions. They took their money and their passports and treated them little better than slaves.

In April 2006, Central Command issued comprehensive labor guidelines for all defense contractors employed by the U.S. Government in Iraq and Afghanistan. General George Casey, the commander in Iraq, ordered that all passports be returned to their owners. Additionally, new policies required that fees for host-nation recruiters had to be paid by the contracting companies; recruiters could no longer charge fees to prospective employees. Casey also threatened "harsh actions" against companies that did not come clean and end abusive practices. The Pentagon also revised the FAR to add a clause implementing federal statutes requiring provisions authorizing the termination of contracts if the contractor or any subcontractor engages in trafficking in persons.

That the United States should suffer such a scandal is ironic, in that the administration had actually been a global leader in combating human trafficking. Under the Bush White House, the Congress had passed two major acts of legislation: The Trafficking Victims Protection Reauthorization Act of 2003 and the Trafficking Victims Protection Reauthorization Act of 2005. In addition, the Department of Justice launched a number of initiatives to investigate, track, and prosecute human trafficking conspiracies worldwide, as well as within the United States.

The administration's efforts in combating human trafficking were commendable, as was the apparent sincerity with which it tackled the abuses of unscrupulous recruiters and subcontractors in Iraq and Afghanistan. Given the administration's sensitivity to the abuses of global human trafficking, the fact that U.S. agencies allowed them to flourish is inexcusable. The problems in Iraq should never have materialized to begin with.

ASYLUM AMNESIA

Another acute problem with contracting in-country has been looking after host nationals whose safety, or whose families' safety, were put at grave risk by working with American companies. Since the outbreak of the Iraq War, an estimated 2 million Iraqis have fled their home country. The United States has accepted only a fraction of these refugees. From October 2006 through March 2007, the United States accepted 15,000 refugees in total, of whom only 68 were Iraqis. U.S. policies are responsible for this small inflow. The Department of Homeland Security enforces tougher security screening procedures for Iraqis. Though the United States has accepted high numbers of refugees from equally threatening countries, including 3,077 Somalis and 2,468 Iranians, the administration fell short of its promise to admit 7,000 Iraqis by the end of September 2007; as of mid-summer 2007, the US had admitted only 133 Iraqi refugees. A majority of stateless Iraqis flee to Jordan, straining the social services of a strong and supportive friend of the United States in the region. Others have fled to Syria, which risks radicalizing the Iraqi diaspora.

One problem with this policy is that some of those fleeing with their families were contract employees working under U.S. government contracts or for subcontractors. These individuals included translators and other key personnel who were instrumental in helping the U.S. forces do their job or who performed important roles in rebuilding the country. Abandoning these individuals and their families to hardships in refugee camps or risk to threats or harm is not only immoral, it does not make sense. It will be difficult for the United States to recruit and retain host-nation personnel who know they may be ignored after having bravely served the American military. Although the government's first priority had to be reducing the violence so all Iraqis could go home, looking to the sanctuary of Iraqi contractors who put their lives on the line for America should have been a priority as well.

THE UGLY AMERICAN

It remains to be seen what book or film will rise to set the image of contractors in combat in the American imagination. Certainly, no one has yet captured the many aspects of the private sector's role in public wars: the challenges of refugees and human trafficking; the difficulties of implementing rules of engagement; and the conditions and demands of service on the battlefield. At best, today Americans remain deeply skeptical.

The ambivalence in the modern American memory of private contractors in public wars reflects, in some part, the discomfort of a generation of Americans that knows America is in transition but does not know where the nation is headed. America has been here before, and we have the movies and books to remind us that we've felt this feeling: sensing the world is changing but unsure of what change might bring. One book that reflected the sense of ambiguity about change was *The Quiet American* (1955).

When Graham Greene wrote *The Quiet American*, few Americans could find Indochina (the French colony that eventually became the two Vietnams) on a map, but they saw an uneasy reflection of themselves in one of the book's chief characters, the young, idealistic Alden Pyle. Pyle is a covert American operative, part of a conspiracy to promote a local militia leader who undertakes a bombing campaign and blames it on the Communists. Its clear from the outset that although Pyle means well, he understands little about the real conditions on the ground, and his efforts may be doing more harm than good.

A film version of *The Quiet American* (1958) turned the book's message on its head. In the film, Pyle is played by the ultimate all-American hero, Audie Murphy (the most decorated soldier in World War II turned Hollywood actor and sometimes country-western songwriter). In the movie, Pyle is a complete innocent and an unambiguous hero. A subtle plot change makes clear that the Communists are actually behind the bombings in Saigon. In the movie, quiet Americans are always in the right.

The fact that Americans could have dog-eared copies of an anti-American book on their bookshelves as they rushed to theaters to watch a pro-American film of the same title demonstrated how closely Americans stood to the edge of both confidence and despair over their country's place in the world as the Cold War settled into place. That dichotomy would describe well today how the nation feels about Iraq (and, concomitant with that unease, America's concern over contractors). A better understanding of the realities of contractor life in Iraq might help Americans to look to the future with confidence—or they may have to wait for the book.

Clearly, the role of contractors in combat is far from perfect. In a way, that is to be expected; the fog of war reminds us that war will never be perfect. Still, the realities of combat offer more than enough fodder for those who want to make a case for or against the place of the private sector in public wars. Arguing for all or nothing, however, is hardly a debate worth having. The truth is that there will be quiet Americans on many battlefields for a very long time, as we will see in the following chapter.

5
Chapter

Why We Can't Go Back

Armies reflect their era.

The ultimate conceit about force planning (deciding how much and what kind of military a nation needs and the amount of contractor support required) is that there are stark choices.[1] The Quadrennial Defense Review (QDR) is a case in point. The congressional mandate (1996) requiring the Pentagon report every four years on the adequacy of its strategy, force structure, and resources to provide for national security over the next twenty years, follows a long tradition. Truman had his NSC-68. Eisenhower had the Solarium Project. Others followed. Like the QDR, they all began with a premise: Evaluate the threat. Discover what the nation needs. Buy it.

That is *not* how it works.

Many factors temper the decision of how much is enough and whether a service should be provided by the public or the private sector—not the least of which is how we think about security. Here, Americans are definitely of more than one mind. At least two competing theories govern how the nation assesses what will make it safe. These theories are so fundamental to making choices about national security that Americans hardly ever reflect on them. Yet they usually rest at the bottom of every defense proposal from either the right or the left. Both are a product of American culture, and both have their roots in Western European ideas.

One theoretical construct for thinking about how to make America safe sounds an awful lot like something that might have been drafted by Machiavelli. Indeed, Machiavelli's writings and those of his intellectual cousin, the Englishman Thomas Hobbes (1588–1697), are often credited as the foundations for national security thinking. The school that builds on their ideas is called "realism." Realists and neo-realists (and the many permutations of these labels that political scientists invent) argue that the structure of the international system places states in ceaseless competition. Conflict is inevitable. Power is the core concept of the real-ist paradigm. States collide because they are rational actors, constantly working to ensure their national security by maximizing power in relation to other states, aligning with other nations to achieve uneasy collective security, or nestling under the wing of a great power hegemon. In each case, state behavior is driven by the unending quest for security.[2] It's kill or be killed—a Hobbesian choice.

In contrast, liberalism (and the many derivative theories of international rela-tions that build on its very different vision of the how world works) contends that state actions represent the collective will of groups within in the society.[3] Foreign policy and national security strategy are the products of the cooperative view of "empowered" elements, including international and multinational institutions and the laws and treaties they promulgate. Liberalism takes a structuralist approach to international relations, believing power to be exercised and distrib-uted thorough formal organizations and institutions. In the liberal universe, con-flict and competition are not inevitable. Institutions can act to ameliorate international violence and promote cooperation, trust, and joint action. The roots of liberalism are not as ancient as realist ideology but are nonetheless rooted in our Western heritage. They, in part, trace their origins to the Enlightenment and its belief in the inevitability of progress in the human condition. Today, liberal ideology is as deeply woven into the fabric of American political discourse as are realist ideas.

When realist and liberal beliefs are debated in public they sound very differ-ent. They make different assumptions and offer different recommendations. They ring as distinct voices on the campaign trail. They bicker on cable news. They each have their own talk radio stations. They seem like they are offering real choices. But in truth, the options are more limited.

Both theories are grounded in a common intellectual heritage, sharing common constraints. They limit themselves to assessing the physical capabilities and limitations of states and institutions. Those factors, as well as cultural influ-ences and ideas (like the West's musings on Machiavelli), define the scope of how societies think about security.[4]

The fact that many factors determine what a military looks like is nothing new. It has always been so. Italy had its *condottiere*. France had its *Compagnies d'Ordonnance*. The British had their Hessians. All these military structures derived from a plethora of social, economic, political, cultural, and technical influences. In that respect, the American way of war is no different from that of any other nation.

In practice, the worldview of Americans, whether from the right or the left, greatly limits America's choices. That's why American foreign and national secu-rity policies are marked by more continuities than contrasts from administration to administration, regardless of whether the administrations are democratic or republican. That also explains why, when the Defense Department issues a QDR and argues it has produced a rational assessment that began with a blank sheet of paper onto which it merely filled in the challenges the nation faces and the best means to deal with them, it is being less than forthright. Wherever different theories and beliefs Americans take from the marketplace of ideas, in the end, they tend to offer solutions that sound a good deal like the ideas they had the day before.

All that said, the realities of how decisions get made ought to make Americans more than a little skeptical about indictments of using contractors in combat that make the practice sound like a conspiracy birthed out of thin air by some neo-conservative cabal. The place of the private sector in public wars has been growing and growing over the course of the past seventy-five years under the leadership of politicians from both the left and the right. Thus, trying to craft public policies about contractors in combat as if they were an aberration, rather than a reality of war in the modern world, would be a tragedy. Fixating on the issue of contractors in combat diverts Washington from focusing on the real issues threatening America's competitive advantages in the twenty-first century.

Accepting that the world is changing in fundamental ways and that changing course on contractors in combat is nothing less than bucking world historical trends is central to crafting common-sense policies for the future. If the nature of war takes a dramatically different turn—if modern militaries look fundamentally different than historical militaries—it will only be because the nature of society fundamentally changes. Until that happens, the third age of war in the Western World will continue on its current path.

As a result of the rise of the private sector over the last three quarters of a century, future wars may never again look like "the good war" of World War II, in which the United States had to dump more than 40 percent of the economy into the fight, put millions of citizens in uniform, and plead with civilians to grow victory gardens, collect tires and tin cans, and buy war bonds. Today, the developed nations can turn to a private sector that can do many of the things governments used to do, and better.

There is one overarching and unshakable truth that makes the case that for the foreseeable future, contractors in combat are here to stay: The prominence of the private sector in public wars is part of living in a "globalized" world.

BRAVE NEW WORLD

Globalization is not new. It comes and goes. Over the course of history, there were many eras of exploration, conquest, interaction, and commerce that built global networks. In fact, the world was well on its way to building an unprecedented global marketplace at the turn of the twentieth century.[5] Then World War I broke out. The Great War, and the dislocation in worldwide markets that followed, stopped globalization in its tracks. Nations gingerly got back on the path to an international marketplace after World War II. As the Cold War progressed, despite the division of nations between free markets and managed states, the process of building an international integrated economy picked up steam. It took a bit of a breather in the 1970s when a global downturn in growth cast doubt on the staying power of the free enterprise system. Then, at the end of the Cold War, the march toward economic freedom went into overdrive. The rich got richer. The poor got richer, too.

This was not supposed to happen. The battle between capitalism and communism was supposed to put the future up for grabs. At least half the world doubted capitalism had all the right stuff. The fact that they guessed wrong is more than obvious. Since World War II, market-based economies have thrived, while virtually every communist state across the globe has collapsed. At least Francis Fukuyama got that part of his *The End of History and the Last Man* right.

There is, after all, no credible alternative explanation for how history happened—though scholars have tried. Some argue, for example, that the world evolved into some kind of American empire merely masked by global markets. The historian William Appleman Williams asserted that America practiced "Open Door Imperialism," a ceaseless quest for economic dominance that led to the establishment of an informal empire.[6] He wrote feel-good histories for left-wing conspiracy theorists. As powerful and evocative as Williams' writings were seen to be in the 1960s and early 1970s, it is questionable how well they have stood the test of time and distance from the raw emotion of the disillusionment that birthed them.

The U.S. economy is neither imperialistic (an empire by definition requires exercising sovereignty over the dominion's far-flung territories) nor monopolistic. It is only one link in the global economic system with the United States dependent on other nations and transnational corporations, which it does not control, for goods and services that are critical to the U.S. economy (global oil supplies are a case in point). America cannot be both imperial and dependent. As the economist Joseph E. Stiglitz famously argues in *Globalization and Its Discontents*, world economic policies cannot be run by "Washington consensus."[7] Contrary to Williams and others who claim America is the world's puppet master, globalization has a life of its own—and right now it is on a winning streak.

No victory is complete or permanent. That is the part Fukuyama got wrong. Amongst the new world disorder there are other candidates rising to the challenge of challenging freedom. It is true that none of them seem any more compelling than the muddled thinking of Marx and Lenin. The latest danger, described in Samuel P. Huntington's *The Clash of Civilizations and the Remaking of World Order* (1996), offers a prime example. Huntington's book is often singled out as a touchstone for debate about the next great threat to Western civilization. His hypothesis is that in the post-Cold War world, global politics are multi-polar and multi-civilizational and that dangerous conflicts will emerge between peoples belonging to different cultural entities. As the West asserts its global influence, Huntington contends, it will do battle with Confucian and Islamic societies attempting to counter with their own economic and military power. The tragedy of 9/11 put *The Clash of Civilizations* on center stage in the security debate.[8]

The Clash of Civilizations does not necessarily see Islamic fundamentalism as a coherent, competitive alternative to Western modernity. Islamic peoples are a threat not because they are united, but because they are divided and chaotic and thus a potential source of trouble. Still, there is not much to Huntington's thesis. Dissension among some disaffected parts of the Middle East, South Asia, and Africa does not inevitably translate into a war between West and the rest of the world. Nor does a "clash of civilizations" explain how a collage of weak and disparate groups can hope to keep pace with the power of the West over the long term. Finally, pointing out that extreme religious fundamentalism is at the root of the discord battling against Western-style capitalism does not portend disaster either. Western capitalism has faced religious extremist movements many times over its history, including radical ideas birthed in the West, such as Christian liberation theology which enjoyed a brief spurt of popularity in Latin America in the 1980s. None have stood up well against the promise of freedom, justice, and the rule of law. Free-market states bested all comers. As with *The Soldier and the State*, in the end history will probably show that Huntington got some things right, but just as much wrong.

Still, there is no argument that Islamists of Bin Laden's ilk would like a war of civilizations if they could get one. The odds are against them. Indeed, as in past attempts to harness Islamic extremism, terrorism linked to Islamism has accomplished little more than bringing misery to the Islamic world. So far the chief victims in al Qaeda's global war are Muslims. Most victims of terrorist attacks are Arab Muslims killed by other Muslims.[9] To keep up with the West, competitors have to do more than have an intense hate. They have to figure out a means to match the raw power of the West to make war.

That is not to say the world is as safe as Fukuyama forecast in *The End of History*. Evil never takes a holiday. Arguably, enemies of the free market nation-state abound (and some certainly have the potential to be very dangerous troublemakers). Nevertheless, they face a pretty resilient opponent. Free nations have a lot of strength for the fight.

HISTORY REVISITED

One important part of that strength is the private sector. A robust private sector is a robust part of national power in a globalized world. In fact, each time the West surged toward establishing global networks, it increased its reliance on employing the private sector for public wars. The dynamic works like this: as the world globalizes, more wealth is created and that wealth spills over into the private sector, in turn the public sector turns to private business, using the private sector's power to help police the world.

During the age of exploration and colonial expansion, for example, countries often turned to privateers to supplement their navies. Likewise, nations also relied on public–private partnerships in the form of trading companies to help rule their colonial empires. Without question, the greatest of these belonged the greatest empire-building nation of them all—Great Britain.

Britain's East India Company had its roots in a royal charter issued by Queen Elizabeth in 1600. Granted to a band of businessmen interested in importing spices from Asia, the company developed its own administrative bodies and military forces over the course of the British imperial age, which it used to rule parts of the empire, guarding them from competitors. The East India Company had broad discretionary power. Representatives could negotiate treaties, collect revenue, and administer justice.

The company was, in fact, expected to pay its own way. In India, by the mid–eighteenth century, it raised such an enormous army to defend company business that the company then embarked on a course of military conquest to pay for the maintenance of the army.[10] Before the Regulating Act of 1773 and the India Act of 1784, shareholders in the East India Company virtually made British foreign policy in Asia on their own. In 1834, the company became a quasi-government agency. Taken over by the Colonial Office in 1857, the government phased out private management in 1873. For hundreds of years, however, the company remained a prominent element of British national power and a symbol of the empire's imperial reach.[11]

History does not simply repeat itself. The private sector in the current wave of globalization differs dramatically from the private companies that supported public wars during past eras of global expansion. There are profound differences between Robert Clive (1725–1774), who made a fortune conquering half a subcontinent for the British East India Company, and the contractors in Iraq and Afghanistan. (1) The size and power of today's private sector is unprecedented. (2) Globally, in the post-Cold War era fewer business operations are owned and controlled by states. (3) Rules of global governance in the modern era define more effectively what type of behavior is permissible. (4) Today's global information environment (the press, the Internet, and so forth) allows for unprecedented transparency and activism in monitoring commercial activities. These world historical differences make the private sector a far better partner in public wars than in the past, accounting, in large part, for why the world has entered into a new era, the third age of war.

BRAIN POWER

There are two reasons that modern free market economies promise to have a lot of staying power. Both reasons have something to say about why the private sector will remain an important part of public combat.

The first reason that free markets are so powerful in public wars is that free markets are free. There is a reason why Milton Friedman was so confident the all-volunteer army would prove a success. He had an unshakable confidence in the value of freedom in free-market economies to create the goods and services that people needed when they needed them. In *Capitalism and Freedom* (1962), Friedman made a simple, compelling argument. He rejected the notion of the Enlightenment—that progress was inevitable. Instead, Friedman argued that in a free society progress was always possible. Progress comes from variety and diversity. Freedom, a combination of liberty and justice, created a space for every individual to make an individual choice. That allowed entrepreneurs the opportunity to offer a range of goods and services to the marketplace. In turn, the market had the freedom to pick what it needed to get the job done.

America's free-market economy has allowed America to recruit and retain a quality force. It has also created the opportunity to turn to the private sector to get what additional capability it required when it required it.

Initiative and innovation are hallmarks of what the private sector can bring to public wars. There is more than enough proof of that in the way the free market responded to the demands of the wars in Iraq and Afghanistan. One great example is the appearance of robots on the battlefield. The Pentagon had been developing robotic systems for decades. When the war started the military had no land robots in combat. By 2004, it had 150. By 2007, it had 5,000. Many of them were PackBots, small, versatile machines used to search caves for insurgents, clear buildings, and defuse roadside bombs. PackBots were an innovation of a small company founded in 1990 called iRobot Corporation. They started out by marketing iRobot Roomba, a robot vacuum cleaner. When the winds of war swirled up the company responded. The first PackBot left the lab in 2001. Within six years they were ubiquitous on the battlefield.

The case of iRobot is not exceptional. There is a reason for that. The free market has eclipsed government's capacity to provide innovative goods and services. That represents a significant change from just a few decades ago. Nothing illustrates this transformation better than the shift in research and development—the font of new products and new capabilities for the marketplace and the war path.

Before the Second World War, on average, government research accounted for 20 percent or less of all the dollars Americans spent on developing new capabilities. World War II and the Cold War changed all that. The success of the Manhattan Project, which developed the atomic bomb, in particular, enamored Washington with "big science." From World War II on, militaries largely pioneered the technologies that were the most critical to military competition. In the United States, for example, from jet aircraft and nuclear weapons to stealth technologies and precision-guided weapons, the Pentagon largely set the course of investments in science and technology, shaped research and development programs, and determined how new technologies would be applied to battle. The impact of the public sector defense research and effort was pervasive and dramatic. Government funded the lion's share. In the 1960s, government spending accounted for a mind-boggling two thirds of all research and development in the United States.[12] That, however, is no longer the case.

The U.S. Government's percentage of the research and development portfolio began to slip in 1980. Since then, the private sector has leapfrogged well ahead. By the mid-1990s, increases in government spending on research did not even keep up with inflation. By 1996, industry was already outpacing government, paying 60 percent of total funding and conducting 70 percent of the research.

Not only is the government effort accounting for less and less of the innovation pie, but increasingly more and more government research is being directed by the Congress through legislative "earmarks," government appropriations targeted towards a specific project by individual members. Almost 30 percent of the appropriated science and technology budget is directed by earmarks. Pork is also bi-partisan: for the 2008 budget, the ranking members from each party on the Appropriations Defense Subcommittee were the top members in the House in inserting earmarks into the budget. The Democrat got $162 million, and the Republican received $161 million.[13] Much of the research that members of Congress support pleases individual constituents but does not well address the armed forces' research priorities. As a result, although the money may not produce bad science, it may not produce the science the armed services really need. So, as government spends less on research and development (as a percentage of the whole), it gets even less for the money it does spend.

It is not so much that Washington's research effort is in dramatic decline. Government spending has been completely eclipsed by the explosion of private sector business creativity. American research and development continues to grow—to about $312 billion in 2004 (over 2.6 percent of GDP). That year industry accounted for 64 percent of the total. Government counted for less than a third. What these research and development trends illustrate is how the private sector and its vanguard, the individual entrepreneur, have become the great wellspring of innovation.[14] This is one reason why it just makes sense for the Pentagon to rely on contractors for cutting-edge capabilities and practices.

CHECKBOOK POWER

The second great advantage that the private sector brings to public wars is capacity. There is a very good reason why companies like KBR are willing to promise to support 50,000 troops anywhere in the world on a moment's notice—because they can. That capacity comes from an expanding global economy fueled by global business. In the modern world, free trade stands as the driving force in global economic growth. Countries that have pursued liberalization have witnessed an increase in GDP. And, as more countries have opted into the global marketplace since the end of the Cold War, the pace of globalization has really taken off.

As countries open their markets, per capita GDP increases. This is a simple fact. The International Monetary Fund (IMF) survey of the literature on trade and growth found that "many cross-country econometric studies have concluded that trade openness is a significant explanatory variable for the level or the growth rate of real GDP per capita." Countries that became global traders made more money.[15]

No nation has benefited from globalization more than the United States. A U.S. Commerce Department report in 2004 concluded that "Growth in trade over the past 50 years, fueled by falling trade barriers, has contributed directly to the most rapid sustained economic growth in U.S. history."[16] Global growth also spurs efficiency. The drive to produce "better, faster, cheaper" improves the competitiveness of manufacturing enterprises and service industries. In turn, competition brings lower prices.

Because the United States is the world's number-one global trader, it has been better positioned than any other country to exploit the global base of industrial goods and services that expanded so rapidly after the Cold War. "The late 1990s in the United States," writes John Steele Gordon in his comprehensive economic history of America, *An Empire of Wealth*, "were the greatest period of wealth creation in the history of the world."[17] No one does globalization better than the United States.

Not only is the United States the world's greatest competitor in a competitive world—there is plenty of competition out there to exploit. America's military industrial base is comprised of private-sector (both privately and publicly owned) and government-owned entities located in the U.S. and throughout the world that provide the full array of goods and services required by the armed forces of the United States and select allies.[18] And what is out there is a lot. As Pierre Chao, an industrial base expert at the Center for Strategic and International Studies, points out, "[I]n this round of globalization, not only are the links denser, but the pipes are fatter." At the peak of the last great round of industrialization at the end of the nineteenth century, industrial production counted for about 12 percent of GDP. Today manufacturing is pressing 25 percent of global production. Capital flows (moving money around the world to invest) counted for about nine percent of global GDP. Today, it is a startling 28 percent.[19] All this global growth has made the world America's shopping mall.

Global business is not only bigger, but the pace of the spread of globalization is quickening. The information age accelerated the process. Computers and digital communication systems have transformed business. At the beginning of the twentieth century, there were 1 million phones in the United States. Today there are over 300 million phones, cell phones, and personal digital communication devices. Twenty-five years ago, no one owned a personal computer. Today, many children, and most businesses, have a hard time envisioning life without them. Soon most people may own pocket-sized computers containing as much information as a modern library.[20]

These technologies have changed how the world talks, and that has had a profound impact on business. A vice president at KBR and the head of the company's laundry services in Baghdad have the same name. They often get each other's company e-mails—a reminder of how business communications have become instantaneous and ubiquitous. Getting information to the people who need it, when they need it, in the form in which they need it, has moved business processes into the speed of light—and that has put globalization on steroids.

One of the largest and fastest growing parts of this industrial base is the portion providing contractor services. It is huge. It is expanding. Between 2001 and 2005, the number of firms servicing the Pentagon grew to 96,000, an increase of 115 percent in four years.[21] In large part, the dramatic growth is because a lot of what the military wants is available for the asking. The twenty-first century private sector is a global supermarket. Many of the goods and services that the Pentagon demands from its contractors are the same things the private sector demands from the private sector—just-in-time delivery of common goods and services, everything from food to fuel.

Business is not only getting bigger, it is getting bigger in a way that is not undermining competition. One of the great risks of relying on contractors is that as companies got bigger from government profits a few big firms would dominate the defense business, driving up costs, driving off competition, and drying up innovation. The evidence suggests, however, that that is not what is happening. From 2003 to 2004, over 22 percent of the Pentagon's business that went to prime contractors wound up in the pockets of small business—about $42 billion. Subcontractors did $86.5 billion in Pentagon work, and 37 percent of that went to small firms.[22]

Services, in particular, remain one of the most diverse components of the defense industrial base. Small companies took in 24 percent of all defense contracts in 2005, and small and medium companies doing government work grew by an average of 20 percent over the course of the year.[23] Considering that this sector of military business includes mammoth contracts such as LOGCAP, the percentage of small and medium firms is significant. The opportunities for up-and-coming companies to bring fresh ideas to the marketplace have remained consistent despite the expansive growth of service contracts.

The dual forces of innovation and capacity provided by a rapidly expanding private sector offer the greatest competitive advantage in the world today, and the United States is its premier practitioner. "The American economy at the dawn of the twenty-first century," Gordon concludes, "was more nearly capable of producing those sinews [of war] than any other economy the world has ever known."[24] America's greatest strength is that it is a great competitor exploiting the advantages of the private sector better than anybody else. The greatest danger to the United States is not al Qaeda or anybody else but the possibility that America will lose that competitive advantage. Ironically, the greatest threats to losing America's competitive edge come not from enemies— but from ourselves.

WARNING SIGNS

Warnings that America could be its own worst enemy are not new. Before the Cold War barely started, George Kennan, the State Department scholar often credited as the father of "Containment" (America's strategy to counter Soviet power), warned that the greatest danger to the United States was that it might lose its competitive edge.[25] In 1946, Kennan penned "the Long Telegram," in which he laid out many of the key concepts for competing with the Soviets. The last three paragraphs (350 words of a very, very long message sent to State Department headquarters from Kennan's post at the embassy in Moscow) provided his most important points. "Much depends," he wrote, "on [the] health and vigor of our own society." Kennan argued, "We must have the courage and self-confidence to cling to our own methods and conceptions of human society. After all, the greatest danger that can befall us . . . is that we shall allow ourselves to become like those with whom we are coping." In short, he warned, if in order to compete with the Soviet Union, the United States became more like the Soviet Union, a "garrison state" with an authoritarian government and centralized decision-making that sacrificed the advantages of a free society and free markets, then America would lose its decisive competitive advantage.

Kennan's caution was repeated by many, including Eisenhower in his "military–industrial complex" farewell address. Perhaps the most extreme warning, however, came from a small, slight dark-haired woman with incredibly audacious ideas—Ayn Rand (1905–1982).

Rand's work read as a rejection of Soviet collectivism, but she intended far more. She proved almost as critical of American political leaders on the right and the left, realists and neo-liberals—even staunch anti-Communists. Anything that compromised individual choice and responsibility and handed power to the "looters" (in other words, big business and big government) Rand saw as fair game.

In 1943, Rand, an émigré who fled from Stalinist Russia, published *The Fountainhead*. It was rejected twelve times before she found a publisher. In a world where the United States bested its enemies by unprecedented teamwork that harnessed government, industry, and every American, no one seemed much interested in an odd-ball story of an idealistic architect who would rather be out of work than compromise his artistic integrity and who ultimately blew up his own buildings. By the close of World War II, however, by word-of-mouth the book became a bestseller.

In 1949, Hollywood made *The Fountainhead* into a film with one of its most bankable stars, Garry Cooper. Directed by King Vidor, it hit the screen to decidedly mixed reviews. "Wordy, involved and pretentious," wrote the *New York Times* film-critic Bosley Crowther, "it came to the Strand [movie theater] yesterday. And a more curious lot of high-priced twaddle we haven't seen for a long, long time."[26] Although Rand's film did not make for compelling cinema, the book and her subsequent bestseller *Atlas Shrugged* (1957) earned her a loyal following. Rand (who counted among the influences on her work the Age of Enlightenment and John Locke) birthed her own philosophy, "objectivism," which emphasized the individual and the pursuit of rational self-interest as the only appropriate measure of social value.

In the end, neither the warnings of Rand, Kennan, or even Eisenhower caused great consternation among the American populace, in large part because much of what they warned about never happened. Neither the state nor big business ever overwhelmed the nation's freedoms. Many of the issues that prompted their concerns, however, still linger, dangers that could threaten, as Kennan warned, the "health and vigor of our own society"—a profoundly capable private sector. And with more competitors in the world than ever, U.S. policies that weaken American competitiveness may be a far greater danger today than when Kennan wrote his telegram or Rand wrote her novels.

ASSAULT ON REASON

By far, enemy #1 in the battle to preserve the private sector is preserving the America's commitment to free trade practices against protectionist government policies. After World War II, the United States led the global campaign to open up markets. Through the 1980s free trade was not even an issue up for debate. Republicans, democrats, liberals, conservatives, right, left—all acknowledged that free trade should be the foundation of American economic and foreign policy. Even when doubts began to be heard, like complaints about foreign cars from Japan and trucks from Mexico, mainstream politicians held the line in both political parties. A republican president, George Bush, signed the North American Free Trade Agreement (NAFTA), a milestone in modern legislation promoting the open movement of goods and services between Canada, Mexico, and the United States. A democratic president, Bill Clinton and a republican Congress, worked hand-in-hand to ratify the treaty in 1993.

Free trade, however, is no longer America's idol. In October 2007, *The Wall Street Journal* found that 59 percent of Republicans surveyed thought free trade was bad for the nation. Democrats liked free trade even less. Adam Smith would not be pleased.

The origins of America's sudden loss of faith in free trade remain hotly contested. There are a number of possible causes, from a wave of anti-globalization demonstrations around the world to economic upheavals from the Asian Financial Crisis (1997) to America's post-9/11 recession to the unsettling rise of China as a manufacturing power and India as a service provider. After a half-century of runaway growth, some in the United States are getting nervous when they see other countries getting bigger in the rearview mirror of competition.

Each year, the Heritage Foundation, a think tank in Washington, D.C., and the editors of *The Wall Street Journal* publish the *Index of Economic Freedom*. The index evaluates and ranks 161 countries across 10 specific measures of economic freedom, including standards such as tax rates, investment and monetary policies, and property rights. In 2007, the United States finished a respectable fourth. Although America's scores have waxed and waned a bit over the last 15 years, they have continued, overall, to climb modestly. This good news is cold comfort. While the United States is hovering with modest gains in efficiency, other countries are making rapid strides, streamlining policies so that they can better compete in global markets. America can in part rest on its laurels, because the United States still has the world's largest economy, but that prestigious position may not last forever. America has to get back in the game.

The best policy Washington could adapt would be to rebuild bipartisan momentum for free trade agreements, international covenants between the United States and other free nations that facilitate the free exchange of goods, people, services, and ideas. The proposal to just with stick free trade may sound like an all-too-simplistic answer to the complex challenge of the global economy, but Clausewitz's maxim applies equally well to global economic policy. While free trade is the right answer, it is a tough task to remain true to free market principles in the face of stiff global competition and anti-globalization sentiment. That, however, is one of America's greatest challenges.

Although the world is getting more competitive and the ripples of globalization can touch the United States in a New York minute, little of the current backlash against free trade makes any sense from either an economic or security standpoint. The near-hysterical debate over outsourcing that preceded the 2004 Presidential elections offers one example.

OFFSHORING SECURITY

Offshoring is the transfer of a business process, such as customer service or the development of computer software, to an overseas provider. In July 2004, headlines screamed after the Department of Homeland Security (DHS) awarded a contract for US-VISIT (a project designed to monitor the entries and exits of non-U.S. citizens across U.S. borders) to Accenture LLP, a U.S. subsidiary of a Bermuda-based corporation. CNN's "Exporting America" ran a segment about outsourcing American security. For months, "Exporting America" tried to tap into public fears by highlighting anecdotal stories while ignoring official statistics that show that concerns about job loss are wildly overblown. Their reporting about potential security flaws was equally wrongheaded.

Economic arguments against outsourcing are the weakest of all. Outsourcing opponents routinely focus on only one side of the issue, ignoring the gains in lower prices, higher efficiency, and "insourced" jobs—work created as a result of overseas business. In 2004, when the Accenture LLP story broke, more Americans were employed than ever before—a record high of 139 million workers, as reported by the Bureau of Labor Statistics.[27]

The notion that sending jobs offshore creates more jobs is counter-intuitive, but true. Job losses from hiring foreign companies to do work tend to be small compared to the number of jobs created. The only official study on the impact of offshoring jobs available at the time (released by the Department of Labor on June 10, 2004) found that only 4,633 job losses were associated with overseas relocations in the first quarter of the year. That represented a miniscule two percent of total layoffs in America.[28] On the flip side, in 2004—as CNN railed about offshoring—studies showed there were 6.4 million jobs across the United States in which the employer is a foreign company. These jobs were and continue to be growing at a faster rate than jobs being lost. According to the Organization for International Investment, "Over the last 15 years, manufacturing 'insourced' jobs grew by 82% at an annual rate of 5.5%; and manufacturing 'outsourced' jobs grew by 23 percent—at an annual rate of 1.5%."[29] The truth is that smart outsourcing can add jobs.

There is no reason that the government should not exploit the advantages of free trade and outsourcing as aggressively as the private sector, if these practices deliver the best value for service. Protectionist policies only stifle innovation and increase costs. Where the contract is fulfilled—whether in Boston, Britain, or Bermuda—does not necessarily add to or detract from the end goal of protecting America. The only demand should be selecting companies that can satisfy all of the contract requirements while also expertly completing projects; and selecting companies with good management headquartered in countries with strong rule of law. In short, both the public and private sectors can achieve the appropriate levels of surety and reliability of service if they insist that contract work meets appropriate standards.

It is particularly important that the U.S. government insist upon stringent standards when dealing with national security–related work. Physical security, data protection systems, robust law enforcement, auditing, and strong legal protections are all important parts of that security. Any contract award that does not provide for these types of measures could compromise U.S. security, regardless of which company is awarded the contract or where the work will be done. In the absence of a stronger protections regime, foreign outsourcing customers have had to incorporate security requirements into a legally binding contract with foreign vendors. Contracts with U.S. outsourcers frequently specify New York as the controlling jurisdiction and require insurance, which is usually provided by a U.S. carrier.

Engaging in mutually beneficial cooperative business ventures with companies in countries that meet appropriate criteria is simply sensible outsourcing. It is good for General Motors and the federal government. It helps provide services in the United States and services in Iraq, Afghanistan, and other countries where American companies support the U.S. government. Sensible outsourcing is just a part of competing in the world today.

The short answer to addressing the fears of a hotly contested global marketplace is not to stop competing, but to become a better competitor in the race to provide better, faster, and cheaper goods and services. If the United States does not invest more effort on refurbishing its competitive edge, the competitive world in which we live will not continue to serve Americans well.

BINDING PROMETHEUS

Not only does America have to remain part of the global private sector to enjoy the advantages of the global private sector, Washington has to rethink how it taps into the wealth of the world. In the 1980s, under Republicans, the U.S. government undertook a major effort to be a better steward of tax dollars. The legacy of Reagan's effort to make the private sector serve government better has had the unintended consequence of making government a worse consumer.

During the Reagan era, a spending binge to refurbish the military after the hollow force of the 1970s, combined with tax cuts, sent the federal deficit soaring.

An administration full of fiscal conservatives had a hard time explaining why they could not balance Washington's checkbook. At the same time, a wave of defense contracting scandals assaulted the credibility of a government that got elected by promising smaller, more efficient government.[30] The White House and Congress responded with a long list of legislative initiatives to discipline how government did business. One of the most significant was the Federal Acquisition Regulation—the FAR.

In addition to the FAR, Washington put a number of other systems in place to safeguard the United States government against unwarranted exploitation. The International Traffic in Arms Regulations (ITAR), for example, regulates exporting sensitive defense technologies and services (such as high-powered computers and cryptographic analysis).

Washington first put export controls in place in 1949, principally focused on the Soviet Union. Though ITAR was a Cold War creation, it has been revised and expanded any number of times since the fall of the Berlin Wall, targeting a growing list of concerns over emerging national security threats. In 1998, for example, Congress tightened rules after a scandal over private-sector space services provided to China. The law added requirements for exporting technical information related to dual-use satellite technologies (technical capabilities that could be used by either the military or the commercial sectors).

There is plenty of pressure to add even more restrictions to ITAR. Some are driven by efforts to impose protectionist policies (laws and regulations intended to make it more difficult to compete with goods and services produced in the United States) clothed as measures to address security concerns. In other cases, they reflect genuine concerns over enemies trying to steal America's secrets. If ITAR restrictions become too restrictive (to the point that they seriously strangle first-class innovation) the problem will be solved. America will no longer have secrets worth stealing. The most dramatic and powerful advances will be made elsewhere.

The Omnibus Trade and Competitiveness Act of 1988 created another Reagan-era initiative, a legislative mandate for the Committee on Foreign Direct Investment in the United States (CFIUS), which has come to be another important regulatory mechanism. The Secretary of the Treasury heads CFIUS. Eleven other agencies participate in its deliberations, including the Departments of Defense, Justice, Commerce, and Homeland Security. CFIUS's task is "to suspend or prohibit any foreign acquisition, merger or takeover of a U.S. corporation that is determined to threaten the national security of the United States." CFIUS made headlines in 2006 when the proposed sale of facilities at six U.S. ports by a British-based company to Dubai Ports World, a government-owned company in the United Arab Emirates, raised hysterical concerns. Headlines trumpeted fears that Arab ownership might offer terrorists a gateway into American ports. Because the deal had been approved by CFIUS, some questioned whether the Bush administration exercised adequate due diligence in reviewing the sale. The concerns proved baseless but prompted shrill cries in some quarters for more protectionist policies.[31]

All these requirements are legacies of the Cold War. The problem is that the global marketplace is significantly different from the global marketplace that was present when all these rules were written a quarter of a century ago. Since then, Congress has blithely tinkered with the laws governing these instruments, but only to add requirements and restraints—ignoring that the nature of global competition is changing while the laws governing how America competes sleepwalk into the twenty-first century.

American laws need to look after American interests, but they have to serve all of the nation's interests equally well—including interests both of security and of economic growth. CFIUS offers a great example: although some foreign companies might want to buy American companies to steal American secrets, most want to invest in America because they recognize that America is a good investment. By the end of 2004, foreign investors held $1.9 trillion in U.S. corporate stock and $2.7 trillion in tangible assets. In 2005 alone, foreign investors increased their holdings in the U.S. by $1.4 trillion. This investment is good for Americans, contributing to low interest rates, bolstering stock values, and generating new jobs. In fact, foreign investment today supports over five million jobs. These are advantages worth protecting. Simply making it harder to invest in the United States is not an acceptable approach to providing security.[32] The longer that legislation such as CFIUS, FARS, and ITAR remains on the books unreformed, the more damage will be done to America's competitive edge.

Most of the rules governing how Washington acquires goods and services were drafted in the 1980s and were intended to add oversight, checks and balances, and transparency to how government does business. They were rules, however, written over a quarter of a century ago, designed for a marketplace that has transformed itself with the birth of the information age. It is hard to imagine any thriving major U.S. corporation for which business remains much the same as when Reagan was in the White House.

Since the end of the Cold War, Congress has been only become more unthinkingly reactive about the burden of layers of bureaucracy over contracting practices, adding more requirements at every whiff of scandal. Indeed, the reaction of congressional critics to complaints of contract abuse in Iraq was to axiomatically argue for even more hurdles to getting an agreement with the private sector. At the same time, individual members of Congress work more vociferously than ever to insert legislative mandates, called earmarks, to ensure that contracts and federal dollars are funneled to favored constituencies. The omnibus spending package Congress proposed for fiscal year 2008 (October 2007 through September 2008) included 11,000 individual earmarks.

Acquisition reform has been the "holy grail" of government reform since President Reagan commissioned the Packard Commission in 1985. It is too much to hope to achieve sweeping changes that could accomplish all of government's objectives—contracting that is fast, efficient, effective, thrifty, fairly competed, transparent, untainted by politics, and pleasing to every political constituency in Washington. On the other hand, the status quo is clearly unacceptable. At minimum, reforms must return the FAR to its original purpose as single family of guidance that governs government contracting, sweeping away the plethora of boutique regulations and requirements set up by individual agencies.

FISCAL POLICIES

Following World War II, even after expending $300 billion and 400,000 lives, the United States started the postwar period well ahead of the pack.[33] It had by far the largest economy in the world. By the end of the 1950s, the U.S. economy was worth more than double what it was before the war. Today, America still has the world's largest GDP, but it can no longer take that advantage for granted. In particular, the United States can ill afford to maintain government fiscal policies that undermine the nation's ability to compete. Under the list of bad policies two top the list by far—entitlement spending and tax policies.

The greatest danger to sustaining a strong national security system is not the private sector greed, it is Washington's indifference to a looming fiscal crisis that comes from the growing cost of entitlement programs like Medicare, Medicaid, and Social Security (discussed in chapter 2). Long-term entitlement spending poses a daunting challenge. Between now and 2050, Social Security, Medicare, and Medicaid costs will rise from 8.7 percent to 19.0 percent of GDP. Consider that an equivalently sized tax increase today—raising taxes by 10.3 percent of GDP— would amount to $13,457 per household.

Government spending on mandatory entitlement programs will crowd out the rest of the federal budget. If Washington does not restrain spending now, in order to pay for Social Security, Medicare, and Medicaid costs in the future, lawmakers may literally have to eliminate every other federal program, including all defense and homeland security. Because every year of delay steeply increases the ultimate costs of reform, addressing this challenge now must be a priority— otherwise there will not be enough defense dollars to either pay the military force or outsource any activities.

Entitlement spending is, in fact, at the root of the government's most serious fiscal ills, from balancing the budget to keeping inflation in check. The growth in these mandatory government spending programs has the potential to literally strangle the federal budget. It is one major challenge to U.S. competitiveness—but only one. If that were all Washington had to worry about, the challenge of formulating sound fiscal policies might not be so daunting. But, another equally troubling challenge lurks right behind it—taxes.

There are Americans today who believe that raising taxes can provide the government with enough resources to solve every problem (including Social Security, Medicare, and Medicaid) and stimulate growth in the economy; the source of their mistaken notion can be blamed in large part on the economist John Maynard Keynes (1883–1946). Keynes (a child of the Enlightenment if there ever was one) believed that government spending could be used to fine-tune the economy and create jobs. During the 1930s, in response to the trials of the great global depression, Keynes posited *The General Theory of Employment, Interest, and Money* (1936), claiming that government spending could be used to pump new money into the economy. He asserted that when the economy's total demand is lacking, government could act as a consumer and make purchases itself. Because the GDP is the sum of all purchases of final goods and services, these government purchases would add to GDP. In turn, the economy would grow.

Keynesnian economics, however, is just a shell game. Every dollar that the government injects into the economy must first be taken from the economy. As *The Wall Street Journal*'s Robert Bartley argues, it is all about "Government Budget Restraint" (GBR).[34] GBR is a measure of how government moves money around.[35] It highlights the futility of government "pump-priming." The government is not priming anything, but merely redistributing wealth—and probably far less efficiently than people could do it themselves.

The problem with Keynesianism, as columnist Amity Shlaes[36] makes clear, is worse than just creating the intellectual justification for high taxes and lots of government spending. The promise of government dole, she argues, was harnessed by the New Deal to put constituent politics in Washington on steroids by promising perfectly legitimate government payouts that would benefit certain electoral groups. In this manner, she writes, "the president [Franklin Roosevelt] systematized interest-group politics more generally to include many constituencies—labor, senior citizens, farmers, union workers." The New Deal helped create a new brand of politics that transcended old political ideology and popularized a kind of "liberal" ideology that promoted groups over individuals.

In many ways, the political implication of Keynesianism turned out to be more insidious than the merchants of death or the military industrial complex. There the enemy was simple greed. In the new liberal politics, Washington could console itself by arguing that it was layering on new taxes and programs in pursuit of social goods like eliminating poverty or alleviating suffering.

Keynesian economics, however, lacked any kind of checks and balances that told the government when spending was doing more harm than good. Indeed, much of the macroeconomic analysis done since Keynes wrote argues that there are legitimate limits to government intervention in the marketplace. In particular, relying on taxes to keep an economy competitive is a bad idea. High taxes only make the problem worse. When tax levels exceed 20 percent of GDP, taxes threaten to extinguish growth in an economy. America's problem is that taxes have been growing for decades. There are still too many people in Washington who take Keynes seriously. There is, according to economist J.D. Foster, "remarkable consistency in the growth of the taxpayer burden year after year. Over the past 40 years, the taxpayer burden has risen at an average rate of just over 2.1 percent per year."[37] The United States is on a path to break the 20 percent barrier and keep right on going.

The level of taxes is not the only problem. The current tax system imposes mammoth costs on economic efficiency. High tax rates discourage entrepreneurship. Discriminatory taxes against capital undermine saving and investment. Special loopholes and penalties undermine efficient allocation of resources. Complexity imposes deadweight. Economic output may be about 15 percent lower than it could be as a result of bad tax law. Annual growth rates could be much higher—*if* the tax system did not punish productive behavior.

America could afford some irresponsible fiscal policies when it had competitive edge to spare. That is no longer the case. Washington, if it wants to continue to rely on the strength of the private sector, cannot ignore the fiscal burden it places upon the economy.

Arguing that trying to turn back the burden of big government is impossible makes no sense, either. Big government is not inevitable. For the first quarter of the twentieth century, when the American economy grew dramatically, government was, as Amity Shlaes writes, "a pygmy. Its size was less than 2 percent of the national economy, smaller even than that of state and city governments." [38] The fiscal burden of Washington is not part of the tradition of liberal democratic government: it is a threat to it.

LEADING SMART

The list of Washington's shortfalls in helping hone the nation's competitive edge is long and getting longer. In addition to major issues that undercut America's global leadership right now (protectionism, obsessive regulations, ballooning entitlement spending, and high taxes) are a host of problems that may prove even more problematic in the long run. All of them have to do with fueling the nation's traditional capacity to exploit the nexus between science, technology, and entrepreneurship. That is important for a simple reason. It is estimated that scientific and engineering knowledge doubles every ten years. From the height of the Industrial Revolution to the decade after World War II, as much as 85 percent U.S. economic growth came from technological change. During the Cold War half of the nation's growth came from technology.[39] If the United States loses its ability to exploit innovation better, faster, and more cheaply than all comers (if America believes it can rest fat, dumb, and happy on the successes of the past), America may well lose its supreme competitive advantage.

High on the endangered list are science, technology, engineering, and math proficiencies. Today, the average American high school senior trails a similarly typical student in 21 other countries in both math and science. Many of the engineers and scientists produced in America's world-class graduate schools are foreign-born, including over one third of the doctoral students in the physical sciences, and half the engineers. U.S. visa policies make it difficult for these students to live and work in the United States after they graduate—and even if they can work here, security requirements generally preclude them from working for the government on defense-, intelligence-, or homeland security–related programs. To make matters worse, the number of foreign students coming to the United States dropped precipitously after 9/11 and is only now returning to pre-2001 levels. Even now, growth is anemic. Other countries are out-competing the United

States in attracting foreign students. When America does train a science professional, for the cost of employing them, a company could hire 5 chemists in China or 11 engineers in India.[40] The United States faces a dual challenge training Americans to compete better and encouraging the best in the world to join America's competitive team.

Trumpeting the importance of education may seem out of place in a list of priorities for harnessing the private sector for the public's wars. But the genius of war and the genius of the marketplace share much in common. They are, writes Robert Bruner, the Dean of the University of Virginia Business School, the "visionaries, inventors, entrepreneurs, and general managers, people who create something larger out of the assembly of resources. They are quick learners, they recognize problems, and opportunities ahead of the crowd, they shape visions and enlist others in support."[41] A competitive society, one that wants to exploit and not just manage the marketplace, needs this kind of genius by the bucketful—and this kind of genius is taught in the sense that a first class education, in matters that really matter, is undoubtedly the best preparation for the future.

Policies that inhibit the growth of a competent, competitive workforce have to be high on the list of anti-competitive government policies that have to change. "If you can solve the education problem," quipped Alan Greenspan, former chairman of the U.S. Federal Reserve Board, "you don't have to do anything else. If you don't solve it, nothing else is going to matter all that much."[42] Education and visa policies need to be a top priority.

In terms of an education agenda, Washington needs to do less, not more. Americans already spend a boatload on educating America's future workforce. The problem is America does not get much return on its investment. What is needed are schools that spend more of their money on educating children. Restoring good governance in education includes returning authority to the states and empowering parents with the opportunity to choose the right school for their children.

Not only does the United States have to start spending the money it spends on education on educating America's students, it has to start teaching twenty-first century skills—particularly in science, technology, engineering, and math. Traditional learning methods have to be replaced by teaching practices determined to be the most effective by cutting-edge scientific education research. America also has to change what it teaches. The old-fashioned ways of training scientists are dead—or should be. Today's boldest scientific advancements are made by understanding how complex systems work, integrating the knowledge of different physical sciences and engineering. Often referred to as "network science," effective research requires understanding multiple scientific disciplines as well as how to work in interdisciplinary teams.[43]

Visa policies also require fundamental rethinking. Over the decades, visa policies have evolved to favor some constituencies over others. They have been tightened to address concerns over unlawful immigration. They have been made more restrictive in response to fears about terrorism. They have been slowed by an immigration services system that fails to provide competent, responsive service. They all must change. The United States must actively encourage high-skilled immigration and ensure that foreign students receiving advanced scientific and engineering degrees have every opportunity to live and work in the United States.[44]

SOCIAL IRRESPONSIBILITY

Perhaps the most insidious threat to the future of the private sector will come not from Washington, but from the private sector. This threat comes from good people trying to do good things for good reasons. The doctrine of "corporate social responsibility" evolved as a well-meaning effort to take the hard edges off of globalization, but it is becoming one of the chief threats to freedom, security, prosperity, and environmental protection.

Corporate social responsibility insists that companies, when making corporate policy decisions, should put social considerations far ahead of making profits. The doctrine holds, according to Professor David Henderson, "that enterprises can best attribute to the general welfare by consciously adopting sustainable development as their objective, and pursuing in consequence a range of self-chosen social and environmental goals."[45] Simply complying with corporate responsibilities defined by laws is inadequate, it is thought. Companies should adopt virtuous conduct.

Two arguments fuel the argument that the private sector should seek to undermine its own efforts to remain competitive in the marketplace: (1) the inequities of global development make the rich richer at the expense of making parts of the world poorer, and (2) growth and wealth inevitably come only at the expense of severe environmental degradation. Profit-oriented activity wreaks inordinate destruction on the planet. In short, the two greatest evils of globalization—poverty and pollution—are caused by companies making profits. Because companies are largely responsible for making the world a miserable place, the private sector, globalization's critics contend, has a unique social obligation to adopt non–profit oriented policies to help redress these problems.[46]

Both arguments for corporate social responsibility, economic inequality and environmental stewardship turn the nature of globalization on its head. They are also flat wrong. Rather than being the source of inequality, globalization is perhaps the best mechanism available to offer opportunities for economic growth to poor nations.

Globalization is also the best tool for improving environmental standards. Mike Moore, former Director-General of the World Trade Organization, points out that, "All serious research shows that poverty is the greatest threat to the environment. People don't live in polluted squalor by choice, nor do they trek miles to strip trees for charcoal by choice. There is a direct connection with rising living standards and better environmental outcomes."[47] Countries enjoy a superior environmental quality when they can afford to establish and sustain environmental standards.

Global free markets create wealth. As incomes rise, more money becomes available to spend on environment issues. More money becomes available to establish and enforce environmental standards, and more money can be allocated to developing technologies and practices that reduce environmental degradation. In short, more globalization means a higher level of environmental sustainability—not less.[48]

Misunderstanding globalization, in turn, leads to thinking that corporate social responsibility (a doctrine that threatens to kill the force that is best suited to address human misery) is a good idea. It is not. Layering business decisions with extra concerns drives up costs and drives down profits. When that happens, companies will be strongly motivated to do whatever they can to hold on to market share and stifle competition, making sure—at minimum—that their competitors are weighted down with the same restrictions. Companies become more willing to adopt anti-competitive practices and press for more government regulation. That, in turn, results in less investment, less innovation, and less growth. Rather than achieving sustainable development, corporate social responsibility leads to a downward spiral of strangled growth and productivity.

Worst of all, the logic of corporate social responsibility pretends as if Adam Smith never wrote a word. Smith warned that the only thing worse than a government telling markets how to work was a corporatist sector setting its own policies independent of marketplace pressures.

Private-sector practices should focus on the private sector's purpose: competing in the marketplace. There is, of course, a place for self-governing rules and standards among private companies. IPOA standards of conduct for military contractors are a good example. A case can also be made for writing socially responsible requirements into a contracts and legislation—such as banning the practice of human trafficking. These, however, differ significantly from the kinds of policies pressed for by corporate social responsibility advocates. It is certainly appropriate for government, for example, to ban companies from undertaking activities that directly result in harmful behavior—like seizing the passports of foreign workers. On the other hand, trying to punish firms for the allegedly "indirect" consequences of their business practices—such as causing poverty—crosses the line as government wrongfully intrudes on free markets. Likewise, industry standards that are established in order to make companies better competitors are sensible. Ones that dictate social policies are not. In a free market, on the other hand, companies should be free to adopt any kinds of social policies they want (as long as they are consistent with the rule of law). They should not, however, be protected from the ways in which the marketplace might chose to punish or reward them for their choices. Nor should Washington be expected to enshrine corporatist polices in law.

THE AMERICAN CENTURIES

In a 1941 editorial in *Life* magazine, Henry Luce coined the term "the American Century." Few would debate that the century did not end as Luce had predicted, with the United States the world's primary competitor in a hyper-competitive free world. The issue now is whether America will own the twenty-first century as well.

Whether or not the United States fails to address the anti-competitive forces pulling against it, everything from outdated regulatory policies to inadequate education, it cannot stem the rise of the private sector's role in public wars. The expansion of the private sector and the forces of globalization could well continue whether the America is a world-class competitor or not. Within a decade, some suggest, over 80 percent of the planet's middle-class consumers will be outside the industrialized world. China alone could have 595 million middle-class consumers, almost twice the entire population of the United States.[49] China, India, and plenty of other nations are learning how to harness the power of globalization and outplay America at its own game.

As long as globalization grows, the private sector will continue to offer a powerful tool for public wars. In turn, the nations that compete best in the global marketplace will be in the best position to exploit the potential of the private sector. When they band together with other nations that share their commitment to freedom and free markets, the rising tide lifts all boats. Today, few countries are better placed to exploit the advantages of contracting in combat than is the United States—but whether it can retain that advantage remains to be seen.

6
Chapter

Why We Hate

Contractors do not wag dogs.

Hollywood makes bad history. Hollywood is no substitute for a schoolroom. On the other hand, Hollywood makes for *great* history. There are few better time capsules reflecting the angst and optimism of American popular culture than American films. The 1997 motion picture *Wag the Dog* offers a great example.

Headed up by veteran "A-list" director Barry Levinson, with an equally A-list cast including Robert De Niro and Dustin Hoffman, the film tells the tale of a Hollywood mogul whom the White House hires to divert attention from a presidential sex scandal. His solution is to stage a war against Albania. "The tail wagging the dog," implied by the title, comes from old adage symbolizing when a matter of lesser significance impacts the course of a much more important issue—like starting a war rather than embarrassing a president.

Levinson adapted *American Hero*, a 1993 novel by Larry Beinhart, which postulated that President George Bush manufactured the pretext for the first Gulf War to aid his reelection campaign. While Beinhart aimed his satire at a republican president, dog wagging soon evolved into a bipartisan sport. In 1998, President William Clinton became embroiled in a sex scandal. That same year, Clinton ordered cruise missile attacks on suspected terrorist targets in the Sudan and Afghanistan. In 1999, the White House sent U.S. troops in support of NATO operations in Bosnia. Administration critics looking to go after the president could not help invoking the "wag the dog" analogy.

Revisionist Hollywood history got so bad that, for some, myth became truth. When Clinton's Defense Secretary William Cohen (a republican) testified before the 9/11 Commission he had to specifically refute the charges. "I would like to say for the record," Cohen declared, "under no circumstances did President Clinton ever call upon the military and use that military in order to serve a political purpose. . . . at no time did he ever try to use it or manipulate it to serve his personal ends. . . . I think it's important for that to be clear because that 'wag the dog' cynicism that was so virulent."[1] The fact that a senior government official had to spend time during a hearing on the greatest terrorist tragedy in American history refuting the belief that presidential policies aped a movie is a great testament to the power of popular culture to shape popular opinion.

Wag the Dog followed in a great Hollywood Cold War tradition of recasting American angst as conspiracy. In *The Manchurian Candidate* (1962), the obscured enemy was a communist scheme to brainwash Frank Sinatra and Laurence Harvey. By 1975, following the wave of disillusionment from the Vietnam War, Robert Redford found that the enemy was "us" when he stumbled on an American plot to take over Middle East oil fields. In the wake of the Cold War, Hollywood had no enemies left, but old habits proved hard to break. Films like *The Long Kiss Goodnight* (1996) with Geena Davis and Samuel L. Jackson, *Conspiracy Theory* (1997) with Julia Roberts and Mel Gibson, and *Wag the Dog* had to invent conspirators to feed dark suspicions that there had to be an unseen enemy somewhere.

The Long Kiss Goodnight, for example, uncovered a CIA operation to stage a 9/11 style attack in order to justify budget increases to combat terrorism. Indeed, after the real 9/11, theories that the CIA had to be behind the attacks on New York and Washington sprouted all over the Internet. Life imitates art.[2]

CONSPIRACY 101

The reflexive post-9/11 impulse to embrace conspiracy concepts proved to be bad news for private sector military service providers, who became fodder for those who wanted to see the unseen hand of the military–industrial complex behind every contract. That Hollywood continually embraces the conspiracy motif should come as no surprise. That contractors would become a target for conjecture should come as no surprise either. Fear of conspiracies is an inherent part of American political culture. Senator Nye's investigations, Eisenhower's military–industrial complex, Sy Hersh's explanation for Abu Ghraib[3]—all resonated, in part, because they appealed to democracy's natural, deep distrust of secrecy and power.[4]

Conspiracy theories, once created, are hard to kill. They come to life first by tapping into the popular culture to find a fear or uncertainty that makes even implausible explanations sound reasonable. Then all that is required is to present a bare modicum of facts to justify a compelling and troubling narrative. That is not hard. It is easy to "connect to the dots" (in the parlance of the 9/11 Commission) when the conspiracy theorists get to pick which dots they want to connect. The rest is just sitting back and demanding proof that the conspiracy does not exist. Indeed, to hard-core conspiracy theorists, vehement repudiation of a conspiracy is certain proof that a conspiracy actually exists.

When civil society—the scholars, journalists, and others who look out for the rest of us—fail to provide the public a fair and balanced assessment of public policy dilemmas, they leave fertile ground for conspiracy theories to flourish.

Unfortunately much of the writing, reporting, and investigating on contractors in combat has done more to feed traditional conspiracy theory-making than to encourage real public policy investigation. Indeed, efforts to investigate and report on contractors in combat often begin with a presumption that company profits drive foreign policy—that tails really do wag dogs. How Hollywood and other aspects of political and popular culture foster these perceptions goes a long way toward explaining what we hate about contractors in combat and why.

Conspiracies will always be part of American culture, but separating fact from fiction is important. Separating unsubstantiated allegations from real problems is part of meeting the challenge of harnessing the private sector for public wars, keeping the United States competitive, and overcoming anti-competitive practices that could hamstring America's ability to effectively fight future wars.

LUMPERS AND SPLITTERS

Making conjecture seem like history is also part of Western culture. The practice comes from imitating the way real historians work. J. H. Hexter (1910–1996) described the process famously when he divided his fellow scholars into "lumpers" and "splitters."

It all started during a 1975 debate between Hexter and his fellow British historian, Christopher Hill, over the legacy of the seventeenth century (the age of Locke, Hobbes, and many of the intellectuals who contributed so significantly to America's intellectual traditions).[5] Hill had a penchant for reducing the consequences of every act to the forces of economic determinism (in classic Marxist terms, a contest over the control of the means of producing goods and services in a society). In a review of Hill's *Change and Continuity in Seventeenth Century England* and a subsequent exchange of letters in the *Times Literary Supplement*, Hexter branded Hill a "lumper." Lumpers organized history into coherent patterns by massing as much evidence as possible in support of their thesis, quietly ignoring facts and trends to the contrary. In contrast, "splitters" eschew patterns, use facts to make distinctions.

For Hexter, the great challenge of writing good history lay in balancing the tension between crafting a compelling narrative (lumping) and stopping to account for all the evidence (splitting) that reveals the complexities of recounting past events. When historians fall to one side (telling a good story at the expense of the facts) or the other (massing facts without coherent meaning and missing the big picture) they produce only caricatures. In short, selectively using sources made for poor history.

What makes for bad history, however, is often business as usual for writing about highly politicized contemporary issues when facts may be in short supply or uncooperatively do not match the story being spun. Noam Chomsky's *9–11* (2001) offers a great example of present-day lumping. Writing in the tradition of William Appleman Williams, the professor emeritus at the Massachusetts Institute of Technology and left-wing cultural critic and activist collected all the facts he needed to make the case that the fault of the 9/11 terrorist attacks lies with capitalist globalization.

Contractors in combat have fared even worse than the story of 9/11. Chomsky's writings were only the first wave. Rising anti-Americanism and anti-war sentiments created a climate that craved conjecture. Adding to this anxiety, in late 2001, Enron, a Houston-based energy company claiming over $100 billion in revenue, crashed in the wake of allegations of accounting fraud. Less than a year later, scandal also bankrupted WorldCom, a major U.S. telecommunications company. Both incidents deeply shook Americans' confidence in corporate America, priming the pump for concerns over contractors in Iraq and Afghanistan. These massive and highly publicized corporate failures made it easy to believe that the private sector simply could not be trusted.

Concerns over cooperate greed were just the start. An unsettled popular culture, drawing on an unsettling cocktail mixing the traditions of Machiavellian misgivings, Adam Smith's suspicions of a monopolistic marketplace, and Eisenhower's military–industrial complex, offered the intellectual underpinnings for doubting the motives of big government and big business. Plummeting public trust coupled with anxiety over the spiraling violence in Iraq made both the private sector and the public war easy targets. As a result, "why and what we have to fear" may not be the contractors themselves, but convenient truths that leave out the inconvenient facts. Lumped and split in scholarly books and documentaries, on Web sites, in the court of public opinion, and on the floor of Congress, the composite picture of contractors presented in popular culture is seriously out of step with how contracting actually works in combat (as described in chapters 3 and 4). None of the sources of civil society that inform our citizens has served us very well.

THE SCHOLARS

Academic works by serious academics (unlike Chomsky's polemics) are, of course, far from conspiracy theories. That does not, however, make them suitable for understanding contractors in Iraq and Afghanistan and the future of war.

Peter Singer, in *Corporate Warriors: The Rise of the Privatized Military Industry,* which came out only months before the war, raised a number of concerns. Arguably, *Corporate Warriors* was the first major scholarly treatment on the topic. Not surprisingly, Singer became a sought-after commentator as the occupation became more troubled. In turn, he ratcheted up the severity of his criticisms.

Singer is a thoughtful and insightful scholar. It is not clear, however, that at the onset of the war, he legitimately represented an authoritative source for commentary on contemporary contracting practices.

Support firms providing logistics and other services comprised the overwhelming bulk of contractor support in Iraq. In a 254-page book (excluding notes, bibliography, and index), *Corporate Warriors* dedicates less than 16 full pages to discussing these kinds of companies.[6] Four of those pages are simply a description of the services military support firms provide. As a result, many of the case studies in *Corporate Warriors* have little direct relevance.

Corporate Warriors' discussion of the performance of service companies is not only brief, it is ambivalent. The chapter on these companies (which focuses on Brown & Root and the successor company—KBR) ranges from mild criticism, wherein he noted that "not everything has gone smoothly for the firm in recent years", to complimentary comments: "In general, Brown & Root has been able to fulfill these [government] contracts successfully" and "The accomplishment of Brown & Root in providing superior, rapid logistics and engineering services has clearly established a template for future military operations."[7] In fact, reading Singer's brief treatment of KBR's major role in Pentagon contingency operations should have suggested that there be no surprise that the company would likely play a major role in any future military deployment—whether it was under a democratic or republican administration.

Singer dedicates much of *Corporate Warriors* to an analysis of private military security firms such as Executive Outcomes, which, for a period after the Cold War, did a thriving business in conflicts across Africa. These companies, however, had by and large gone out of business before 9/11. Some of them have been reorganized and renamed. It is also known that some South Africans, including former employees of these companies, are employed by subcontractors in Iraq. Their number, in terms of the overall contractor force, is very small. Several of the major private security firms serving in Iraq, such as Blackwater, were not even in operation during the period covered by the book. As a result, many of the case studies in *Corporate Warriors* have little to tell us about Iraq (though 2008 saw an updated edition containing some information concerning contracting operations since 9/11).

Nor does Singer escape accusations of lumping. Richard Lacquement, a professor of strategy and policy at the U.S. Naval War College, wrote in a review of the book that Singer

> tends to lump together all flavors of private military corporations, suggesting guilt by association with a small number of admittedly distasteful companies. This tendency to associate loosely all firms with the sins of the most egregious ones (almost always provider firms) seems even less fair given the fact that elsewhere Singer notes that such firms constitute a small fraction of the overall private military firm population. Many of his accusations do not apply well to support firms.
> The book contains some significant flaws, but they generally stem from the groundbreaking effort to comprehend the significance of these firms. There are also many loose assertions, insinuations, and innuendos that are unlikely to withstand closer scrutiny, but for now, as an opening argument, they should be taken seriously."[8]

In other words, *Cooperate Warriors* was the first, but hardly the last word on the subject.

The press' insistence on portraying Singer as an expert on contracting in Iraq after the outbreak of the war was also problematic. Singer did not have any unique knowledge of contracting practices in or after the war in Iraq. Indeed, few in Washington did. Many of the oversight mechanisms that provide authoritative information on contracting in Iraq, including federal auditing agencies, Inspectors General, and the Government Accountability Office, had not even begun their operations when Singer published the book. Any Washington analyst speaking on the efficacy of contracting in Iraq at the time could largely only conjecture on the conduct of contracting. Interestingly, since publication of *Corporate Warriors*, Singer has not produced any substantive scholarly research on the subject. His most recent books are on child warriors in Africa and robotics.

But Singer has not remained entirely silent. He has produced some writings and papers covering contractors during the occupation period, including preparing an updated edition of *Corporate Warriors*, in which he discussed contracting in Iraq. In September 2004, he wrote a piece for the *Washington Post* examining the scandal at Abu Ghraib. This analysis, however, differs in character from the academic tone of *Corporate Warriors*. Singer started out with the Army's report that 16 of 44 documented incidents of abuse involved contractors. He then added a laundry list of unsubstantiated allegations regarding other incidents of contractor misconduct. Singer also lumped in some additional unsupported assertions, including (1) a claim that "nothing is being done to make sure that such a fiasco [Abu Ghraib] doesn't happen again" (at the time of the article, the Pentagon had already initiated a long list of investigations and corrective actions);[9] (2) an allegation that the "fact" that outsourcing saves money is a "common myth" (this assertion can only be made by dismissing out of hand many studies that show the opposite);[10] and (3) an allegation that contracting "has never been about saving money. It's more about avoiding tough political choices concerning military needs, reserve call-ups, and the human consequences of war" (this assertion will be dealt with in chapter 7).[11] From this list, he offers a general indictment of government contracting in Iraq, crossing well over the line from scholar to pundit.

Deborah Avant, Associate Professor of Political Science and Director of the Institute for Global and International Studies at the Elliott School of International Affairs, George Washington University produced the next major scholarly contribution on the subject. *The Market for Force: The Consequences of Privatizing* updates the image of the contractor with a few references to Iraq and Afghanistan, noting for example the incidents at Abu Ghraib and the murder of four Blackwater contractors in Fallujah.[12] Nevertheless, Avant covers much the same ground as *Corporate Warriors*. In addition, as Singer's, her study primarily focuses on contractors that provide military-like security services rather than companies like KBR and DynCorp that offer logistical support. On the other hand, although Singer mostly imitates the historian's craft, Avant tackles contracting from a political scientist's theoretical perspective. Much as realist and neo-liberal scholars try to organize foreign affairs under various international relations theories, she offers a framework for evaluating the impact of contracting in combat on governance, civil society, and military effectiveness.

Though Avant's investigation takes a different course, she ultimately shares many of Singer's concerns. Avant begins with a premise that would make Machiavelli proud, arguing that the monopolization of violence stands as a defining feature of sovereignty. She is also a structuralist. Avant believes that nations best serve the public good when they play by the rules. "The control of force has been most stable, effective, and legitimate when all three aspects have reinforced one another," she writes, "when capable forces have been governed by accepted political processes and operated according to shared values."[13] An overreliance on private security firms, Avant concludes, threatens to undermine the trilogy of the safe, secure, and appropriate use of military force. Private sector alternatives to national militaries could undercut their spirit and effectiveness, in turn leading to loss of political control.

Avant falls short not by lumping facts, but in how she fits the facts to theory. Avant has no faith in the marketplace to moderate the behavior of for-profit companies—a debatable presumption. Likewise, the notion that governments can ever have a "monopoly" on violence can also be disputed. Economics professor Bruce Benson notes, in a review of *The Market for Force,* that "even if a bureaucratic organization, such as [a] police force or an army, produces a good or a service, the individuals who work in that bureaucracy are private parties under contracts negotiated either individually or through a collective bargaining organization, such as a union. The individuals are not 'owned' by the state. . . . Seen in this context, the normative idea that 'government' should have a monopoly in the production of violence, out of the fear that private entities might abuse such powers, does not make much sense because contracting out must occur at some level."[14] Privatization, Benson argues, has long been a fact of life in providing public services. As a result, Avant's presumption that more privatization endangers loss of political control is questionable.

Through 2005, most scholars, other than Singer and Avant, had been relatively silent regarding trends concerning the private sector in public wars. There are few studies of comparable depth and scope. The fact that academia has been much absent from the debate not should be seen as too surprising. Interdisciplinary studies are often the most difficult to tackle, and as an academic topic, this subject sits at the fault-line of a number of disciplines—military and business history, economics, international relations, law, philosophy, national security, and public policy, to name a few. Undertaking a study requires proficiencies and knowledge in multiple areas. Studies on Iraq and Afghanistan are complicated by the fact that both are active war zones, making it hard for scholars to access the information they need to prepare authoritative studies. Once the work is done, it can difficult to find peers qualified to review the study. Academic departments, journals, and conferences have a hard time classifying the research. Even the best work could be easily overlooked, dismissed, or misunderstood. Worst of all, few pick up the challenges raised by the scholars—testing their conclusions, refining theories, adding new evidence: in short, all the effort needed to build and broaden academic studies so that they provide a robust body of research on a subject. All these things have been missing in the debate over contractors in combat—and when the academics are absent, the other voices that impact modern memory move in quickly to fill the gap.

THE MOVIES

Just as academia has been slow to rise to the challenge analyzing the issues surrounding contractors in Iraq, Hollywood has proved to be even more sluggish. That void created an unprecedented opportunity for independent filmmakers.

Hollywood has changed since World War II. Even before Pearl Harbor, Hollywood released a spate of films interpreted as encouraging American intervention in the war. They prompted congressional hearings, where Senator Gerald Nye accused Hollywood of wanting to enter the war to protect its business interests in Great Britain.

When war finally came, Hollywood enlisted. U.S. Marines at Wake Island held out against an overwhelming Japanese invasion following the bombing of Pearl Harbor in 1941; the movie *Wake Island* sprang to the silver screen just nine months later (interestingly, the over one thousand contractors on the island did not rate a place in the largely fictionalized account of the siege). *Wake Island* was just one of many war movies to hit the theaters. According to culture historian Richard Sklar, "In the three full years of war, 1942–1944, the studios averaged around four hundred and forty features a year."[15] Many of the films were for or about war effort.

In contrast, Hollywood's first spate of Iraq war movies did not come out until 2007. Most of them were critical or at best ambivalent about the American adventure in Iraq. None did much box office business.[16] They were also a little late to the screen. Independent documentary filmmakers had already birthed a number of major documentaries on the war, including critically acclaimed films such as *Fahrenheit 9/11* (2004) and *Gunner's Palace* (2004). These features, rather than mainstream Hollywood movies, established the first celluloid symbols of Iraq and Afghanistan in modern memory.

Without question, the most significant film of the era was Michael Moore's *Fahrenheit 9/11*. The award-winning movie was Moore's fifth production. His previous work included the documentaries *Roger & Me* (1989) and *Bowling for Columbine* (2002), as well as *Canadian Bacon* (1995), a comedy with a plot similar to *Wag the Dog* (the U.S. president engineers a war with Canada to boost his ratings). According to a review in *Time*, *Fahrenheit 9/11* argued that "the collusion of big corporations and bad government [has exploited] the working class, here and abroad, for their own gain . . . in the process [depriving] citizens of their liberties."[17] After its release, the film quickly became the highest-grossing documentary of all time. It also generated immense controversy. Media response was rampant. Typical was a searing column by the writer Christopher Hitchens, who declared the film riddled with inaccuracies and lies.[18]

More than one commentary on the film drew upon references to Eisenhower's military–industrial complex in describing the logic behind Moore's movie. Nevertheless, the subject of contractors in combat hardly rates a mention. That is not surprising. Attention to the issue did not dominate the headlines until the spring of 2004, and by that time the film was already in the can and headed for movie theaters.

Other filmmakers, however, were quick to build on Moore's motif to frame the war as a story about big business and bad government. *Why We Fight* (2005) screened at the Sundance Film Festival 44 years after Eisenhower's farewell address. That speech figures prominently in the documentary's explanation of why America went to war in Iraq.

The title, *Why We Fight*, draws from a series of documentaries commissioned by the War Department during World War II. Army Chief of Staff George C. Marshall needed to explain government war policies in simple terms to millions of American soldiers drafted into uniform. Those documentary films were made to serve that purpose. The task of making the films fell to a big-time Hollywood director, Frank Capra, who then served as a major in the U.S. Army Signal Corps. Among others, Capra enlisted the support of Walt Disney, whose studios provided cutting-edge animation to illustrate the global struggles against fascism. The documentaries were so popular that they were distributed to commercial theaters as well as overseas to American allies in Britain and Russia.

In co-opting the title "Why We Fight," filmmaker Eugene Jarecki accomplishes a number of symbolic goals. First, he intimates that the film is picking up Capra's mantle, the responsibility for explaining to the American people why their sons and daughters are in harm's way. Second, the title implies an irony, contrasting American participation in the "Good War," as opposed to military adventurism since World War II. Both reinforce Jarecki's indictment of a corrupt Washington and a self-serving corporate America.

In another manner, the choice of title is appropriate. Jarecki attempts to accomplish essentially the same task as Capra—placing the decision for war in a simple, compelling moral context. That was certainly Capra's supreme achievement in his wartime documentaries. There was a reason why Marshall had confidence that Capra would make the kind of movies Washington needed to make the case for war. The story Washington was selling was the same kind of tale that Capra had been putting on the silver screen since the 1930s in movies like *Mr. Smith Goes to Washington* (1939), a film that celebrated faith in the traditional American values of patriotism and democracy. Filmmakers like Capra and Disney, Sklar writes, "demonstrated remarkable skill at infusing social myths and dreams with humor, sentiment, and a sense of shared moral precepts and responsibilities."[19] In his film, Jarecki attempts to follow the same formula, but misses the target.

Politically charged documentaries, like the anti-war *Why We Fight*, take lumping to its highest level. Jarecki includes multiple explanations for why America undertakes corrupt crusades, including an obsession with military technology, corporate profits, and outright hubris. He also adds various allegations to undermine any claim that Washington has any moral authority. Some of the most manipulative moments include the use of personal vignettes. Interviews in the film include one with William Solomon, a 23-year-old New Yorker who enlisted in the army for six years and was shipped to Iraq. Solomon claimed to have joined the military out of depression and desperation. His mother had died and he was deeply in debt. From this vignette, the film implies that the burden of fighting wars for the military–industrial complex falls on a "poverty draft" of volunteers who join the military because they have no other choice (Moore makes a similar charge in *Fahrenheit 9/11*). Though the idea of a "poverty draft" is a hotly disputed contention,[20] *Why We Fight* does not include any vignettes or other facets to show the other side. Indeed, the entire film seems to artfully avoid those facts that do not fit the story Jarecki is trying to tell.

Filmmaker Robert Greenwald, to an even greater degree than Moore or Jarecki, has taken on the role of a modern Capra-esque filmmaker. When Capra exalted traditional American values as he did in films like *Mr. Smith Goes to Washington* and *It's a Wonderful Life* (1946), he had to do so in part by indicting the establishment as a foil for the determined, idealistic individual to stand up against. In the case of *It's a Wonderful Life*, the bad guy is a greedy banker. In *Mr. Smith Goes to Washington*, it is a cabal of businessmen and corrupt senators. When *Mr. Smith Goes to Washington* came out, it was actually highly controversial. Congressional voices argued that it should not be seen overseas because it would be interpreted as an indictment of American democracy. Indeed, Vichy France (the unoccupied portion of the country after its defeat in 1940, ruled by a fascist government) banned Hollywood films but gleefully made an exception for *Mr. Smith Goes to Washington* because the regime considered the film anti-American. Greenwald adopted the same approach, creating a series of films denouncing, among others, conservative media (*Outfoxed: Rupert Murdoch's War on Journalism*—2004) and corporations (*Wal-Mart: The High Cost of Low Price*—2005), as well as defense contractors in combat, in *Iraq for Sale: The War Profiteers* (2006). All are stories of the little guy being duped by big, bad corporations and an indifferent government.

Greenwald and Capra, though polar opposites in their relationships to the wars of their times, share common ground. Neither were disinterested parties. Both had a dog in the fight—and dogs do wag tails. When Capra crafted the "Why We Fight" series, he wore an American military uniform. His films were designed to gain support for the war effort. Greenwald is a co-founder of a group called "Artists United to Win Without War," part of a coalition of national organizations called "Win Without War," that advocates, among other policies, a "prompt withdrawal of troops" from Iraq. His films are designed to erode support for the war. Indeed, the underlying premise of *Iraq for Sale* is not merely exposing corrupt contracting practices but, in the tradition of *Fahrenheit 9/11* and *Why We Fight*, challenging the U.S. military effort in Iraq as well. Indeed, in 2003, Greenwald released *Uncovered: The Whole Truth About the Iraq War*, which attacked the legitimacy of Washington's decision to invade the country. Thus, it is difficult to argue that the motivation for *Iraq for Sale: The War Profiteers* does not come, at least in part, from Greenwald's anti-war activism. Greenwald's politics make it difficult to believe that the film represents an objective assessment of contracting practices in Iraq.

Iraq for Sale: The War Profiteers offers a compilation of all the significant allegations made against contracting in Iraq, from U.S. policies being driven by corporate greed to undermining military effectiveness and exploitation of employees by contracting companies. The film, however, is an exercise in overactive lumping that is so severe that even film reviewers commented on it. "There's no objectivity in this film," Walter Addiego writes for the *San Francisco Chronicle*. "Greenwald's goal is not to offer balanced coverage but to roil the waters. It should also be said that most of the charges aired here have been reported before. But Greenwald is skillful enough to spark a fresh sense of outrage."[21] Jeannette Catsoulis for the *New York Times* describe the film as a mix of "facts, liberal outrage and emotional manipulation (like his colleague Michael Moore, Mr. Greenwald knows the visual power of a grieving mother), 'Iraq for Sale' has an us-versus-them sensibility that's extremely effective."[22] Culling and illuminating the most compelling elements of a narrative, such as featuring emotionally charged individual interviews and repeating even the most outrageous allegations, are the hallmarks of cinematic lumping.

Greenwald's assertion that the film offers a thoughtful and probative study of the subject rests primarily on a practice of bombarding company officials with e-mails and phone calls requesting interviews. All of Greenwald's requests were summarily denied (as illustrated with outtakes at the end of the documentary where filmmakers make countless efforts to talk to company officials on the record). Given Greenwald's reputation for politically charged and biased work, it is not surprising many declined to be interviewed for *Iraq for Sale*, but this meant that Greenwald did not present any viewpoints that might have come from his detractors. Doug Brooks, the president of IPOA, whose members include companies discussed in the film, tracked down the filmmakers and requested to be interviewed. Brooks appears very briefly in the film, and his interview is posted on the *Iraq for Sale* Web site, but none of the major points he raised about contractor performance and accountability are addressed in the documentary.[23]

It is also clear that as many of Greenwald's films, *Iraq for Sale,* rushing to be relevant, has the feel of a film rapidly slapped together and released. *Iraq for Sale,* for example, includes incidents that occurred little more than a month before the movie hit the silver screen. Politics may well have driven the production agenda. "At the [Washington] D.C. premiere," relates one report, "[Greenwald] made it clear that the film's agenda is to affect the 2006 election. In a Q&A following the film, Greenwald and Robert Borosage, co-director of the Campaign for America's Future, talked about producing the film in time for the election."[24] The movie's production company even established a Web site called "Brave New Theaters" as a resource for organizing and promoting screenings of the film.[25] Greenwald also worked with anti-war political action groups such as MoveOn.org to help speed sales and distribution.[26]

Politicized documentaries are nothing new. Arguably, Moore, Jarecki, and Greenwald follow an established American liberal tradition. In the 1930s a group of filmmakers formed the Worker's Film and Photo League to make politically and socially progressive documentaries. During the Depression, the U.S. government produced films to trumpet New Deal programs like rural farm assistance. In the 1950s and 1960s, documentary filmmakers adopted techniques from *avant garde* films schools like Direct Cinema, *Cinéma Vérité,* and the British Free Cinema, which relied on location shooting, nonprofessional actors, minimalist scripts, and hand-held cameras. The appearance of "raw" filmmaking they invoked gave documentaries a greater feeling of immediacy and being rooted in real life events. The politically charged decades of the 1960s and 1970s and issues such as civil rights, the Vietnam War, and the women's rights movement inspired a dramatic expansion of interest in politicized documentaries.

That said, the current spate of politicized documentary films is in a league of its own. Today's independent filmmakers have access to production technologies that rival what can be done in Hollywood. Additionally, as demonstrated by films like *Iraq for Sale,* independent producers are no longer bound by traditional means for marketing and distributing their features. *Fahrenheit 9/11* showed that these films can be commercially viable, reaching very large public audiences. These features make the politicized documentary a potent part of modern popular culture. In some respects, documentaries may prove to have even more pervasive impact on the modern memory of wars than does traditional Hollywood fiction.

Documentaries have an unprecedented opportunity to influence public policymaking as well. There are dangers there. Documentaries live in a shadow-land of scholarship. Unlike traditional Hollywood fare, they can claim that they present real facts and real history because they deal with undeniably real subjects. On the other hand, documentary filmmakers are not bound by the same rules of scholarship that generally guide historians and political scientists. Nor do documentary filmmakers have to adhere to the standards of journalism followed by reporters. Thus, while readers of academic or scientific material from a professional journal (like the *American Historical Review* or *International Security*) might have confidence that the author at least knew about professional standards and their published work had been peer reviewed, a movie patron can't have that same confidence. Documentary makers frolic in a "Lumpers" playground with little concern that they might be held accountable for the veracity of their research. Ticket sales, rather than quality of scholarship, stand as the most important measure of a film's long-term influence.

THE BOOKS

As conditions in Iraq deteriorated, contractors in combat consistently garnered front page headlines, and DVD sales for *Fahrenheit 9/11* skyrocketed, mainstream publishers had proof enough that the issue of mixing profit and patriotism could produce bankable books—the result was a small library on the subject. These works differ qualitatively from *Corporate Warriors* and *The Market for Force,* both of which were published by university presses.

Publication by a college academic press is often considered as a mark of at least some promise of responsible scholarship. Typically, these works are heavily footnoted. In other words, authors must provide documented sources for each piece of evidence presented. Notes are usually from "open sources" (ones accessible to anyone through publications, libraries, the Internet, or public archives), allowing other scholars to check the notes and determine for themselves the veracity of the material being cited. In addition, manuscripts submitted to academic presses usually undergo a peer review. The publisher will send the text to from one to three scholars knowledgeable in the field. Typically, reviewers are asked to comment on the quality of the scholarship, the use of sources, and how the author's work fits into the larger body of writings on the topic. It is highly unlikely that a university press would accept a book for publication if the author's peers cast serious doubt the value of the work.

Many universities recognize that acceptance by an academic press is indicative of a sufficient degree of rigor in the scholarly research, making such publication often sufficient to meet the requirements for obtaining tenure. No respectable university press would print a book that merely compiled assertions and allegations without any assessment of the worth and relevance of the criticisms leveled at the subject. For this reason, Singer and Avant's books, published by two of the more well known and respected university presses—Cornell and Cambridge—are given much credence. Other, recent books on contracting in combat (all from commercial presses) do not face the same scrutiny.

Although tales of contractors in Iraq are not authoritative, they are influential. The Web site of *Iraq for Sale* lists several under a section called "facts and research."[27] Alongside *Corporate Warriors* and *The Market for Force,* Greenwald lists a half-dozen books by commercial publishers. In 2007, one tell-all book on contractors reached *The New York Times* bestseller list for nonfiction, hardcover.

Like Hollywood, commercial publishers proved to be slow off the press when it came to the issue of contractors in combat. Commercial books on Iraq appeared within months after the war ended, but contractors were not a major theme in any of them. The first wave of contractor books appeared in 2006. A trio of works garnered particular attention. Gerald Schumacher's *A Bloody Business: America's War Zone Contractors and the Occupation of Iraq* is perhaps the least problematic of the three.

Despite its inflammatory title, Schumacher, a retired Special Forces colonel and freelance author, commentator, and business consultant, does not set out to indict the practice of contractors in combat. "Many Americans believe that war should be the exclusive purview of soldiers," he writes in the introduction. "This thinking ignores the realities of insurgent warfare, the requirements of nation building, the complexities of battlefield technologies, and the willingness of volunteers to join a downsized military in the absence of a national draft."[28] Rather than grapple with the rights and wrongs of contracting practices, Schumacher stated his primary interest was in crafting an unvarnished story of what life for contract employees was really like. Two companies, MPRI and Crescent Security, allowed him to serve as the equivalent of an imbedded reporter observing their overseas operations.

Schumacher's assessments are strengthened both by the fact that he has extensive professional experience in military operations on the battlefield and that he actually accompanied contractors in combat. Still, *A Bloody Business* offers only a small sliver of insight into contracting practices in Iraq and Afghanistan. Schumacher covers only three kinds of activities: convoy, training, and security operations. These make up a small percentage of operations (albeit the ones most likely to find themselves in combat). He is less well qualified to make a broader assessment on contractor operations and the nature of the war and war strategy. What's more, *A Bloody Business* contains no footnotes or references. Schumacher's reporting has to stand on its face value; it is unfair to try to draw larger lessons or conclusions from what amounts to a personal account of life with contractors in combat.

Robert Young Pelton's *License to Kill: Hired Guns in the War on Terror* covers the subject of contractors much more broadly. Pelton seeks to paint a portrait of the activities of security contractors in Iraq, Afghanistan and elsewhere since 9/11. He also relies on first-person vignettes as the heart of his book. Like Schumacher, he collected many of his stories first-hand, on the battlefield. In many respects, *License to Kill* is similar to *A Bloody Business*—a war story about gritty, dangerous life on the front line. Pelton is a journalist, filmmaker, and explorer; his book reads as much like a travelogue as like a study of contracting in combat.

A difference between *A Bloody Business* and *License to Kill* is that Pelton is less inclined to act as a cheerleader for contractors and contracting practices. He shares the concerns of Avant and Singer that the most significant danger is the loss of government's control over military operations. Pelton quotes from a conversation with Singer in the book. "It's not about economic cost savings," Singer states, "it's about political cost savings. When things go wrong, you simply blame the company."[29] Lack of contractor accountability and the consequences of contractor misconduct are themes Pelton returns to throughout the book. In turn, Pelton earned a blurb of praise from Singer for the book's dust jacket:

Licensed to Kill is smart, funny, sometimes scary, and always interesting. Pelton truly captures the cast of characters that make up our new 'coalition of the billing' in the War on Terror."
– P. W. Singer, author of *Corporate Warriors: The Rise of the Privatized Military Industry*

Likewise, Pelton speaks warmly of both Singer and Avant's critique of government contracting.[30]

In the end, however, Pelton adds little to the debate. He, for example, criticizes Order 17 as creating "a virtually nonexistent standard of accountability for security contractors in Iraq that has persisted, though the specific legal grounds have since shifted."[31] Like *A Bloody Business*, Pelton's work lacks notes and references. He offers no consideration of alternate viewpoints. Other than his personal opinion, the status of legal oversight of contractors lacks much authority as a forceful critique.

The third major book to come out from commercial houses in less than a year was *Blood Money: Wasted Billions, Lost Lives, and Corporate Greed in Iraq*, by T. Christian Miller. Miller is investigative reporter for the *Los Angeles Times*. Like Pelton and Schumacher, he writes from the perspective of a first-person observer. Miller has considerable experience in international reporting.

Like the other books, *Blood Money* has a sensationalist title. As Miller's title also suggests, however, his story includes much more than a combat narrative. *Blood Money* puts contracting in combat in the context of the administration's overall policy and strategy for fighting the war and winning the peace. "In his dazzling new book," writes John Freeman in a review for *The Seattle Times*, "failures are part and parcel of the new and improved kind of war the U.S. hoped to fight in Iraq. Following the swift fall of the Taliban in Afghanistan, Secretary of Defense Donald Rumsfeld wanted to go in fast and quick in Baghdad with a light force, Miller explains, then outsource the rebuilding to corporate America."[32] In short, *Blood Money* falls more in the tradition of *Iraq for Sale* than *Why We Fight*. His indictment is much more modest. Rather than go after a corrupt globalist, capitalist system, Miller lays the blame squarely on an administration guilty of hubris, dishonesty, and incompetence.

Blood Money departs from *Bloody Business* and *Licensed to Kill* in that Miller includes the trappings of an academic study, including footnotes and an extensive list of on-the-record interviews (meaning the person being interview agreed that their remarks could be quoted in public). To have done anything less would have seriously undercut the book's credibility. It would have been difficult to accept that the author could be both a globetrotting investigative reporter and at the same time have had occasion to deeply research all the strategic and political aspects of the story that would have required putting the White House, the Pentagon, Wall Street, and a number of other places under careful scrutiny as well over the brief years of the events described in the book.

Still, even the modicum of notes and sources provided eschews the notion that Miller has any grand new insights to offer. Although the list of interviewees is long (including Peter Singer, on multiple occasions), with few exceptions, such as Douglas Feith (the Pentagon's Undersecretary for Policy in the run-up to the war and during the initial years of the occupation) and perhaps a dozen others, the names are not recognizable experts with unique and unimpeachable insights into the great geo-strategic issues surrounding the war. The footnotes are equally unimpressive, citing some of the interviewees, but mostly secondary sources including press accounts, published government studies and reports, and a few original official letters and memoranda obtained by the author.

To his credit, however, Miller documents his sources. Yet, it is difficult to see where he has added much new "big picture" information about contracting. "Billions have gone missing, as Miller reveals," Freeman gushes in his review in

The Seattle Times.[31] That is not an accurate comment (Freeman appears to have come to his conclusion by rephrasing promotional material on the inside flap of the dust jacket). Miller's investigative reporting does uncover some allegations of fraud, waste, abuse, and theft, but *Blood Money* does not "reveal that billions have gone missing"; rather, the book (for the most part) repeats allegations made by other sources, placing them in context of Miller's reporting.

Commercial presses exist to make money. In that regard, the wave of contractor books that hit store shelves in 2006 and the plethora that followed in their wake could well be successful. They all make for fine reading on a long distance flight, with stories of men against fire and salacious Washington politics. They do not, however, add much to understanding the issues surrounding the role of the private sector in public wars. Given the lack of serious academic scholarship and the distortions of the most popular documentaries on Iraq, controversial best sellers are not what is most needed to inform public policy making.

THE ORGANIZATIONS

Nongovernmental organizations and other research institutions, particularly through Web-based publications and postings, have played a role in shaping the debate over contractors as well. These contributions are many and varied. Unlike many public policy issues, however, the "think tank" community has largely failed to move the debate over contractors in combat.

It is not surprising that the nongovernmental organizations that have shown the most interest in the issue are based in the United States and Great Britain, the largest employers and consumers of private-sector military services. The British American Security and Information Council—often just called BASIC—offers a case in point. A self-described "progressive" think tank with offices in London and Washington, it lists two reports, both by David Isenberg, a veteran security analyst who works primarily on arms-control issues. Isenberg focuses almost exclusively on security contractors and issues of oversight and accountability.[33]

In contrast to BASIC, the International Institute for Strategic Studies (IISS) based in London commissioned a paper by an outside author for its prestigious Adelphi papers series. Authored by Sarah Percy, a university lecturer at Merton College, her paper also focused on accountability issues, though her recommendations place more focus on industry self-regulation.[34]

Matthew Uttley at King's College prepared a similar study as an independent research project for the Strategic Studies Institute, the academic research arm of the U.S. Army War College. Uttley compared American and British contracting practices with an emphasis on addressing the issue of determining the cost advantages of "insourcing" vs. "outsourcing" and identifying the best practices for ensuring efficient and effective contracting services.[35]

All three studies emphasize the practical requirements for managing contract services. Each argues that it is wrong to equate private security firms with mercenaries. Rather, they focus on improving existing regulatory regimes. These efforts represent reasonable scholarship. They are, however, unique products. None of the institutions from which these studies sprang established sustained research programs in this field. Indeed, no institution has yet established a sustained research program addressing contractors in combat. Not only are these studies one-of-a-kind, they have not sparked much interest (despite the ongoing public controversy over the subject) by major American think tanks from either the right or the left.

The lack of substantive engagement by the research community is not surprising. Although Isenberg, Percy, and Uttley authored fine work, they did not advance the conceptual ball much further than Singer and Avant did, except for updating the issue to address conditions in Iraq. That did not do much to assist major research projects.

There are other reasons that may explain the reluctance of think tanks to deal with contractors in combat. Although research studies do suggest that there is arguably a role for regulatory reform, in comparison to the other weighty topics confronting the defense community (from the precarious situation in Iraq to confrontation with Iran and the war on terror), contractors (despite the heated public rhetoric) hardly seemed the most dramatic or dynamic issue that they could tackle.

Additionally, it is difficult to envision where the research community could make additional major contributions. It is unlikely that its members can compete with government organizations such as the Government Accountability Office and Inspectors General in massing authoritative data. Nor are they likely to be able to match the access achieved by investigative journalists in the field. At the same time, in addressing the subject from an analytical perspective, think tanks face the same challenge as university academics. Contracting in combat is a multi-faceted public-policy issue that crosses over a number of disciplines. In-depth study could well demand a team of researchers drawing from these multiple disciplines—a major commitment even for major think tanks. Such a project would require considerable resources. Here, the issue to be confronted was the constituency and support for a major research project. Opponents of contracting have so highly politicized the issue that they have no pressing demand for substantive research. The stakeholders with the greatest interest in serious research might be the companies themselves. It would, however, be difficult for think tanks to take money from companies and then provide objective research on the topic.

More responsive to the research challenge has been the Federally Funded Research Development Centers (FFRDC). The government's 36 FFRDCs are chartered by Congress to provide technical and scientific expertise not available from public or private entities. FFRDCs perform fee-for-service work for government agencies. RAND and other research centers that primarily serve the Department of Defense have been tasked periodically over the years to address issues related to contracting and outsourcing producing a wealth of studies. In 2005, for example, RAND analysts Frank Camm and Victoria A. Greenfield authored a study that developed a risk assessment process to determine when the employments of contract services were appropriate for military operations.[36] However, although FFRDCs usually produce work of a routinely high quality, the sponsor of the research has ultimate control, determining the scope of the research and whether to accept the findings. The customer's—the government's—interests always come first. Thus, FFRDC studies routinely shy away from intensely politicized subjects.

In contrast to the modest response from the mainstream research community, advocacy groups have been far more vociferous in tackling the contractor issue. In 2003, the Center for Public Integrity report, "Windfalls of War," proved to be a catalyst in sparking media attention by repackaging publicly available information about the political donations made by companies providing military services to the Pentagon. Since the initial report, the center has developed an expanded Web site listing documents, investigations, and news on the topic.

Although the facts the center presents are undeniable, the context in which the information is presented is not. The report and the title of the site presume that companies are reaping inappropriate war profits—the military–industrial complex redux. Merely listing political donations, as done in the original report, however, hardly proves that these companies are receiving any benefits. Although the biggest contributor on the Web site's list of government contracting companies was Kellogg, Brown, and Root (at the time a subsidiary of Vice President Dick Cheney's former company, Halliburton), that fact alone means little. KBR is not new to the military contracting arena; it, as its predecessors, had been one of the nation's largest military service provider companies under both democratic and republican administrations going back to the 1960s. Additionally, the list of contributors is not complete. Because it only includes companies who provide military services to the Pentagon, it omits those companies who provide other types of defense goods or services. Thus there was no comparison between donations made by these companies and other defense companies. Furthermore, it omits any comparison between the donations made by companies who provide services to the Pentagon, which, combined, total almost $23 million, and companies in other industries. These statistics would make the donations appear far less ominous. In 2000, for example, pharmaceutical companies gave almost $27 million to political campaigns.

The list of donations that the center provides is not linked to any allegations of impropriety on the part of government contracting officials or company representatives. Indeed, even now after six years of war and countless investigations, there is no documented evidence of systematic collective fraud by the 14 companies that accounted for almost $23 million in donations. Finally, publicly traded companies like KBR list their stockholder reports and financial statements on their Web sites. Their profits are transparent, and they do not appear excessive.

Equally troubling is the work of the Campaign for America's Future. The campaign is a 501c(4) non-profit organization. In contrast, most think tanks (like the Brookings Institution in Washington, D.C. where Peter Singer is employed) are 501c(3) tax exempt non-profit organizations. These Internal Revenue Codes define what activities are permissible under an organization's tax exempt status. The campaign is in the same category as groups like MoveOn.org and the National Rifle Association. Unlike think tanks, these organizations can engage in an unlimited amount of lobbying and also conduct political campaigning. Much of their work reflects their commitment to political action.

The Campaign for America productions about contractors in combat are highly politicized. The campaign worked with Greenwald and Brave New Theater in promoting *Iraq for Sale* before the 2006 congressional mid-term elections. Its September 2006 report, "War Profiteers: Profits Over Patriotism in Iraq," compiles pages of a disjointed series of allegations, mostly from press reports, all unfavorable to service providers and the administration. The report finishes by claiming that few Republicans supported proposed congressional measures for investigating or prohibiting contractor activity and concludes, "As citizens, we can't provide oversight for the private contractors in Iraq. But we can hold our leaders accountable." [37] The report is simply advocacy for advancing a political agenda.

THE PRESS

America's media is a favorite target for criticism, another great American tradition and one enjoyed by both right and left. Robert Greenwald's *Outfoxed: Rupert Murdoch's War on Journalism* claimed that Fox News demanded that reporters and producers espouse right-wing political views in their reporting. The conservative Web site Townhall.com trumpets a blog demanding "Freedom From the Liberal Press." In truth, the American press is a diverse collage of writers, bloggers, television, radio, and press reporters and commentators. Despite their diversity, none have served the issue of contractors in combat particularly well.

The most serious problem is not biased writing, although there are cases of that. Nationally syndicated columnist Maureen Dowd blasted the owner of Blackwater for being a conservative, a Republican, and evangelical Christian, a combination that was apparently proof enough he headed a company of desperados. "Once there was the military–industrial complex," Dowd writes, "Now we have the mercenary–evangelical complex." [38] Although quips like that delight the left and infuriate the right, they add nothing to a serious debate about contractors in combat.

Press coverage of contractors in combat falls short because of the episodic nature of the media business. In today's 24-hour news cycle, where "what bleeds leads," even the best investigative reporting does not provide the kind of sustained attention to an issue that is necessary to really inform a public policy debate. David Phinney, and Cam Simpson of *The Chicago Tribune* (whose series received the George Polk Award for International Reporting), highlighted the exploitation of third party nationals by subcontractors in Iraq. There has, however, been little follow-up reporting on how companies work to rectify the problem and prevent further abuses.

Lack of follow-up makes all the difference. On February 12, 2006, the CBS news show *60 Minutes* ran a program titled "Billions Wasted In Iraq? U.S. Official Says Oversight Was 'Nonexistent,'" featuring allegations of contractor abuse by the company Custer Battles. The report is featured on the CBS Web site with a postscript added stating, "Shortly after this story aired, a federal jury found Custer Battles guilty of 37 separate fraudulent acts. It demanded the company repay $10 million dollars in damages and penalties to the U.S. government and whistleblowers."[39] When the judgment against the company was later dismissed, CBS did not do a follow-up report, and as of December 2007, the story was not even updated on the Web site to reflect this development.

Indeed, few major press outlets have given sustained coverage to the issue. One notable exception has been National Public Radio (NPR). National security reporter Eric Westervelt and other reporters at NPR have authored a number of pieces for network's flagship news shows including *Morning Edition*, *All Things Considered*, *Weekend Edition*, and *Talk of the Nation*. The work by Westervelt and other NPR reporters and producers, however, is not the norm.

Another serious challenge for the press is lack of expertise. Few issues demand researchers skilled in more fields. Yet, increasingly, the press is backing away from keeping subject experts on staff. "At a time when it is most needed," observes veteran reporter Walter Pincus, "the media, and particularly newspapers, have dropped the idea of having experienced reporters provide analysis and content." Pincus notes:

> It was not always that way. From the 1950s through the 1980s, I could name reporters and columnists whose experience on their beats or in their areas made them thoughtful and respected commentators. Younger reporters today are regularly shifted around from beat to beat, never really having enough time to master totally complex subjects, such as health, public education, and environmental policies. Coverage then depends on statements and pronouncements by government sources or their critics.[40]

Even when reporters get the story right, there is no guarantee that they really have mastered the content they are reporting on.

Expecting the public media to grapple with the serious and complex issue of the role of the private sector in public wars is unrealistic. Competition among media outlets is fierce and increasingly segmented as cable stations, online magazines and blogs, and other boutique media outlets fight for advertising dollars, market shares, and the capacity to reach ever narrower constituencies. In the globalized media marketplace, the media will continue to do what the media do best—provide vivid, targeted first impressions of news events, giving customers what they want. That is an important role for informing the public but an inadequate instrument for crafting an understanding of public policy.

The media are not the only ones falling short. Congress has done little better.

THE CONGRESS

Capital Hill does more than legislate. The Congress also plays a key role in communicating information, ideas, and opinions to the American people. They speak to America through many voices. Reports by the Government Accountability Office and the Congress Budget Office, which are responses to information requests by members of Congress, are publicly available and widely used by the press, academia, and think tanks. The Congressional Research Service (CRS) also delivers reports to Congress. Although the CRS does not publicly release its reports, many members of Congress make them available on their Web sites. Congressional committees can also issue reports themselves. Members can also address issues by giving speeches on the floor of the chamber. These are covered by C-SPAN, a free public information cable channel that is carried by all cable service companies. Congress even uses legislation to send messages. Members know that some of the bills they propose have little chance of passage, but they introduce them hoping to "send a message" on their stands on certain subjects.

All the techniques at their disposal have been employed by members of Congress to speak out on the issue of contractors in combat. In June 2006, the democratic minority staff of the House Committee on Government Reform, for example, issued its report (prepared for Congressman Henry A. Waxman, at the time the ranking minority member on the committee) titled "Dollars, Not Sense: Government Contracting Under the Bush Administration." The report served as an instrument to criticize contracting in Iraq and Afghanistan, as well as other government practices, flatly concluding that federal contracting was riddled with fraud, waste, and abuse.

The preparers state that the findings draw on over 500 reports, audits, and investigations. What they do not say is that the information is intentionally packaged so that the data is presented in the most inflammatory manner possible. "Dollars, Not Sense," included, for example, the conviction of Custer Battles.[41] Although the conviction had not at that point been overturned, the report failed to note that that the judgment was under appeal and that Custer Battles and had countersued its accusers for making false claims.

Although the preparers did not provide an objective report, they did, like the producers of *Iraq for Sale,* manage to get their report out before the congressional mid-term elections. When the democratic majority took over the committee, one of its first acts was to put a link to the "Dollars, Not Sense" report on the homepage on the committee's Web site.

No technique has been used more to frame the issue of contractors in combat than congressional hearings. Standing congressional committees have jurisdiction over various federal activities. The majority party represented in the

Congress selects the committee chairs. In the last few decades, Committee chairs have become increasingly powerful, having greater authority and autonomy to shape the committee's legislative and hearing agenda. Included in their authority is the power to initiate legislation and hold hearings on the proposed bills and other subjects.

Although the objective of hearings is to inform the legislative making process, they can also be used to shape public opinion. The committee chair can select the topics and scope of hearings and determine when they will be held, how long they will last, and who will be invited to testify. Testimony can be sought from government officials and other selected experts—even other members of Congress. Normally, individuals who testify provide written statements before the hearing. During the hearing, they offer opening verbal remarks and answer questions from the committee members. The members can also make opening comments. In particular, it is not unusual for the committee chair to issue a long initial prepared statement to frame the issue. C-SPAN provides coverage of many, albeit not all hearings. All the elements of the hearing together provide the majority staff, in effect, with a public theater for shaping how the public sees an issue.

Congressional activism (whether it results in legislation or effective oversight, or not) serves a powerful political purpose—helping to build momentum for a political agenda. The Campaign for America's Future's "War Profiteers: Profit over Patriotism," for example, trumpeted democratic efforts to highlight the issue in the Congress, reporting:

> Since the mid point of the 108th Congress, numerous anti-profiteering bills and amendments to defense appropriations have been introduced in Congress to combat war profiteering. Six hearings have recently been held that exposed the harsh reality of contractor waste, fraud, and abuse during the occupation of Iraq. Members of Congress have called for a Truman Commission style investigation of the gross misuse of funds. These efforts have gone nowhere, often not even getting out of committee. Partisan division has too often undermined national interest. . . . catastrophic conservativism has made us less secure, sacrificed too many lives, and wasted billions.[42]

As the report illustrates, even a party out of power can use Congress get its message out.

When the democrats took control of both houses after the 2006 elections, the issues of contracting in combat moved to the top of the hearing agenda. In the year before the democrats took over control of the Capitol, even though Congress had already held a number of hearings on the subject, apparently that was not nearly enough. Committees in both houses have looked for opportunities to scrutinize the issue. Only days into the new congressional session, for example, on January 17, 2007, the Senate Committee on Armed Services held a hearing "[t]o receive testimony on abusive practices in Department of Defense contracting for services and inter-agency contracting." In October 2007, the Senate Committee on Homeland Security and Government Affairs held a hearing titled "Is DHS [the Department of Homeland Security] too Dependent on Contractors to Do the Government Work?"

Without question, however, the most aggressive hearings were by the House Committee on Oversight and Government Reform under Representative Henry Waxman, who is now serving as the committee's chairman. On October 1–2, 2007, the committee held extensive hearings on contracting in Iraq and Afghanistan. To accompany the hearings, the majority staff issued a 14-page statement listing allegations against Blackwater.[43]

Both sides, of course, play politics with political issues. As the dealing with the issue of contractors in combat demonstrates, however, not all battles are engaged identically. Although progressive attacks on contracting practices have been vociferous, opposing views have been expressed far less forcefully. The Republican Study Committee, an influential conservative House caucus that includes over one hundred members, often takes the leading in opposing the democratic agenda and maintains a Web site highlighting its activities and priorities. From 2005 to 2007, virtually no entries defending contractors in combat are evident.

In part, the lack of a concerted political response from the right may be because of the nature of some political debates. Some debates are "asymmetrical," in which one side has all the advantages. Contracting in combat is one of those issues. The arguments against contractors are framed much like a good conspiracy theory, just daring anyone to prove that fraud, waste, and abuse do not exist! That is a virtually impossible task. When opponents to contracting practices can point to even one allegation that has been made suggesting the inappropriate application of the private sector in the public's war, they have the high ground in the debate. Because Americans are rooted in beliefs that lead them to distrust the combination of big government and big companies to begin with, combating allegations of contractor waste, fraud, and abuse is a monumental challenge.

Making war against the military–industrial complex is simply too easy. In these kinds of debates the other side always has to play defense. As a result, rather than engage in a substantive discussion, the other side plays "damage control," talking about the issue only when necessary and as soon as possible shifting the argument to an issue easier to engage. These are time-honored Washington tactics. The result, however, is that when Congress plays asymmetric political warfare the American people do not get the full hearing of an issue that they deserve.

BEYOND CONSPIRACY THEORY

If nothing else, debating the place of the private sector in public wars has served as a reaffirmation that dog-wagging is a bipartisan sport. The right wing, it is claimed, went after the Clinton presidency—Hillary Clinton claimed the White House was the victim of a "vast right-wing conspiracy." After Iraq, it is said, the left wing went after Bush (conspiracies are back), and contractors are at the center of the storm.

In part, the over-the-top allegations of contractor excess are part of America's open political traditions that encourage left and right to battle for the center. The instruments that inform public debate, from the ivory towers of academia to the floor of Congress, have done little to moderate the dispute that is to be expected. The loudest voices are heard first.

The virtue of democracy, however, is that the debate is always open. There is always opportunity for reasonable reflection to be heard. When this happens—when academic disciplines catch up with the challenge of studying contractors in combat, when think tanks can no longer ignore what could become one of the most pressing national-security issues of the twenty-first century, when the media and the Congress recognize and act upon what is really driving the role of the private sector in public wars—the people will get the information they need to make their own informed choices. Likely as not, that will happen—over time. In democracies, sooner or later, the truth of a matter rises to the top.

Even as analysis becomes more dispassionate and depoliticized with the passage of time, one problem will linger: a nagging concern that has plagued the West since before Machiavelli penned *The Art of War*. At the root of this enduring doubt is the suspicion that profit and patriotism are not compatible—that as the role of the private sector grows, the world we have known will be lost. Addressing that worry—explaining why we don't have to repudiate the place of the private sector in public wars—is the topic of the next chapter.

7
Chapter

How We Have Changed

Contractors are citizens too.

Francis Fukuyama was right to pin his hopes on the modern liberal nation-state as mankind's best hope for *The End of History*. The victory dance was just a little premature. And, in truth perhaps there should be no dance at all. It is folly to believe that the world is at the end of anything. No human political order can permanently endure. Yet, surely a case can be made that nationhood has a long history ahead of it. "We live in a democratic age," writes Fareed Zakaria in *The Future of Freedom: Illiberal Democracy at Home and Abroad* (2003) and he is right.[1]

At the dawn of the twentieth century, Zakaria notes, democratic rule was the exception rather than the norm. Today it is the other way 'round. States with governments brought to power by elections are by far in the global majority. Freedom can even be quantified. Since 1973, Freedom House (a non-profit organization with offices in Washington and New York) has issued an annual index grading every country in the world on its level of freedom. The trends it documents leave little question but that peoples across the globe are enjoying more authority in making decisions that govern their daily lives.

The superstars of the state system practice what Zakaria characterizes as "liberal democracy": a political system marked not only by free and fair elections but also by the rule of law, a separation of powers, and the protection of basic liberties of speech, assembly, religion, and property.[2] Among the many reasons why these states turn out to be the most successful is that they, over the long term, turn out to be the best competitors in a global marketplace, most adept at managing Adam's Smith cherished free markets: they are the nations with the most invisible hands guiding the tiller of the nation. These are the countries where corporatist cabals are least likely to determine the course of statecraft.

In the end, the best bulwark against private sector abuse in public wars is having members of the private sector who are citizens of responsible states.

Sustaining the character of citizenship is the single and most important guarantor that Eisenhower's military–industrial complex will not become a reality.

Ironically, the proliferation of the private sector in public wars is often cited as the chief threat to undermining citizenship. This is a centuries-old objection to contracting in combat that reaches back to the writings of Machiavelli. This argument is plain wrong. There may be threats to nurturing citizenship in America's liberal democracy (and for that matter elsewhere in the world); addressing those issues, however, has little to do with contracting for combat.

On the other hand, it is true that the expanding role of the private sector is changing the nature of our society—though not in the way critics contend. In fact, these changes may be seen as largely positive, portending shifts in our society that may make America a better competitor in the twenty-first-century marketplace—changes that create a workforce with new knowledge, skills, and attributes that might make the nation even more safe, keep it free, and contribute to increasing prosperity in the decades ahead. Unleashing this potential starts with understanding how the role of the private sector is changing us and dispelling the myths of how it is not.

PROFIT AND PATRIOTISM

Although fraud, waste, and abuse are commonly cited as the chief crimes of contracting, the most troubling criticisms go far deeper. They contend that the expanding role of the private sector in public wars is destroying democracy. In short, they argue that profit and patriotism are not compatible. Those are charges that have to be taken seriously, because if they were true then all the mechanisms traditionally used to combat abhorrent practices (like fraud, waste, and abuse) would be useless. In an illiberal democracy, the rule of law is turned on its head, crushing rather than empowering transparency, accountability, and oversight. Citizenship cannot stand against a corrupt system. Fortunately, concerns that the American system has been corrupted by big business are wildly overblown. Thus, attention should rightly be paid to the concerns of critics that touch the core of constitutional government.

The first concern about employing contractors for combat is a fear that the practice can become an instrument that adds a layer of secrecy and unaccountability to foreign policy. In this manner, an administration could undertake a covert foreign policy, paying contractors to do things that Congress or the courts would not let government soldiers or diplomats do. Alternatively, an administration might overtly advance a policy by putting contractors in harm's way, hoping that Washington would receive less criticism if its policies failed or only contractors were killed or taken hostage instead of American servicemen. Singer, Avant, and many others repeatedly advanced these concerns.

Arguably, using contractors as surrogates is something that an administration might try. Indeed, there is nothing new about the idea—the British East India Company took practice to its extreme, at times altering British foreign policy to serve its corporate objectives. There is, however, a big difference between the practices of the eighteenth- and the early nineteenth-century British Empire and the modern American state. British rule through the first half of the nineteenth century did not enjoy full protections of a fully liberal democracy (such as universal suffrage), and these shortcomings (including the excesses of the British East India Company) reflected the endemic weaknesses in Albion's old political system.[3]

In contrast, modern America is not in danger of having its foreign policy determined by KBR any more than by the overseas franchises of Kentucky Fried Chicken. Fear that an administration can use covert contracting to subvert democratic rule is equally untenable. That charge can only be made by ignoring the systems of checks and balances in American governance.

Covertly contracting foreign policy is one of the least likely avenues for advancing a covert administration agenda. Government contracts are subject to the full gamut of government and public oversight. The administration must, for example, comply with the requirements of FARS, have money appropriated by the Congress, make its practices open to oversight by Inspectors General, government auditors, the Government Accountability Office, and Congressional committees, and comply with "sunshine laws" such as the Freedom of Information Act (the FOIA, passed in 1966, ensures public access to government documents and is enforced by U.S. federal courts) and "whistleblower" protections (the Public Disclosure Protection Act of 1998 provides legal protection for individuals who expose illegal activities). Indeed, the Center for Public Integrity would not have been able to obtain the information it used to compile its inflammatory *Windfalls of War* report without free access to information provided openly by the government. Attempting to drive a covert policy through the maze of Washington's contracting requirements and oversight is no easy task. Russian roulette offers better odds.

AN AFFAIR TO REMEMBER

There are a few high-profile cases in recent history of covert foreign policy programs being run in a manner that attempted to evade the system of Constitutional checks and balances.[4] The most notable is the Iran–Contra Affair. Iran–Contra happened because the system worked. Congressional legislation blocked initiatives by the White House to combat Communist expansion in Latin America. In late 1982, the Democratic-controlled Congress enacted the Boland Amendments, prohibiting federal agencies from providing military aid to the Contras, anti-communist groups fighting against the government in Nicaragua. The administration circumvented the law by using National Security Council (NSC) staff (not explicitly covered by the legislation) to continue to funnel aid to the rebels. NSC staffer Lieutenant Colonel Oliver "Ollie" North directed these operations raising both private and foreign government funds to finance the activities.

At a press conference on November 25, 1986, when Attorney General Edwin Meese acknowledged the existence of the program, including an effort to divert profits from an arms-for-hostages deal with Iran (to obtain the release of seven U.S. citizens kidnapped in Lebanon) to the Contras in Nicaragua, he revealed the scope of what became known as the Iran–Contra affair. A withering blitzkrieg of investigations followed. Reagan established a Special Review Board to investigate the actions of the NSC. He appointed what became known as the "Tower Commission," with former Senator John Tower, Edmund Muskie, and former National Security Advisor Brent Scowcroft among other Washington notables. The Tower Commission roundly criticized the administration, as did a separate report prepared by the Congress. Several key NSC staffers were prosecuted. North was convicted on three felony counts. His conviction was later vacated by a federal court.

After receiving the Tower Commission report, on March 4, 1987, Reagan spoke to the nation about the Iran–Contra affair. During the speech he accepted "full responsibility" for his own actions and those of his administration.[5] The Tower report did not recommend wholesale changes to the national security system but did recognize that "[t]he NSC system will not work unless the president makes it work."[6] Reagan admitted the Tower Commission was right.[7]

The Iran–Contra scandal offers an object lesson in the real threat to democratic control—the subversion of government practices—not their exercise. As cumbersome, bureaucratic, convoluted, and complicated government contracting mechanisms appear to be, in the end the one thing they do not offer is a prime instrument for running secret foreign policies. Such abuses are much more likely to happen, as Iran–Contra illustrates, when government agencies try an end-run around Constitutional checks and balances.

DARK HISTORY

There are other variations on the theme of unaccountable government. They appear equally untenable under closer scrutiny. One holds that the American polity would be less sensitive to abuses, misadventures, or causalities incurred by government contractors than it is to those incurred by military personnel. Thus, an administration might adapt a more reckless foreign policy when the lives and reputation of U.S. troops are not on the line. Singer claims, for example, that contracting allows an administration to adopt a "[w]hen things go wrong, you simply blame the company" policy.[8] That assertion hardly stands up at all given the U.S. experience in Iraq.

Some of the most widely publicized and criticized incidents in the troubled occupation of Iraq regarded contractors. At Abu Ghraib, for example, CACI International supplied more than half of the analysts and interrogators. Titan provided all the translators. Contractors were implicated in over a dozen of the charges of criminal behavior. Even if the White House had wished to craft a case that contractors were responsible for conditions at Abu Ghraib it is hard to imagine that the argument would have been taken as credible. The notion that government can somehow divorce itself from the conduct of its contractors can only be made by ignoring the federal laws and requirements under the Uniform Code of Military Justice that dictate the duties of federal officials and military personnel.

The public responses to the death of four U.S. contractors in Fallujah and widespread condemnation of the treatment of third-country nationals by subcontractors in Iraq both demonstrate that the American public is far from indifferent about the fate of those paid by American tax dollars—even when the payment comes from a contract rather than a government payroll. In neither case did the government escape widespread criticisms, even though in both instances U.S. officials were not directly responsible for overseeing the operations (both the incidents involved companies contracting services with the United States who were in turn subcontracting operations to other companies).

Admittedly, poor contractor performance, malfeasance, or flat-out criminality can tarnish America's image or undermine U.S. policy. The abuses by contractors at Abu Ghraib are a case in point. That, however, is hardly a problem restricted to contractors. After all, a majority of the abuses at Abu Ghraib were committed by uniformed military personnel, not contractors. In addition, overwhelmingly, the responsibility for creating the conditions that allowed the abuses to take place falls on the military as well. Members in the chain-of-command were subjected to various punishments for either their failure to appropriately supervise soldiers or for actually permitting abuse to occur.

Ultimately, responsibility for the cause of Abu Ghraib should be placed directly on the shoulders of the senior military commander General Richard Sanchez. Sanchez's failure was not so much that he condoned torture or abuse of detainees as is so often alleged in the press. Rather, it was Sanchez who, in the face of spiraling violence in Iraq, sanctioned military sweeps that rounded up vast hordes of suspects and dumped them into military prisons. At the same time, Sanchez did little to establish adequate procedures to process the detainees or expand the facilities and personnel to ensure adequate supervision of detention operations. Although contractors may have been at fault at Abu Ghraib, the senior military commander on the ground bears the lion's share of responsibility for this dark chapter in American military history.

It would, however, be unfair to condemn the entire military for the abuses at Abu Ghraib. Indeed, few do. Here Americans seem to have learned at least some lessons from Vietnam.

On March 16, 1968, a company of American soldiers entered the small Vietnamese village of My Lai. In the course of a few hours, they killed most of the men, women, and children in the village. Some were beaten. Some were raped. Some were mutilated. No one fired at the Americans. One soldier was injured. He accidentally shot himself in the foot.

Not every soldier took part in the killing (in 1998 the Army bestowed Soldier's Medals on a helicopter crew that rescued some of the villagers), but many did, and still others participated in the cover-up. When news of the massacre erupted a year later (aided by the energetic reporting of Sy Hersh) the incident sparked widespread condemnation. It also fueled a broader effort by the anti-war movement to indict all military operations in Vietnam as criminal.

Among other initiatives following the news of My Lai was the "Winter Soldiers Investigation," a project sponsored by the Vietnam Veterans Against the War. In 1971, the project gathered testimony from over 100 veterans (and military contractors) detailing instances of abuse and war crimes. A documentary on the event, *Winter Soldier,* was produced the following year. Despite numerous investigations, the project did not uncover any documented pattern of widespread systematic war crimes. Today, the veracity of the project remains highly debatable. Some dismiss it as largely a fabrication. Others defend the sincerity of the effort.[9]

Most of America's soldiers fought admirably in Vietnam, even if the cause for which they fought remains to this day controversial. That should come as no surprise.

The lesson that should be learned from My Lai or Abu Ghraib is that it makes no sense to condemn whole institutions, either governmental or in the private sector, based on single incidents. Such indictments take lumping to a whole new level. This lesson does, in fact, seem to have been learned. Even the harshest war critics now frequently commend American troops for their service to the nation (though some Iraq war veteran groups have tried to resurrect the Winter Soldier project, claiming widespread abuses).

The military is unlikely to willingly participate in widespread criminality, something explained in *The Soldier and the State*. Not only is the military bound by law to do the right thing—it is, as Huntington notes, a profession with standards of moral and professional conduct that make illegal behavior unacceptable. "Duty, honor, country," the West Point motto, and other expressions of the military ethos encapsulated in the oath of allegiance sworn by military personnel when they join the armed forces, and other codes and creeds used by the services, demand honorable service from military members. These credos have real influence in ensuring that the vast preponderance of military personnel serve their nation well.

As for contractors, it is wrong to assume, as critics so often do, that they are not bound by codes of conduct as well, codes that keep them from putting patriotism over profit. They are sanctioned by the kinds of codes that Adam Smith first envisioned as the best strictures of moral behavior for governing a free market—codes that are informed by and spring from enlightened self-interest. IPOA, for example, has an extensive code of conduct for its member companies, a code that has been systematically revised and updated over the years to account for the growing missions and responsibilities of its members.

The establishment of corporate values (as opposed to standards of corporate social responsibility as described in chapter 5) is commonplace and appropriate. In 2007, for example, Blackwater posted its company code on its corporate Web site the follow values:

- Integrity: We are committed to the highest standards of ethical and professional behavior and endeavor to instill universally recognized and accepted core values of proper conduct in all our employees and independent contractors.
- Teamwork: We operate as a coordinated body of collective wisdom and experience. Every day our employees and independent contractors strive to

discover and implement cohesive solutions to challenges by using the best minds
we can assemble.

- Innovation: We value, encourage and empower our independent contractors and
  employees to dream, to innovate and challenge conventional wisdom. We strive to
  raise expectations and break through barriers others deem impossible to breach.
- Respect: We honor the rights and beliefs of our fellow associates, our customers,
  our employees and our community. We treat others with the highest degree of
  dignity, equal opportunity and trust. We respect the cultures and beliefs of people
  around the world.
- Accountability: We act ethically and legally as we work to meet our contractual
  commitments. We take responsibility for our behavior and our performance. We
  are accountable everyday. We support quality assurance and personal discipline
  in all our endeavors.
- Excellence: We meet or exceed all professional and contractual expectations and
  obligations. We strive to deliver superior quality products and services on time
  and under budget. Our employees and independent contractors are dedicated,
  loyal and honorable.
- Efficiency: We create value with limited resources everyday. Our employees create
  exceptional products and services in response to specific customer needs. We
  operate a streamlined organization that prides itself on solving issues in a lean,
  economical manner. We deliver great value for a great price.

By industry standards, a list of core company values like this is fairly
unexceptional.

Blackwater even requires its personnel to take an oath identical to the oath
sworn by officers accepting commissions in the U.S. military services which
include the requirement to protect and defend the Constitution of the United
States. The military oath states:

> I (insert name), having been appointed a (insert rank) in the U.S. Army
> under the conditions indicated in this document, do accept such
> appointment and do solemnly swear (or affirm) that I will support and
> defend the Constitution of the United States against all enemies, foreign
> and domestic, that I will bear true faith and allegiance to the same; that
> I take this obligation freely, without any mental reservation or purpose
> of evasion; and that I will well and faithfully discharge the duties of the
> office on which I am about to enter, so help me God.

Employing a similar oath for a private sector company is an exceptional
practice.

The reason legitimate companies are likely to adhere to these voluntary codes
is that it is in their interest to do so. It would be difficult for any company with a
reputation for operating outside the rule of law to sustain a significant business
share in the highly competitive field of military service providers. There is a reason
that companies like Executive Outcomes were forced to disband or reorganize.
They had terrible "name recognition," making it unlikely that any reputable

government would engage their services. Even companies like Custer Battles, which was cleared of charges of defrauding the U.S. government, have a difficult time restoring the reputation of their firms.

Although certainly not an absolute check on fraud, waste, and abuse, the desire to continue to do business with the U.S. government, with other governments, and with NGOs around the world is a powerful incentive for legitimate companies to offer legitimate services and root out cases of criminality in their ranks.

An added incentive exists to play by the rules: these companies know the world is watching. They have been scrutinized, subpoenaed, and sued. Few companies would relish the opportunity of Erik Prince, the chief of Blackwater, for an in-depth interview with *60 Minutes* after confrontational hearings before Congressman Waxman's committee in the House.[10] Companies crave profits. Part of making profits in a transparent, global competitive economy is avoiding scandals that attack the credibility of the company.

Given the plethora of public and private oversight, it is difficult to envision how any major service provider could believe it could get away with widespread illegal practices and not get found out sooner or later. Even Enron found out it could not fool all of the people all of the time. Any military service provider that tried a similar tactic would likely meet a similar fate. Shareholders and federal prosecutors would not be pleased.

ROGUE FOREIGN POLICY

Other concerns about contracting combat also appear less threatening under closer scrutiny. That the United States might actually use the private sector to directly or indirectly advance its publicly stated policies is neither a practice that is new nor objectionable. Before Pearl Harbor, Pan Am helped camouflage U.S. war preparations, ferrying material to build U.S. air bases in Latin America, West Africa, and the Pacific. During the Reagan presidency, a major American labor organization, the AFL-CIO (funded in part by the federal government in the form of grants from the National Endowment for Democracy) supported Lech Walesa's Solidarity movement in Poland, a key effort that led to the collapse of the Iron Curtain. In these cases and many others there was very little evidence of "the tail wagging the dog." More often than not, business and labor work well with the government in war and peace because they recognize a mutual interest.

In *Corporate Warriors*, Singer makes much of the fact the U.S. government encouraged the Croatian government to hire MPRI. That, as history shows, is unexceptional. The desire of the Clinton administration to encourage Croatia to act as a block against Serbian expansionism was no secret. Indeed, there was wide bipartisan support for the policy. Not every effort of Washington to harness Wall Street has been a ringing success or even a good idea, but the practice is clearly neither novel nor unconstitutional.

Government does not even need government contracts, or for that matter any money to pass hands, in order for Washington to get companies to cooperate in matters of foreign policy and national security. Many federal laws and regulations, for example, dictate what companies can and cannot do overseas and who they can and cannot do business with (such as economic sanctions on foreign countries like Cuba, Iran, and North Korea). Additionally, government can demand access to certain business records (without even requiring a warrant) where matters of criminality or national security are of concern. In many instances, all the government is required to do is present prima facie evidence (a legal term meaning evidence sufficient for presumption of fact that will stand unless rebutted) that it requires the information. This power was highlighted recently during a controversial program the government initiated to tap international communications after 9/11 that required the cooperation of telecommunications companies.[11]

Critics might look forward to a day when multi-national corporations doing business with the United States hold the interests of other more rich and powerful states in higher esteem—a world in which America no longer commands the attention of the world's business. That is a legitimate concern. After all, that is the nature of competition in the modern globalized marketplace. The best safeguard against such a threat is making America the place where people most want to do business—nothing builds loyalty like success.

Equally important is keeping the state sovereign. If international institutions are allowed to undermine the authority and responsibility of the nation, global companies will be accountable to no one and will become governments unto themselves. Equally important, common sense and due diligence must be used when deciding with whom America does business. The practical application of instruments like CFIUS, ITAR, and the Arms Export Control Act just makes sense in cases in which business practices really do affect U.S. national security interests.

At the same time, America should, by and large, seek to do business with businesses in nations that share the common values of a liberal democracy. Not only do the countries with which the United States shares a long record of trust and confidence make the best allies—the companies that do business in those countries are likely to be most dependable as well.[12]

Doing business only with nations that have institutions as strong and transparent as the United States may not always be possible. This has proven particularly true when subcontracting for services with some host countries or third-country nationals. On the other hand, simply not contracting with companies from developing nations is no better an idea. In fact, contracting can be used as means for stimulating both economic growth and strengthening civic institutions in these countries. For example, U.S. outsourcing to Indian services companies for software services sparked an industry-wide effort in that country to upgrade security and privacy protections.[13] In the absence of strong rules of law in other countries, foreign outsourcing customers have had to incorporate requirements for legitimate business practices into legally binding and enforceable contracts with their vendors.

The notion that the private sector can somehow be excluded from impacting on foreign policy is also fallacious. Today, business is global and every company that does global business in one way or another affects U.S. foreign policy or foreign perceptions of U.S. policy. The foreign influences of corporations during the Cold War were so persuasive it had its own name: "Coca-colanization."[14] An activist business community overseas was part of what animated William Appleman Williams to formulate his conception of an informal American empire.

But Williams got it wrong. Despite Wall Street's long-standing interest in government's business around the world, government contracts may be among the least important factors driving how U.S. business seek to shape American foreign policy. The U.S. private sector invests in overseas companies and markets and has many billions more tied up in importing and exporting goods and services. Boeing offers a case in point. The company is consistently on the list of *Fortune's* top 50 U.S. Companies (ranked #28 in 2007). Although the company is one of the nation's largest defense firms, its defense business is dwarfed by its commercial aircraft sales. The company is, in fact, one of the nation's leading exporters of goods and services. As a result, Boeing's commercial aviation, rather than defense-sector, business largely drives how the company views the world. And Boeing is in a league of its own. No other defense company or military service provider firm even cracked the top fifty. The vast wealth of corporate America may have its say about the course of American foreign policy, but manipulating policy to suit contracting in combat is not high on their list.

The notion that companies cannot be trusted is a notion that cannot be trusted. For every example of contractors that hoodwinked the government in peace and war there are innumerable of examples of private sector firms that provided quality service for fees. Still, concerns about war profiteering have been a consistent theme in American history going to back the days of the colonial frontier.[15] That sad history, however, is vastly surpassed by the legacy of the American free enterprise system that has fueled the engine of war in every war the nation has fought. The United States has never lost a fight because the free market let it down—a fact that the detractors of contractors in combat frequently ignore.

SOLDIERS OR CITIZENS

The second major concern raised by the critics of contractors contends that replacing soldiers with civilians on the battlefield destroys government's traditional monopoly over the practice of violence and the meaning of military professionalism. This argument is so riddled with intellectual inconsistencies that it is a wonder that it is made so vociferously—and accepted so widely.

Western governments, from the Middle Ages to the present, have never had an exclusive monopoly on violence—in the sense that only government-owned and government-operated assets were combatants on the battlefield. War has always been a mix of public- and private-sector entities since the days when royal troops and militia fought side by side on Flodden Field to the days when they fought on Wake Island to the days when they guarded the Green Zone in Baghdad.

Likewise, in war the assets that are "contracted" on the battlefield are increasing both inside and outside of government. Levees and draftees (even though paid) should not be considered contract employees since their employment is not voluntary. Militaries based on conscription, however, are in decline. The United States ended requirements for mandatory military service in 1973. When the Cold War ended, many of its allies followed suit. "Several have shifted from conscript systems to all-volunteer forces," wrote defense scholar Cindy Williams in 2006, "and two more plan to do so within the next few years."[16] Even though military volunteers (and to some extent government civilian employees) certainly have more restrictions on their contract than private sector contractors, they are still "contract" employees. Indeed, there are virtually no government activities (outside those performed by elected and appointed officials) that are not bound by formal written contracts.

Additionally, military service per se is not an immunization against bad contracting behavior. Most contracting scandals in every American war have involved uniformed military personnel. Iraq and Afghanistan are no exceptions.

The notion that only soldiers can provide ethical service to the nation on the battlefield is equally unsupportable. World War II offers perhaps the best illustration. America had 190,000 men in Army uniforms before the prewar military buildup. By the end of the war over 8 million Americans wore olive. Most American servicemen, whether GIs in Normandy or leathernecks on Iwo Jima, lived their lives before Pearl Harbor untouched by war. A twenty-year-old struggling up the sands on Omaha Beach was born six years after World War I ended. By D-Day, Army regulars were outnumbered by draftees and wartime volunteers 40 to 1. America fought the war with a citizen army and, although every soldier had a uniform, swore allegiance to the flag, and had at least a modicum of military training, most were still civilians under arms. In fact, the skills and attributes they brought with them into their military service immeasurably improved the quality of the force.[17]

In World War II, the military did not make citizens out of soldiers. In the rush to war, there was hardly time enough time to teach soldiers to fight let alone to indoctrinate them with the character, spiritual values, and patriotic fervor of citizenship (in fact, the notion that the military should perform this function turns Machiavelli on his head. Machiavelli argued the case for a citizen militia was that it already had the requisite basis for the virtues of a citizen army). Citizenship training in the Army, such as the *School of the Citizen Soldier,* a series of lectures ordered by one the chief army generals responsible for stateside training, was laughingly superficial.[18] In contrast, when General Marshall ordered the film series "Why We Fight," he did so not to school soldiers in how to be citizens, but to explain to citizen-soldiers why this particular conflict was worth their commitment and sacrifice. Marshall understood that merely putting American citizens in uniform was not enough to gain their allegiance. Americans had to believe that their military service was consistent with the practice of citizenship—not the other way 'round.

Even in the early years of the Cold War, when the military had much more time to spend on indoctrination and felt (in the face of suspected communist subversion and without the immediate threat of a real shooting war to inflame the public's passion) a greater responsibility to teach soldiers citizenship, the Pentagon's efforts were monumentally unsuccessful. The military's overzealous interest in citizenship training waned when officers and soldiers began to affiliate with extremist right-wing anti-Communist groups. In response to the concern of the military becoming "politicized" Washington ratcheted back its citizenship programs.[19] The army and the other services reverted to their more traditional missions, not teaching soldiers how to be citizens, but teaching citizens how to be soldiers, inculcating the values and ethos vital to efficient, effective military service.

In fact, after the war, Congress explicitly rejected the idea that military service was a required instrument for teaching citizenship.[20] Even though Roosevelt declared, "that we must have universal military training after this war," and Truman labored for seven years to enact legislation, including asking Congress to act on the proposal on 17 occasions, the initiative went nowhere—and for good reason.[21] After mustering millions under arms and winning a global war in less than three years, Congress was hard pressed to accept an argument that American citizens were not fit material to become soldiers. Likewise, the performance of America's citizen army during the war made it problematic to suggest that American citizens lacked the attributes for good soldiering.

When America reinstituted the draft during the Korean War, it did so in anticipation that the battle in Northeast Asia was merely a prelude to a larger global conflict and that the U.S. military machine might have to ramp up to fight World War III.[22] The draft was sustained even after it became apparent that a global ground war was not imminent. In the greater austerity of postwar Korean War budgets, the military convinced itself that conscription was a cheaper source of manpower than a volunteer force.

President Johnson maintained the draft throughout the Vietnam conflict rather than calling out the National Guard, in part because he believed the draft would be less politically volatile and economically disruptive.[23] At no time over the course of warfare in the twentieth century was a case ever convincingly made that military service was an essential tool for teaching citizenship or that responsible citizenship must include a stint of military service.

It is remarkable how contemporary advocates for a return to the draft turn history the other way round. Politicians who decry contracting as a crude cost-saving measure and demand a return to conscription miss the point that the United States maintained Cold War conscription as a crude cost-saving measure. Likewise, proponents that argue military service is necessary for teaching citizenship ignore the fact that the generation that fought the greatest war of the twentieth century rejected that idea out of hand. Finally, the argument that somehow a draft would be more equitable also misreads the history of World War II, when the size of the military required virtually every able-bodied man of age to suit up for Uncle Sam. Today, because of (1) the size of the military, (2) the size of the draft-age population in the United States, and (3) the number of long-service volunteers in the military who would like to stay in the military, any draft would require such a small number for annual service that conscription would seem like little more than something akin to winning or (depending on one's point of view) losing a lottery.

Some ideas, however, never die. The Universal Military Training and Service Act of 2001 would have required "the induction into the Armed Forces of young men registered under the Military Selective Service Act, and [the authorization of] young women to volunteer, to receive basic military training and education for a period of up to one year," and it was introduced in the House three months after 9/11. The act failed, as did every other post-9/11 effort to reinstate the draft.

An argument for the draft can only be made on the most superficial reading of the nature of American citizenship. The World War II experience is a clear case in point. Rather than making the argument for the necessity of a draft, wartime experience suggests that conscription is unnecessary except in the direst of circumstances (like World War II). It is not clear why there should be any less an expectation that Americans today (who are fundamentally no different from the World War II generation), when asked to serve their country in any capacity in or out of uniform, would not serve their nation as well as their forebears.

By extension, proposals that some form of required "national service" (with college graduates perhaps completing a tour of duty with the Department of Agriculture or the Internal Revenue Service) should serve as an alternative to military time or somehow provide a loyal manpower pool that could replace contractors is an equally ill-considered notion. The argument that somehow national service is essential to teaching citizenship is as anemic as proposing that only attending boot camp would make an American trustworthy enough to safeguard America's interests overseas.

From a practical standpoint, the notion of mandatory "volunteer" service makes even less sense. Critics of the private sector's place in public wars who complain about putting the U.S. foreign policy in the hands of contractors could hardly find greater solace in handing out missions to unqualified youth who were drafted in national service and sent off to "do good" with only a modicum of preparation. The notion of a Peace Corps might be acceptable where there is actually peace—it makes much less sense when citizens are sent in harm's way.

BACK TO THE FUTURE

It is remarkable that any proponent of mandatory national service would not acknowledge that this proposal in the end dilutes rather than reinforces the notion of citizenship as it was first understood by John Locke and the founding fathers. In fact, taking the idea to its natural conclusion—that service should be mandatory to achieve the full rights of citizenships, shows how anti-democratic the proposal actually is. Hollywood again serves to illustrate this paradox best—in the movie *Starship Troopers* (1997), adapted from Robert Heinlein's 1959 novel, which, like much of the science fiction of the period, served to play out America's Cold War fears. Imaginary enemies stood in as surrogates for the Soviets. In the case of *Starship Troopers,* the principal enemy was "the bugs," a species engaged in a war of extermination with earth.

Both the book and the film were controversial—and for the same reason. In the earth of the future, only individuals who volunteer and complete Federal Service qualify for full citizenship. The unquestionable theme of Heinlein's novel is that social responsibility demands personal sacrifice. It is clear where Heinlein's sentiments come from. He was a dedicated anti-Communist and concerned that Americans have the political will to go toe-to-toe with the Soviets throughout the long years of Cold War.

On the other hand, there is unstated irony in the work. In Heinlein's future world, only citizens can fight. Thus, with earth locked in a cataclysmic struggle against an alien race, much of earth's population is excluded from the struggle. Heinlein's future war is the antithesis of America's World War II experience. After Pearl Harbor, the entire nation mobilized for war to meet the gravest threats to national security that could only be mastered by mobilizing the entire nation. When Arachnids attack earth, the Terran Federation responds by sending out an elite group of volunteers to do battle in space and on far-flung planets. Noncitizens get to stay, fat, dumb, and happy, at home.

Heinlein confuses the concept of national service in much the same way as contemporary critics of administration policy. Arguments for a draft, or engaging all Americans in the war on terror in the manner that the United States rushed to arms to fight "the good war" make no sense at all. Virtually the entire U.S. economy was drafted to fight the Second World War. It had to be. In this war, as in most American wars including most of the Cold War, dedicating too many resources to the fight would put the nation more, not less at risk. That was the essence of George Kennan's warning in "The Long Telegram." It was a crucial distinction that Heinlein missed. Heinlein was wrong to equate the challenges of the long Cold War years after the Korean War with the battles of the Terran Federation. Likewise, if he had read the lessons of World War II aright, he would have argued for mobilizing all of society (citizen or not) for the war on the Arachnids. On the other hand, if he had understood the nature of the Cold War correctly he would have eschewed the notion that only those that served were worthy and that combat service alone was the mark of a healthy citizenry.

It was wrong to equate not being a soldier with being less than a citizen. It is too big a burden to place the mantle of citizenship on the back of military service. It is noteworthy that when the film version of *Starship Troopers* came out, the debate over the alleged militaristic and fascist overtones of Heinlein's story reenergized the critics of his work. America, on the other hand, seemed to care less for the issue or the film. At a time when America was unthreatened by major conflict, the years between intervention in Bosnia and war in Kosovo, Americans did not seem to care much about the debate over citizenship and service. Perhaps, they should have paid more attention.

SOLDIERS ARE OUR CREDENTIALS

It is, in fact, somewhat ironic that critics of contracting for combat argue so vociferously that military forces are inherently more virtuous than the private sector. Suggesting, for example, that the United States should have a million-man standing army and eschew contractors all together ignores that part of America's republican tradition distrusts an unnecessarily large standing military. Pointing out the shortfalls of one institution, the marketplace, and exalting the importance of another, the military, hardly merits discussion as serious public policy.

Others want it both ways. The activist organization MoveOn.org lambasts Washington's reliance on contractors and at the same time sows distrust of the military as well. In September 2007, before the much-anticipated congressional testimony of General David Petraeus on military efforts to counter the growing discord, MoveOn.org took out a full page advertisement in *The New York Times*, labeling him "General Betray Us." The organization's political action wing claimed the general distorted reporting of incidents to exaggerate the success of military operations. Thus, MoveOn.org recalls the oldest conspiracy theory of all—trust no one.

None of the critics have it right. Neither conscription nor a professional military is a silver bullet safeguarding democracy. Neither is the salvation of the nation. On the other hand, neither is necessarily a threat to the republic. History demonstrates both have their place.

The fact that military service is not essential to citizenship or even service on the battlefield does not diminish the value or importance of military service. After a bitter battle in September 1944, the 8th Infantry Division's assistant division commander, Brigadier General Charles Canham, entered the bunker of the German commander to discuss the enemy's surrender. Through an interpreter, the German general demanded, "I am to surrender to you. Let me see your credentials." Pointing to a crowd of scruffy, unshaven GIs standing by the entrance to the bunker Canham replied, "These are my credentials."[24] In this true story, often told, Canham's comments say a great deal about the real value of military service.

Military service defines how a nation sees itself. There is a long-standing debate among scholars over whether wars make nations or nations make wars. One school of thought is typified by historian Victor David Hanson. In *Carnage and Culture: Landmark Battles in the Rise of Western Power* (2001), Hanson argues the former, contending that there is a particular Western way of war shaped by cultural influences that extend back to the battles of the Greeks. Civic militarism (in which citizens understanding their rights and responsibilities under a consensual constitutional regime), he argues, typifies Western warfare. In short, Hanson believes, in war, virtue matters—most.

In contrast, in *Battle: A History of Combat and Culture from Ancient Greece to Modern America* (2003), historian John Lynn makes the dissenting case, rejecting the notion of universal themes that define how the west fights. In *Battle*, Lynn states that his goal is "to bury the universal soldier, not to praise him. Only if this concept of universality is put to rest can those men and women who bore the toil of combat of war escape from obscurity and reclaim their different and human faces."[25] Military fights can only be understood, Lynn argues, by studying the specific time, place, and culture when nations go to war.

Hanson is a lumper. Lynn is a splitter.

Like most great historical debates, both sides undeniably grasp a bit of the truth. Virtue does matter. It is impossible to imagine how America could have mobilized an entire nation for war and asked for such great sacrifices without a resilient citizenry. It is worth remembering that before Pearl Harbor, even with fascism clearly on the march in many parts of the world, many Americans opposed U.S. involvement in the war, and anti-war activists like Senator Nye enjoyed a strong following. Yet, when war came, the Americans responded with alacrity. Likewise, after 9/11, the vast majority of Americans favored taking the battle to the enemy with scant dissent. Voices like Noam Chomsky, who saw the fault for 9/11 more with "us" than "them," got little hearing. A strong citizenry heeds the call to arms when a nation is threatened. America has demonstrated that again and again over the course of its history.

On the other hand, Lynn argues convincingly in *Battle* that there are too many exceptions to the rule to accept an overly prescriptive description of Western war as the enduring expression of civic militarism. Additionally, it is equally hard to buy the argument that virtuous warfare is a uniquely Western practice. Just as international relations theories imperfectly define international relations out of the context of time, people, and places engaged in international relations, historical theories that leave out the particulars of historical circumstance fall short as well.

There is a reason America can fit both Hanson's definition of universal civic militarism and Lynn's insistence on historical particularism. America is a free society and able to define how it defines itself. In regard to warfare, the primary instrument that America employs to define itself is its military. This is the absolute value of a free nation's military institutions. They help articulate the nature of virtuous warfare.

VIRTUE AND WAR

Both Hanson and Lynn acknowledge that the character of war cannot be legislated. Governments can, for example, pass laws defining lawful conduct on the battlefield. Multinational and international institutions can sign compacts enumerating standards of conduct. This does not mean that these efforts will entirely shape the way wars will be fought. As America has found in the long war combating global transnational terrorist networks, it has found an enemy that does not play by the accepted rules.

That is where military institutions come in. Generals are fond of saying that the purpose of the military is to fight and win the nation's wars. That is flat wrong. It is the nation's job to fight and win its wars. Responsibility for war belongs to the people. That responsibility cannot be outsourced to soldiers or contractors. The military, however, is the vital component the people have chosen to exercise part of that responsibility. The military is the nation's bridge between its aspirations in war and the reality of war. The purpose of military institutions is not just to fight the nation's war, win through to peace, and conduct the missions vital to country's needs. The armed services also prepare the nation for war and, once the people are at war, provide the professional expertise and knowledge to help guide them the conflict.

A healthy relationship between the military and democratic society is symbiotic. The nation fields a military based on its aspirations for how the nation will serve in war. In turn, the practical experience of the military informs the nation on how closely its aspirations match reality.

The military's knowledge and skill in military operations is not unique or exclusive as Huntington suggests in *The Soldier and the State*. Huntington argues military professionals have a near intellectual monopoly on the exercise of violence. That is wrong. In fact, the military has many competitors before, during, and after war, all claiming to have the right answers to questions of how to use military force. In truth, no nation has more armchair generals than a democracy. On occasion, these voices are correct. Sometimes they are just silly. Still, the old adage is right: "war is too important to be left to the generals." When democracies fight wars, wars are too important to be left to anyone. The sovereignty of the nation does not devolve onto the state even in wartime. That is why constitutional checks and balances remain in place even when the security of the state is threatened. War is the people's business whether the practice of war is being exercised by soldiers or by businesses.

On the other hand, an equally famous maxim is also true—"democracy is not a suicide pact." The founding fathers recognized that an element of "unity of command" was essential in the practice of foreign policy and national security. They therefore placed additional powers in the hands of the executive to act as commander-in-chief. In turn, the president is charged with organizing, managing, and leading a military with funds appropriated by the Congress, and laws agreed to by the Congress and the president and sanctioned by the courts. Thus, although the armed forces are not the exclusive instrument of national power, they were envisioned by the framers of the Constitution as the principle instruments defining how Washington employs military power.

In war, as in virtually every other task of government, Washington can meet its Constitutional responsibilities and still outsource virtually every government activity—except responsibility and oversight. In making wars and winning peace, the nation's military institutions are essential components of both those essential activities of governance. In short, Washington can outsource every requirement for war but the genius for war, for which the nation relies on its armed forces.

The American military, in short, is the nation's self-chosen yardstick for measuring how the public fights its public wars. It performs that role through many tasks. The services perform the yeoman's service of determining what forces are needed and how to fight. Those tasks are accomplished through intellectual exercises, such as writing doctrine and sponsoring scientific research, and through practical experience, such as conducting realistic training. The military also develops requirements used to test and deploy the equipment, goods, and services that the nation needs for war. Additionally, the services maintain a complement of military forces that can be sent to war or employed to meet other vital national interests.

How robust a military a nation needs, and of what nature, is determined by the national security needs of the nation, not by some notional requirement for sustaining citizenship or maintaining Washington's monopoly on making foreign policy. That hardly implies that a modern American military can have few or no forces at all. The United States, after all, is a global power with global responsibilities. It cannot rely only on "rent-a-cops." America needs military forces. In turn, the armed services cannot realistically determine how to fight unless they can fight. Saddling the nation with a hollow military and a Pentagon that lacks the capacity to conduct current operations, maintain trained and ready forces, and prepare for the future puts national security at risk.

If the fundamental purpose of the military is put in danger in the future, it will not be because of the increased employment of contractors. Rather, it will likely result from the same shortfalls that threatened the utility of America's military institutions in the past—chronic underfunding in the absence of war. After the victory parade, Washington is always all too willing to make imprudent funding cuts, giving in to overly anxious impulses to reap "peace dividends" before all the bills have been paid and the military prepared for the next call to arms.

BLOWING IN THE WIND

Contracting in combat may usher in many changes in American society after the wars in Iraq and Afghanistan, but the conduct of foreign policy, the nature of citizenship, and purpose of the American military are not likely to be among them. The role of the private sector in public wars will probably have its greatest effect on the private sector.

The cyclical impact of major wars and the private sector has been an enduring feature of American history. Their influence on one another has been particularly dramatic since the onset of the Industrial Revolution.[26] When major wars occur, the American military draws on the American citizenry to energize the American military machine, adopting the best civilian practices to military purposes. In turn, the military trains its citizen soldiers in the application of these skills. After the war, the nation's citizen-soldiers return to the workplace and apply their new knowledge, skill, and talents to the marketplace. The result is an explosion of innovation, economic growth, and cultural change.

At the outbreak of World War I, the United States stood as the world's pre-eminent industrial power. When America entered the war, it harnessed industrial age practices to the purpose of war better than did any other nation on earth. In turn, the military unleashed over three million veterans schooled in industrial-age warfare on the American marketplace. At the same time, it helped kick-start new industries, such as commercial aviation. American industrial dominance in the world not only grew, but, by the advent of the Second World War, had trained a new generation of soldiers for the battlefield.

GIs differed from doughboys in that the generation that fought the second war to end all wars was the first generation of soldiers who went to war comfortable with modern technology. Unlike their fathers, the technology of the twentieth century was a ubiquitous part of their lives—telephones, cars, radios, and electricity were common place. GI soldiers likely tinkered with jalopies in their garages, fiddled with ham radios, or read comic books about the fantasy worlds that modern technology might bring. They were a generation well suited to harnessing the unprecedented armada of machines that World War II saw brought to the battlefield. Their tinkering, innovating spirit made the American military the master at adapting and improvising with technology on the battlefield.

In turn, the technologies of the Second World War empowered intermediate levels of command in a manner unprecedented in military history. At Normandy, not far beyond the beachhead, a commander of a few hundred men could control ground once held by an entire medieval army and call in more air and artillery support than could a corps commander during World War I. The increasing independence of military commands at the company, battalion, and brigade level called on the military increasingly to employ the principles of "middle management" developed in the private sector.

In the postwar period, the military once again unleashed its veterans on the marketplace, 12 million strong, armed with a confidence in technology, and possessed of leadership and work skills ideal for postwar industries. This work force, bolstered further by the education opportunities created by the GI Bill (government grants of payments to veterans for attending college or trade schools) and new industries evolving from technologies developed during the war, started the nation on the greatest economic expansion of its history.

The Korean conflict was close enough in time and space to be considered an extension of the World War II experience. Vietnam, on the other hand, was something different. In some respects, the war in Vietnam was America's first post-industrial military experience. By the advent of the conflict, industrial-age warfare and the ubiquitous place of technology on the battlefield was old hat. What Vietnam did bequeath to the veterans of that generation, however, was a life-long lesson in individual responsibility. In Vietnam, more than in any other modern American war, very junior officers and soldiers had a tremendous amount of individual responsibility. In addition, the changing nature of the war over the years and the varying character of combat from province to province precluded military leaders from becoming dogmatic in the practice of leadership. The school of war in Vietnam made an ideal breeding ground for individual entrepreneurs for the post-industrial age.

Unlike the economic expansions after the great world wars, however, the contributions of Vietnam veterans went largely unnoticed. Two factors account for that. The first was the great global economic downturn of the 1970s—hardly a market conducive to showing off the capabilities of new age entrepreneurs. The second was a lack of opportunity to exploit new markets and new opportunities. Both those conditions changed in the 1980s. The U.S. economy rebounded and the advent of commercial computers created the opportunities of the information age.

The traditional image of Vietnam veterans as drug-crazed losers or apathetic dropouts suffering from post-traumatic shock syndrome is largely a myth. They became the foot-soldiers in the information revolution. For every Steve Jobs and Bill Gates that graced the cover of trendy magazines, there were innumerable Vietnam-era veterans that served as corporate leaders fueling America's leap into the post-industrial age in the computer industry as well as in many other business sectors.

THE NEW BRAVE NEW WORLD

What the generation of veterans from the long wars in Iraq and Afghanistan will bring back to American society remains one of the most intriguing questions of the day. We do know that the contributions of this generation will be different.

This will be America's first veteran generation in which all the veterans will not have worn uniforms. Many of them will be veteran contractors. Unlike returning military veterans, contract veterans already have both feet in the private sector. Thus, the "cycle-time" of good ideas from the battlefield to the home field might be far faster than in previous wars.

The impact of technology on veterans, both in and out of uniform, may prove to be different as well. Technology in combat today is not only ubiquitous— it is networked. In other words, technologies exist as part of integrated systems that share information and capabilities. Technology is in many cases virtually invisible as users manipulate, improvise, change, and adapt complex systems with virtually no conception whatsoever of the fundamental science behind the equipment they are employing.

Network warriors, whether civilian and soldier, are approaching technology in fundamentally different ways than their fathers, or, for that matter, their older brothers or sisters. They are comfortable in chaos, learning networks, and self-organizing communities that build groups based on interests rather than rules.

Combined with their fresh vision of technology is a new level of entrepreneurship unseen since Vietnam. Iraq and Afghanistan are corporal's wars in which significant responsibility is routinely devolved not just to junior officers, but to small groups and even to individual soldiers. Individual warriors walk away from modern battlefields with more confidence in their individual talents and potential than have those of any other generation in history.

How soldiers and civilians will harness the skills of the information age honed in war remains to be seen. The outcome is likely to be dramatic.

I ROBOT

As in past modern wars, technological innovation sparked by wartime needs will now rebound upon the private sector, creating new opportunities and new markets. In this war, many of those breakthroughs will come the pioneering initiatives of individual contractors. Several potential candidates are already apparent, but it is worth highlighting at least one in order to illustrate what dreams may come.

Robots have stepped out of the science fiction pages and onto the battlefield, in large part because of an unprecedented surge in private sector contributions to military robotics.[27] Thousands are deployed in Iraq and Afghanistan supporting military operations on land, at sea, and in the air. Some robots cost as little as several thousand dollars each. Controlled remotely by soldiers, sailors, and airmen, they perform tasks such as disarming roadside bombs, scouting dangerous territory, and patrolling the sky.

The challenge of imagining the future of war is often a question of timing. Promising technologies are often derided or dismissed simply because their proponents' imaginations outpace the capacity of science and technology to deliver (that has long been the case with robotics). World War I offers a case in point. The nascent technologies described by nineteenth-century science fiction writers and military futurists were not ready for prime time and were incapable of breaking the gridlock of attrition warfare. Although H. G. Wells and Jules Verne are often praised for their foresight in envisioning the proliferation of weapons like tanks, airplanes, and submarines, the machines that they described were little more than fanciful, completely out of the reach of foreseeable technologies. Military writers were more conservative in their appreciation of how machines would change warfare, but even they missed the mark.[28]

In World War I, the future arrived too fast, before new technologies had matured to the point at which they could reshape the face of conflict. Had World War I been avoided and the great powers not tested these new technologies until the 1940s, when they were more mature, the guesses of both science fiction writers and military futurists might have proven nearer the truth.

Timing may not be everything, but it can dramatically affect the process of turning imaginative vision into reality. This may turn out to be the case for robotics. The vision of robots in combat, popularized in science fiction since the cliffhanger movie serials of the 1930s, did not reach fruition in the succeeding decades. The Pentagon had little to show after decades of research, causing the promise of robotics in battle to be largely derided and dismissed as a failure of overly exuberant imagination. Iraq and Afghanistan have demonstrated, however, that dismissing military robotics as a failed future vision may be premature. After decades of military research and development, robotic technologies have finally matured to where they now represent real combat capabilities.

The military is employing thousands of robots in the air, under the sea, and on land. According to press reports, the military has deployed "nearly 5,000 robots in Iraq and Afghanistan, up from 150 in 2004. . . . Soldiers use them to search caves and buildings for insurgents, detect mines, and ferret out roadside bombs." By the end of 2005, robots reportedly had rendered safe or exploded more than 1,000 improvised explosive devises (such as roadside bombs).[29]

No doubt the expansive experience gained for using robots in combat will contribute to developing more commercial applications. In addition, military investments in robotics research are furthering the development of robotic technologies with capabilities for autonomous action. Autonomy will enable robots to sense, react, and even make decisions without human intervention. If these innovations come to fruition, they could well revolutionize military practices and the private sector marketplace.

NOTHING TO FEAR—BUT FEAR

New technologies, new entrepreneurial spirit, and new qualities of leadership have great potential for recharging America's competitive edge in the new century. We'll see. These, however, are the most likely—and most momentous—effects that the wars in Iraq will have on the nature of American society.

Fears that the widespread use of contractors in the long wars in Iraq and Afghanistan will somehow destroy America's military spirit, civic virtue, or democratic governance lack much merit on close inspection. If America does cease to be America, it will be because Americans abandoned their fundamental commitment to the virtues of a liberal democracy—not because they wrote contracts.

8
Chapter

How We Make It Better

There is a war to be won.

That common refrain from World War II has meaning for the long war, though not the same one it had for GI Joe and Rosie the Riveter. Gas rationing, bond drives, and what commodities could be substituted for butter and sugar monopolized conversations at the corner drug store during the global war against fascism. Americans wanted for a good deal because the war effort wanted so much. Today, however, America has resources to spare in fighting the long war against radical extremists and their mad dreams of building global terror networks to kill U.S. citizens and their friends and allies around the world.

That America has the resources for this fight is hardly cause for complacency. Wars are not always won by the side with the biggest battalions.

With a long war still to be won, and other national security challenges likely to emerge in its wake, Americans should not be sanguine over the state of contracting for combat. Though the private sector might not represent a mortal threat to citizenship, foreign policy, or West Point does not mean that there is nothing to worry about.

By any but the most generous standards, it can be fairly argued that America could have fought much better wars in Iraq and Afghanistan. There is plenty of fault to share. Republican and democratic administrations, the Capitol dome and the White House, the military and its civilian masters—all have a share of responsibility for the sad state of unpreparedness for the long war when the long war came.

Unfortunately, there are no "do-overs" in war. And because contracting appears to be at present an inevitable part of the changing face of modern war, the United States would do well to ensure that its practices are as good as they get. Washington has plenty of reasons to more effectively organize for combat for the future years of the long war than it has to date.

There are lessons to be learned from the first years of fighting terror, lessons that will make the private sector a better partner for the public's war. They are at least three, and they are simple—which should come as no surprise. The great nineteenth-century Prussian military theorist Clausewitz wrote in his most well-known work, *On War*, that "everything in war is simple." These three proposals follow that rule:

- Bring back America's competitive edge.
- Fight better wars.
- Make government a better customer.

It is just that simple.

Clausewitz also added in *On War* that although everything in war is simple, in war, "even the simple is difficult." So it goes with the best prescriptions for contracting in combat. They are simple—but difficult.

Here is what needs to be done for the long war to be won.

BRINGING BACK AMERICA'S COMPETITIVE EDGE

Job #1 in Washington starts with ceasing to do things that undermine the competitive advantages of American society. Chapter five included a long laundry list of major concerns threatening the nation's capacity to harness the capacity of a global private sector. If these public policy issues are not addressed (arguably the most significant challenges facing Washington in the years ahead) then any efforts at military and contractor reform are merely wasted effort.

Unless Washington adopts an unashamedly pro-competitive agenda in the near term, America will cease to be a first-rate global competitor in the long term. Not even the most competitive liberal democracy can hope to overcome a government that works against the best interests of its citizens. It would be like world-class sprinters who tie their own shoe laces together. It makes no sense, but it can happen (that is what Ayn Rand tried to warn the world about in her nightmare novels about the "looters" who wage their ceaseless campaigns against the individual).

Sustaining America's competitive edge is a vital part of ensuring that the United States can exploit the advantages of a rich and powerful global private sector. To do that the list presented in chapter five offers a good place to start. That list includes: reemphasizing free trade; reforming acquisition rules; adopting fiscal and education reforms; and resisting corporatist social policies. The goal here is clear. America has to work to maintain its greatest competitive advantage, the ability to tap the global private sector in the service of the public's wars.

FIGHTING BETTER WARS

Keeping America competitive is only a start. Having access to the global private sector is worth little if a nation is not ready for the fight. Indeed, contracting in combat would not have moved from a historical item of interest to front-page scandal had the White House run a better war.

Poor contracting practices themselves are not even close to the most signifi-cant obstacle to running a better war. Contractors, like soldiers in the foxhole, are just the point of the spear. All the people and processes behind them have to be fixed first to make the boots on the ground as good as they can get.

TEAM WASHINGTON

After 9/11, most of Washington did not go to war. The Pentagon went to war, and most others stayed home. The reason for that is that most often government does a mediocre job in marshalling all the resources required to do operations overseas beyond dropping bombs and invading countries.

The Departments of Defense, State, and Treasury, as well as the FBI, CIA, and other government agencies each have separate and unique capabilities, budgets, cultures, operational styles, and Congressional oversight committees. They even operate under different laws. Getting them all organized on battlefields, after dis-asters, and during times of crisis can be like herding cats. In meeting the dangers of the twenty-first century, including by winning wars, interagency operations will be more important than ever.

LEAVE THE CONSTITUTION ALONE

The pressing demand for interagency reform does not require that the federal government be reorganized. There is nothing wrong with the underlying principles of American governance. Especially essential are the Constitutional "checks and bal-ances" that divide federal power between the executive, legislative, and judicial branches. This division entails not only sharing responsibility within and among the branches of government, but ensuring accountability and transparency in the act of governing. Shortcutting, circumventing, centralizing, undermining, or obfuscating Constitutional responsibilities does not make democratic government work better.

Respecting the principle of federalism is also imperative. Embodied in the U.S. Constitution, the imperatives of limited government and federalism give citizens and local communities the greatest role in shaping their own lives. The 10th Amendment states that "powers not delegated to the United States by the Constitution, nor pro-hibited by it to the States, are reserved to the States respectively, or to the people." In matters relating to their communities, local jurisdictions and individuals have the preponderance of authority and autonomy. This makes sense: the people closest to the problem are the ones best equipped to find its solution.

REPEATING HISTORY

For its part, Washington can certainly do better—in large measure simply by improving interagency operations. For in the long history of interagency opera-tions, the same problems spring up again and again.[1]

Why? Government undervalues individuals. Human capital refers to the stock of skills, knowledge, and attributes resident in the workforce. Throughout its history, Washington has paid scant attention to recruiting, training, exercising, and educating people to conduct interagency operations. Thus, at crucial moments, success or failure often turns on happenstance—whether the right people with the right talents just happen to be at the right job.

Washington lacks the lifeline of a guiding idea. Doctrine is a body of knowledge for guiding joint action. Good doctrine does not tell people what to think, but it guides them in how to think—particularly in how to address complex, ambiguous, and unanticipated challenges when time and resources are both hard pressed. Unfortunately, throughout our nation's history, government has seldom bothered to exercise anything worthy of being called interagency doctrine. The response to Katrina offers a case in point. The U.S. government had the equivalent of a doctrine in the form of the National Response Plan. Unfortunately, it had been signed only months before the disaster and was barely practiced and little understood when disaster struck.

Process cannot replace people. At the highest levels of government, no organizational design, institutional procedures, or legislative remedy has proved adequate to overcome poor leadership and combative personalities. Presidential leadership is particularly crucial to the conduct of interagency operations. Over the course of history, presidents have had significant flexibility in organizing the White House to suit their personal styles. That is all for the best. After all, the purpose of the presidential staff is to help presidents lead, not tell them how to lead.

The Iran–Contra affair serves as a case in point. When Ronald Reagan spoke about the affair on March 4, 1987, he told the nation that he accepted "full responsibility" for his own actions and for those of his administration. The president described his efforts to restore public trust in the presidency and outlined a plan to restore the national security process, mainly by adopting the recommendations of the Tower Commission report.

Leadership from the Congress, especially from the Committee Chairs, is equally vital. There is no way to gerrymander the authorities of the committees to eliminate the necessity of competent, bipartisan leadership that puts the needs of the nation over politics and personal interest.

And, in the end, no government reform can replace the responsibility of the people to elect officials who can build trust and confidence in government, select qualified leaders to run the government, and demonstrate courage, character, and competence in crisis.

Fixing these problems requires a scalpel, not a sledgehammer. It would be a mistake to think of interagency operations as a uniform, one-size-fits-all activity requiring uniform, one-size-fits-all reforms.

WORKING IN WASHINGTON

The highest rung of the interagency process is that that of making interagency policy and strategy. These are the tasks largely accomplished inside the Washington beltway by officials from the White House and heads of federal agencies in cooperation and consultation with the Congress. Over the course of modern history, this has actually become the strongest component of the interagency process. When it does fail, failure can often be traced to people and personalities (inattentive presidents or squabbling cabinet officials) more than to process.

Improving performance at the highest level of interagency activities should properly focus on the qualities and competencies of executive leadership as well as upon getting the best-quality information to the leaders so that they can make the best informed decisions.

OPERATING OVERSEAS

Operational activities stand on the second rung of the interagency process. These activities comprise the overarching guidance, management, and allocation of resources needed to implement the decisions made in Washington. Arguably, it is at this level of government where government's record is most mixed. Outside the Pentagon's combat command structure (which has staffs to oversee military operations in different parts of the world), the U.S. government has few established mechanisms with the capability to oversee complex contingences over a wide geographical area. Processes and organizations are usually ad hoc. Some are successful. Others are dismal failures.

Doing better than getting lucky requires more permanent, but very flexible organizations that do not make national policy but that can coordinate large, complex missions. One potential solution is to build on the concept of the military's regional combatant commands, but with a new organizational structure that better supports the nation's national security needs. That organization should probably emphasize facilitating interagency operations around the world while still ensuring effective joint combat action.

Of course, we'd still need permanent military commands under the direction of the Pentagon, but the number of combatant commands should be reduced to three. In Europe and Northeast Asia, the United States has important and enduring military alliances. There is a continuing need to integrate our military commands with them. To this end, EUCOM (Europe) and PACOM (Asia) should be replaced by a U.S.–NATO command and a U.S. Northeast Asia headquarters. NORTHCOM (United States, Canada, and Mexico) should remain as the military command responsible for the defense of the United States.

In addition, three "Joint Interagency Groups" (InterGroups) should be established.[2] Joint Interagency Task Forces (JIATFs) have already been used very effectively on a small scale to conduct counternarcotics operations in Latin America, the Caribbean, and off the Pacific coast of the United States. They incorporate resources from multiple agencies under a single command structure for specific missions. There is no reason that this model could not be expanded, in the form of InterGroups, to cover larger geographical areas and more diverse mission sets. InterGroups should be established to link areas of concern related to national security missions for Latin America, Africa and the Middle East, and South and Central Asia.

Each InterGroup would have a mission set specific to its area. The Latin America InterGroup, for example, should focus on the trafficking of drugs, humans, and arms, as well as upon counterterrorism, civil-military relations, and trade liberalization.

Each InterGroup should include a military staff tasked with planning military engagements, warfighting, and postconflict operations. In the event that military operations are required, the military staff could be detached from the InterGroup (along with any supporting staff from other agencies required) to become the nucleus of a standing Joint Task Force (JTF). Using this model, operations in Iraq and Afghanistan would have been commanded by a JTF dispatched from the InterGroup to run the war and oversee the peace.

BOOTS ON THE GROUND

The third component of interagency activities is field activities. That's where the actual work gets done—rescuing people stranded on rooftops, handing out emergency supplies, administering vaccines, supervising contractors. Here success and failure usually turns on whether government has correctly scaled the solution to fit the problem. Most overseas interagency activities are usually conducted by a "country team" supervised by ambassadors and their professional staffs. Likewise, inside the United States, state and local governments largely take care of their own affairs. When the problems are manageable, such as in the case of coordinating tsunami relief within individual countries, these approaches work well. On the other hand, when the challenges swell beyond the capacity of local leaders to cope, as the case studies of pacification programs in Vietnam and the response to Hurricane Katrina illustrate, more robust support mechanisms are required. Arguably, what's most needed at the field level are (1) better doctrine, (2) more substantial investments in human capital (preparing people to do to the job before the crisis), and (3) appropriate decision-making—instituting the right doctrinal response when a crisis arises.

A generation ago, the U.S. military faced similar professional development challenges in building a cadre of joint leaders—officers competent in leading and executing multi-service operations. The Goldwater–Nichols Act of 1986 mandated a solution that required officers to have a mix of joint education, assignments, and board accreditation to become eligible for promotion to general officer rank.[3] Goldwater–Nichols is widely credited with the successes in joint military operations from Desert Storm to the war on terrorism. The recipe of education, assignment, and accreditation (EA&A) can be used to develop professionals for other critical interagency national security activities.[4]

An EA&A program that cuts across all levels of government and the private sector must start with professional schools specifically designed to teach interagency skills. No suitable institutions exist in Washington, academia, or elsewhere.

The government will have to establish them. Although the resident and nonresident programs of many university and government schools and training centers can and should play a part in interagency education, Washington's institutions should form the taproot of a national effort with national standards.

Qualification will also require interagency assignments where individuals can practice and hone their skills. These assignments should be at the "operational" level so leaders can learn how to make things happen, not just set policies. Identifying the right organizations and assignments and ensuring that they are filled by promising leaders should be a priority.

Accreditation and congressional involvement are crucial to ensuring that these programs succeed and continue. Before leaders are selected for critical (non-politically appointed) positions in national security, they should be accredited by a board of professionals in accordance with broad guidelines established by Congress. Congress should require creation of boards that (1) establish educational requirements and accredit institutions needed to teach national and homeland security, (2) screen and approve individuals to attend schools and fill interagency assignments, and (3) certify individuals as interagency-qualified leaders. Congress should also establish congressional committees in the House and Senate with narrow jurisdictions over key education, assignment, and accreditation interagency programs.

THE CLOCK IS TICKING

In Washington the important is often sacrificed for the urgent. The important, like reforming the interagency process, is put off till later, but later never comes.

That is unacceptable.

Good contracting practices cannot be built on a foundation of sand. The private sector cannot be led in public wars if Washington cannot lead itself. Fixing this problem requires building interagency competencies that are not broadly extant in government. Until Washington starts doing things differently, what it can effectively get out of the private sector will always be, at best, second best.

FRIENDS FOR THE FIGHT

Getting Washington organized is not enough. Washington is always going to require friends for the fight. The threats of the new century are international in character and indeterminable in length, and they require an international response. Alone, the United States cannot win the long war against transnational terrorism, and neither can it respond effectively to the other emerging national security concerns of the twenty-first century. America needs allies. America's greatest strength lies in numbers: the number of free nations that share its commitment to peace, justice, security, and, above all, freedom.[5]

Many thought that in the post–Cold War world "coalitions of the willing" (groupings of states to deal with particular problems) would become far more commonplace means for dealing with the new world disorder.[6] The first Gulf War, in which the United States successfully fought with an ad hoc alliance, appeared to validate the utility of employing temporary coalitions. The 2002 *National Security Strategy of the United States* made specific reference to the growing importance of coalitions of the willing.[7] Such coalitions were to be the coin of the realm for international relations in the twenty-first century whereby the problem would determine the coalition.

That thinking was wrong.

As the experience of the past decade shows, the problem is not the defining factor. The most concerted efforts to promote stability in the post–Cold War world and combat transnational terrorism have been by the United States and its traditional Cold War allies. America's strongest military partners in Iraq have been its longest-standing military allies, Great Britain and Australia. Meanwhile, in Northeast Asia, South Korea and Japan have remained steadfast U.S. partners. Even Canada and European nations, which have differed significantly from the United States in their policies toward Iraq and how the war on terrorism should be fought, in practice have offered significant cooperation in combating transnational terrorism and supporting operations in Afghanistan.

Not only have America's traditional allies been more important than ever, but so have other countries that have worked more closely with the United States in recent years. India and Poland have demonstrated greater interest in developing deep political, economic, social, and cultural ties rather than just participating in casual military and security cooperation. In short, they have shown an inclination to be more partners in an enduring alliance than participants in an ad hoc coalition.

Building alliances is not about gaining consensus in international action or allowing U.S. sovereignty to be overseen by multinational institutions. Indeed, abrogating the state's responsibility for national security is the surest way to undermine a nation's capacity to secure the safety, prosperity, and freedom of its citizens over the long term.[8] Rather, building enduring alliances requires proactive initiatives that build common interests between states by developing deep cultural, economic, social, and military ties between established free-market democracies.

Building enduring alliances should be the centerpiece of long-war strategy, but these alliances will not appear by happenstance. It will require a concerted U.S. effort to build bridges between peoples, facilitating safe and secure travel and interchange between America and its friends and allies. Washington will have to make a more concerted effort to establish a shared common vision, enhancing public diplomacy so that America can better make its case on the world stage. Finally, the United States must invigorate its efforts to promote mutual security by creating new opportunities for security cooperation (much of this effort has to involve stopping anti-competitive practices such as excessive ITAR and visa restrictions). In short, America can do a much better job at building enduring bilateral alliances.

LEARNING HOW TO WIN THE PEACE

Arguably, if Iraq and Afghanistan had been Clinton's War or Gore's War or a war fought by any other Democratic or Republican president, the initial results of postwar effort might have been not that much different.[9] There is no doctrine to guide the President and his Cabinet in planning for and conducting military interventions and post-conflict operations. There are institutions organized and prepared to lead winning the peace. As a result, there should be little wonder that the White House and the Pentagon struggled to get their footing.

Admittedly, that is no excuse. America has a long history of conducting occupations, going back to the American Revolution. What is more, the U.S. military has conducted an operation related to peacekeeping, peacemaking, or post-conflict occupation roughly every two years since the end of the Cold War. Ironically, despite this long history, after the battle Washington always falls back on its most time-honored tradition—forgetting what is required after the shooting stops.[10]

The military's reluctance to think deeply about the place of peace operations in military affairs derived from a rich tradition of Western military theory, typified by Clausewitz, in *On War*. Clausewitz emphasized the primacy of winning battles and destroying the enemy's conventional troops. He was a veteran of the Napoleonic Wars and thus could perhaps be forgiven for not even mentioning peace operations in his classic treatise. After all, peacekeeping operations were something new and novel in his time, first conducted by allied forces dismantling Napoleon's empire in 1815.[11] Washington, which could look back on over a century of these operations by modern states, had less excuse. Nevertheless, tradition has always won out over history, and as a result America starts all of its occupations from scratch. If it wants to do better, that has to change.

GETTING THE RULES RIGHT

Changing starts with establishing a real interagency doctrine that describes how to win the peace.[12] A good place to start in crafting this doctrine would be to go back to America's World War II experience. In planning for the postwar occupations, the military developed something called the "disease and unrest formula." It goes like this: When planning to occupy a country, there are three things that have to be done before the occupation ends to avert conditions from devolving into mass death, chaos, and revolution: (1) prevent a humanitarian crisis, (2) establish a legitimate government, and (3) create security forces that can support that government. Achieving those goals lays the foundation for the state's populace to determine its own future. Once that is done, it is up to the country to rebuild itself. This formula makes sense.

The disease and unrest formula is not nation-building. Indeed, the term "nation-building" is just silliness. Nations do not rebuild other nations. Nations rebuild themselves. Europe certainly rebuilt itself after World War II. The Marshall Plan did not come along until 1948, after legitimate governments had been established in the postwar countries of Western Europe and basic security restored. The

Europeans themselves directed how funds available under the Marshall Plan would be spent. Marshall got all the credit, but Europe did all the heavy lifting.[13]

By eschewing the disease and unrest formula, the United States had to relearn these lessons in Iraq. In the first months that Washington fumbled to get organized, so did Washington's enemies. Washington forgot that in war, the enemy gets a vote. In occupied Iraq, the enemy voted first—and not for peace. Because of the failure to move quickly to reestablish a sovereign government and field security forces to protect the country, the forces in the region that are intent on sowing violence and chaos had sufficient time to mobilize themselves and make the task of turning Iraq over to the Iraqis a daunting challenge.

Although a postwar doctrine needs to have a number of principles—principle number one, without question, must be putting only one person in charge of winning the peace. By its nature, regime change is a multi-agency operation and usually involves a coalition of other countries as well. Despite the multiplicity of actors, a single agency or headquarters must command the operations. Splitting authority for operations in Iraq between military commanders and a civilian administrator was a mistake and complicated the problems of implementing the disease and unrest formula. In contrast, the post–World War II operations remained under a single command authority, a decision that contributed to their success. Unity of command allowed the occupying forces to learn more quickly from their mistakes and adapt better to unforeseen circumstances.

Unity of command would, without question, have made the challenge of managing contractors in Iraq easier. At least three federal entities managed major contracts in Iraq. In addition, other federal agencies let contracts as well. Some agencies even borrowed contract vehicles from other agencies. Thus, one federal department could easily find contracts being managed through its accounts even though department officials were absolutely clueless as to what the contracts were for or how they were being managed. Afghanistan is little better, and perhaps worse. At least two major U.S. military regional commands manage operations in the country, in addition to civilian agencies and an alphabet soup composed of NATO and other international organizations. In this chaos, it is a wonder anything is accomplished at all.

In future U.S. operations, the military should remain in charge until the security situation in the country is stable. Once the stability of the country is no longer at risk from armed conflict, authority should be turned over to a civilian administrator, but this decision to make the transfer to civilian authority should be made by the President.

ORGANIZING FOR PEACE

As well as getting principles right, the United States needs the right kind of organizations to implement those principles. The United States simply lacked an organizational structure adequate for the initial occupation of Iraq.

Currently, the Department of State is setting up an Office of Reconstruction and Humanitarian Assistance to create a core planning capability and a cadre of planners for postconflict duties. The office will conduct initial planning for operations and then deploy its planners to serve in the field. However, the State Department's initiative, although well-intentioned, is inadequate. In fact, it is little more than a "Potemkin Village."

Successful postconflict operations cannot be planned effectively in Foggy Bottom or the Pentagon. Planning and implementation must be done in-theater, in concert with the military combatant commands, where planners can gain a first-hand appreciation of the challenges. The current U.S. embassy system provides each ambassador with an interagency "country team," but the ambassador's authority extends only to the borders of the country to which he or she is accredited.

Instead of building another bureaucracy in Washington, the administration should be building interagency regional teams like the InterGroups. The skills needed to conduct effective postconflict tasks must be brought together under regional teams. These skills are available across the American government and include the ability to manage hard and soft power—such as the capacity to destroy the old regime and then restore security, avert or alleviate a humanitarian crisis, and reestablish a legitimate government.

InterGroups should have components of their staffs dedicated to postconflict planning in the same manner as current operational staffs plan for warfighting contingencies.[14] In the event of war, the postconflict interagency staff can be attached to military joint task forces (a command that includes all the forces from the armed services participating in a particular campaign) to provide the nucleus of an occupation staff for the joint force commander.

As part of its national security education system, Washington also needs special schools specifically designed to teach the operational concepts and practices relevant to postconflict missions. The services already have advanced schools (such as the Marine Corps's School for Advanced Warfighting) for instructing in the operational arts at their staff colleges. These courses train the military's finest planners. The curriculum in these courses should be expanded to include postconflict missions. Similar education needs to be established for planners and supervisors in civilian agencies.

The Department of Defense should retain force training and force structure packages appropriate to postconflict tasks. There are three ways to do this: (1) by training and equipping allies to perform these duties, (2) by retraining and reorganizing U.S. combat troops for the task, and (3) by maintaining special U.S. postconflict forces.

As a great power, the United States needs all three of these options to provide the flexibility that will enable the nation to adapt to different strategic situations that might require different levels of commitments from U.S. forces. Special postconflict units could be assembled from existing National Guard and Reserve units, including security, medical, engineer, and public affairs commands. Because many of the responsibilities involved in post-war duties are similar in many ways to missions that might be required of homeland security units, these forces could perform double duty, having utility both overseas and at home.[15]

The Pentagon's forces for these missions would look like large constabulary units. Among the virtues of these forces is that they would be a better fit for the Guard and Reserve than conventional combat units would be; they would be structured from existing units, have great utility for the breath of military missions, and be a more fitting partner for private sector contractor assets.

The Army, Air Force, and Navy play a part in transforming the National Guard to provide the kinds of capabilities needed for the right force. These forces are needed not just to optimize part of the military for missions other than war, but also to establish units better suited to partner with the private-sector support that will be needed.

ON LAND

The land force needs to be large enough to maintain some units on active duty at all times for rapid response and sufficient to support missions at home and abroad. For response to catastrophes, four components would need to be particularly robust: medical, security, critical infrastructure, and oversight.

Medical

The United States does not have the capacity to provide mass military medical assets that are well suited for dealing with catastrophic casualties at home or massive civilian postwar needs overseas. The current defense medical support available for homeland security is small and ill suited for the task. Rather than field hospitals that take days and weeks to move and set up, the military needs a medical response that can deal with thousands of casualties on little notice, deploy in hours, assess and adapt existing structures for medical facilities, and deliver mass care to people in place instead of moving them to clinical facilities.

Security

A bitter lesson learned in Iraq is that public safety and security in postwar environments has to be task number one. Likewise, virtually no American community is prepared to deal with widespread disorder after a disaster inside the United States, particularly in an environment where infrastructure is widely disrupted or degraded. Dealing with safety and security in these situations will require a military response by specially trained and equipped personnel who are used to working with civilian agencies. These troops should prove equally adept at conducting counterinsurgency operations in urban terrain overseas, where neutralizing the enemy and protecting civilian lives and property are equally important. This force should look much more like a constabulary unit than tradition infantry forces or military police.

Critical Infrastructure

The U.S. military has the command, control, and assets, as well as units capable of providing for the immediate reconstitution and protection of critical resources. The U.S. Army Corps of Engineers has the capacity and expertise needed for managing large-scale contracts under difficult, stressful conditions. The Federal Emergency Management Agency (FEMA), which frequently partners with the military for disaster response, has the expertise to conduct needs assessments and coordinate community recovery. They should be able to work together to perform these tasks anywhere in the world. Response teams reinforced with a large cadre of Reserve contracting officers could be paired with the Corps of Engineers and FEMA to provide an effective infrastructure protection and recovery force for disasters at home or overseas.

Oversight

Any large-scale response will raise concerns about inefficiency, fraud, waste, and abuse. Maintaining the credibility of the response from the outset is essential. The response will undoubtedly involve multiple agencies. A Special Inspector General should be instated to inculcate trust and confidence in the public that operations are being performed in an appropriate and transparent manner. This inspector general capability should be built into the force from the start, and its mandate should include looking at intergovernmental and interagency coordination, program management, acquisition and contract management, and human resources.

IN THE AIR

Contingency forces for deployment overseas and home should be self-deployable and self-sustaining, capable of operating in austere environments where critical infrastructure is significantly degraded. The Air Force's efforts to enhance its expeditionary airfield capability overseas will be well suited to domestic security in the United States and postconflict operations overseas. Now the Air Force needs only to develop a strategic plan to base its Air National Guard forces that support these missions in coordination with the land response forces.

AT SEA

The emerging potential for maritime response for both homeland security and contingency mission overseas augurs the need for an organizational structure that better uses the Navy's capacity and makes it more fitting partner for the U.S. Coast Guard in these kinds of missions. Several states with maritime interests already have state naval militias. In fact, the New York Naval Militia assisted in the response to the terrorist attacks of September 11, 2001. Creating a naval guard, however, should be a national program.

Creating a Navy Guard to include all coastal states would offer several advantages. A Navy Guard would provide coastal states with more resources to address their state maritime security and public safety requirements. Unlike the Coast Guard, the Navy Guard would focus on state needs when not on active federal service. It would also provide an organization within the National Guard and the Navy that treats homeland security missions as an inherent responsibility and would work to develop the requisite competencies and capabilities to fully support these tasks. Finally, a Navy Guard would provide a suitable partner for the U.S. Coast Guard to ensure seamless daily integration of the Defense and Homeland Security departments' maritime operations, as well as responding to contingency missions overseas.

From reorganizing military units to writing the right doctrine, there is much that could be done to get Washington better organized for the task of winning the peace. These reforms are vital part of winning the public's wars and important for establishing the right context in which to employ private sector assets.

A MILITARY WORKFORCE FOR THE TWENTY-FIRST CENTURY

Beyond organizing military forces to do the job right next time, much can be done to make sure the military is a suitable partner for the private sector. Much of that effort goes to correcting poor personnel policies.

One reason the Pentagon turns to contractors so frequently is that the cost of military manpower is pricing military manpower out of the market. Soldiers are becoming too expensive. Personnel policies are also preventing the Pentagon from effectively tapping private-sector talent. Career options for military service personnel are not keeping pace with skyrocketing defense manpower costs and the rapid changes in the American workplace. The Pentagon needs a new plan.

The Pentagon needs a new paradigm for compensating its military personnel that allows them to move seamlessly through active duty, the Reserves, the National Guard, and civilian employment without concern for how their career decisions will affect their health care and retirement benefits. A "rucksack" of benefits that they select themselves and can carry with them would be a critical tool in recruiting and retaining a trained and ready volunteer military. At the same time, Congress needs to address spiraling military manpower costs. In short, the rucksack for America's armed forces needs to be both transportable and affordable.

CHANGING TIMES

An effective military workforce strategy must address three critical contemporary challenges: military manpower, active reserve, and a changing nation.

Military Manpower

Manpower costs consume the largest part of the Pentagon's budget. Indeed, future increases in the per capita cost of military compensation could crowd out needed spending on military modernization in the core defense budget because

Congress and the administration plan to permanently increase the Army and Marines complement in the near term by about 100,000 active duty personnel. Evidence suggests that the current compensation system is too heavily weighted in favor of in-kind and deferred compensation over direct cash compensation.

Active Reserve

Unlike during the Cold War, today's National Guard and the Army, Navy, Air Force, Marine, and Coast Guard Reserves are operational forces that conduct missions at home and around the world during wartime and peacetime. For example, from September 11, 2001, to the end of 2003, over 319,000 citizen soldiers—27 percent of the Reserve Components—went on active duty. The reserves have proven themselves an effective means of rapidly expanding military capacity to meet changing national security requirements, but this requires reserves that have the flexibility to deploy when the nation needs them.

A Changing Nation

Demographic shifts will further alter the character of the military. Although the rate of U.S. population growth will continue to slow, the total population will continue to grow and age, which means that a smaller proportion of the population will be suitable for military service. The cost of military manpower will also increase as the armed forces find themselves competing with the private sector for talented young people. The total size of the military relative to the nation as a whole will likely continue to decrease in the years to come.

At the same time, the American workplace is changing. Workers change jobs, careers, and geographic location with increasing frequency. They leave and reenter the workforce and the schoolroom throughout their lives.

THINKING DIFFERENTLY

The key to recruiting and retaining a quality, all-volunteer force is to adopt career models that are consistent with both the changes in the American workforce and the nation's national security needs. The chief characteristic of this system must be flexibility that allows individuals to decide when and how to volunteer their time and talents. The Pentagon calls this concept "continuum of service," providing more opportunities to move back and forth between active and reserve service and civilian employment, to shift career fields within the military, and to choose options for voluntary deployments.

Among other things, establishing an effective continuum of service will require a package of incentives that best serve the nation and the individual. The right mix will require a combination of immediate targeted compensation (e.g., cash bonuses, career options, and educational opportunities) and the confidence to accept voluntary deployments knowing that the decision will not adversely affect health care and retirement. The Pentagon needs to be able to offer each soldier a "rucksack" that could accompany that individual whether or not the soldier chooses to serve on active duty or in the ready or inactive reserve. In short, health care and retirement should be portable and follow soldiers.

Congress can speed this process by using the military to pioneer entitlement reform. Congress should create a more flexible military retirement system. For example, the military would be an ideal population to pioneer the use of voluntary retirement accounts, which allow individuals to set aside a portion of their Social Security taxes. In addition, the Pentagon might create a variety of retirement contribution options. Right now, personnel who are separated from active service before 20 years receive no retirement benefits. The Department of Defense needs to offer a greater variety of options that are completely portable, following the soldier from active duty to reserve duty and civilian life.

Washington should also move the military health care system toward a defined contribution plan and away from a defined benefit plan (for medical services other than those related to operational missions and deployments). Such programs are both more economical and more flexible. Military and civilian health care systems share a common problem: in many cases, they preclude individuals from assuming at least some of the responsibility for making decisions about their care. As a result, they encourage beneficiaries to treat health care as a free good or service. Structuring the military health care system as a defined contribution plan would allow participants greater freedom of choice and more control. Greater individual control would likely impose more discipline on the system's use of its resources, allowing individuals to build personal health care programs that could accompany them from active duty to reserve duty to civilian employment.

Creating a rucksack for health care and retirement would help the Pentagon get the military that it needs when it needs it while helping to rein in spiraling manpower costs. The rucksack not only would serve the military well, but also could become a model for the civilian workforce of the future.

FOUR PERCENT FOR FREEDOM

The final and most important change that needs to be made is that Washington needs to consistently fund the military at an adequate level.[16] Despite intense military activity since 9/11, defense spending is at a historical low and has been so for far too long. Current and future administrations and Congresses should commit now to spending 4 percent of the GDP on national defense even after any drawdown of U.S. forces in Afghanistan or Iraq—both to prevent recurring hollow forces and to meet the military's immediate needs.

Washington is running a large budget deficit, and the principal reason is the growth in entitlement costs, not increased defense funding since 9/11. Since 1970, the historical ratio between defense spending and entitlement spending on Medicare, Medicaid, and Social Security has inverted. In 1970, military spending totaled 7.8 percent of GDP—almost twice the 4.1 percent of the GDP spent on the big three entitlement programs. Today, defense spending has fallen to 3.9 percent of the GDP, and entitlement spending has more than doubled to 8.8 percent of the GDP. Defense is not the problem with the budget, and cutting defense is not the solution. As a nation at war, the U.S. is spending remarkably little on defense. Devoting 4 percent of GDP to defense imposes a reasonable burden on the U.S. economy and is significantly below the mean of roughly 7.5 percent of GDP that the U.S. spent on defense during the Cold War.

Moreover, underfunding defense actually costs America more in the long run, including reducing the defense industrial base to a dangerously low level. This leads to an undercapitalized base that is not competitive, driving up costs for the U.S. government and taxpayers. Not spending enough on defense also creates the reality—and the perception—of American weakness, increasing risk, hindering economic growth, and lowering stability in the world. In the end, smart defense spending saves money.

And smart spending needs to start sooner rather than later. In the past, when America's military has begun to become hollow, the strain showed first in the National Guard. The same warning signs are evident today, including an austere lack of equipment, heavy reliance on cross-leveling to fill out units preparing to deploy, and a reduction in the levels of unit readiness. However, this problem is not exclusive to the National Guard. The Army and Air Force are already showing signs of funding shortfalls for equipment modernization. Although today's military is not yet hollow, it could become so in less than a decade if funding for military modernization is not adequate over a sustained period of time.

Spending 4 percent of GDP on national defense will allow the U.S. to keep the nation and its service members properly trained, equipped, and ready. In the long term, continuing to underfund defense and allowing wild fluctuations in defense budgets during times of war will only cost the country more and compromise national security. Without smart defense spending, all the contracting in the world will not help much. Contractors will not have an American military worthy of that name for them to serve.

BEING A BETTER CUSTOMER

Even with a well-funded military backed by solid manpower programs that keep the ranks of the armed services filled with highly qualified personnel, the Pentagon will still do lots of contracting in the future. The reason is simple. Empirical evidence proves again and again that the private sector offers government an effective source of services.[17] The challenges that the Pentagon have to overcome are (1) getting smarter about when to contract and (2) having the capacity to oversee the contracts so awarded. Accomplishing these two goals will go a long way toward taking contractor issues off the front pages and out of Congressional committee hearing rooms.

WHEN TO RENT

Contractors may be the best choice for some missions.[18] They are, however, not a perfect fit for every mission. The A-76 process has proven to be a controversial and admittedly imperfect instrument for determining the difference. The Pentagon can do better. The best option is to take a risk-based approach.

A risk-based approach is beneficial because it helps to avoid unnecessary risks while incorporating financial and intangible benefits and drawbacks into the calculation. Risk–benefit analyses are not new in the defense world. For instance, the U.S. Army field manual on risk management contains a standardized approach for assessing and managing risk that can be applied to all activities. This risk-based approach should be applied to contractor sourcing decisions. The approach consists of five steps:

1. Identify hazards.
2. Assess hazards to determine risk in terms of probability, severity, and risk level.
3. Develop ways to mitigate the risks and make decisions about risk.
4. Implement the mitigation processes.
5. Supervise and evaluate.

The field manual also provides useful definitions of "risk" and "hazard." The manual defines "risk" as "the probability and severity of loss linked to hazards" and "hazard" as "a condition or activity with potential to cause damage, loss or mission degradation and any actual or potential condition that can cause injury, illness, or death of personnel; damage to or loss of equipment and property; or mission degradation."[19] These ideas offer a reasonable start point for building the right decision-making framework.

Considering contracting from the perspective of risk mitigation raises all the right questions, including requiring judgments on, for example, the degree to which contractor shortfalls could hinder mission success, the safety implications for contractor employees and equipment and for the U.S. military, and the effect that using contractors may have on the military's ability to comply with laws, regulations, and high-level policy guidance and to collect information. The greater the hazards and risks identified by asking these questions, the greater the scrutiny and attention that should be applied to the decision-making process.

A RAND report focusing on Army decision-making and contractors suggests that there are five distinct organizational venues where and when the assessments should occur.[20] They cover the problem areas where issues usually occur:

1. Outside the military—decisions to use contractors are often influenced by Congress's and the administration's determinations of the appropriate size and operational tempo of military forces.
2. Acquisition venues—policies that "the Army uses to choose contractors, design contracts and quality assurance plans, and oversee and support contractors in theater heavily affect the residual risk associated with their use."[21]

3. Force design and management issues—when reserve component capability is small, for example, contractors may be used more heavily to avoid continually mobilizing the same group of people.

4. System requirement plans—program planners and leadership may encourage dependence on long-term contractor support depending on the vision and the need for highly skilled support personnel: "More generally, officials use spiral development to field systems early and collect operational data on them from the battlefield to refine their designs over time. This encourages the presence of contractors on the battlefield."[22]

5. During specific contingencies—where the military requires a quickly assembled force, it may also require greater contractor support.

Hardwiring assessments on the kinds of contracting that will inevitably prove the most "politically" divisive to begin with is one way to stop scandals before they start.

OPERATIONAL RESEARCH

There is also a way to seriously depoliticize even the most divisive political decisions—making clear that the requirements are clearly driven by military necessity. The military actually had a great tool for doing that, but like a lot of other great attributes of the force it got washed away in the great downsizing that followed the Cold War.

During World War II, the U.S. military discovered an instrument for improving the efficiency of some military operations. It was actually a tool that had long been in use in the private sector: exploiting an emergent field of math to determine new ways of achieving business efficiencies by analyzing complex systems, discovering critical paths that determined productivity, and adjusting the allocation of resources to boost production. During the war, the Pentagon applied "operations research" to all kinds of difficult problems for determining how to organize transatlantic convoys to maximizing bombing runs over the Third Reich.

Operations research became part of American military culture, applied over the years to many of the Pentagon's problems. Indeed, there has been a Military Operations Research Society for over forty years. Operations research was employed effectively during Vietnam, one of the many forgotten successes of the application of military force in a conflict where allegedly, and quite wrongly, it is assumed that the military got everything wrong.[23] The experience of operations was so positive that during the era of the Reagan build-up, every command and military installation had its own team of military operations research professionals, including university-trained officers.

The Army's corps of military operations research professionals was one of the first communities on the chopping block during military downsizing. The fact that the military lost an important capability was proven during the recent Iraq war when it had to be reinvented. Faced with the perplexing problem of dealing with a plague of improvised explosive devices (like mines and booby traps), the Pentagon established a joint interagency task force to study the problem. The task force developed a number of strategies, practices, and innovations to help deal with the challenge. Many of the techniques were derived using classic operational research analysis techniques.

A robust corps of operational research analysts would be ideal for evaluating and determining the private sector needs of the military in future operations. Developing and maintaining this corps of professionals ought to be a Pentagon priority.

CAPACITY BUILDING

In the end, however, the single greatest shortfall in contracting practices in Iraq and Afghanistan was that Washington lacked the capacity to oversee the unexpected massive volume of contracts it handed out. For instance, the Special Inspector General for Iraq Reconstruction "found that the shortage of personnel (and the widespread lack of required skill and experience among those available) affected all facets of reconstruction assistance."[24] This is a problem that would likely have surfaced even if the Pentagon had had a brilliant plan for winning the peace. It is an obstacle that would have loomed large for any administration, Republican or Democrat. Operations in Iraq simply placed a demand on military contracting that (considering the size of the current military force) probably dwarfed contracting during World War II. Nothing the military has done in the post–Cold War world—whether in Desert Storm, Somalia, Bosnia, Kosovo, or Haiti—comes even remotely close. It was if the Pentagon went from sand-lot contracting to contracting in the World Series—overnight.

In hindsight it is clear that fixing that problem would have resolved the majority of serious difficulties encountered in managing contracts. Even the most partisan critics would have had a hard time finding something to complain about. All the controversy might have been avoided if the military were a better customer. But, it was not, and it will not be in the future, either, under a Republican or Democratic president, unless it learns how to do contracting in combat better.

For starting to address all these practical problems, the Army, in particular, could do no better than reading its own report. In October 2007, a commission set up by the Secretary of the Army issued its findings in a study titled "Urgent Reform Required: Army Expeditionary Contracting." Chaired by former Undersecretary of Defense Jacques S. Gansler, the commission found that almost every component of the institutional Army, from financial management to personnel and contracting systems to training, education and doctrine and regulations, needed to be beefed up to handle the volume of work involved in military operations in Afghanistan and Iraq.

The commission found that only three percent of the Army's contracting personnel were on active duty and that the Army did not have one career Army contracting general officer position. The commission found only about half of the contracting officials to be certified to do their jobs. At the same time, during the long war, the Army has experienced a sevenfold increase in work.[25] The solution to these shortfalls is simple. The military must increase the size and quality of its contracting force—and it has to have the capacity to expand that force to meet large-scale contingencies.

A more robust contracting force must include a corps of contracting officers specifically prepared and trained in "expeditionary" contracting. In other words, unlike writing a contract to provide lawn mowing services at Fort Sill or buy new headgear, the military's contingency contracting corps must be prepared and ready to deploy in support of operations in places such as Iraq and Afghanistan. There must also be clear chain-of-command for contracting and contractor support for deployed forces running from the foxhole back to an office in the Pentagon. That will not only make contracting more responsive, it will make sure individuals can be held responsible for conducting the people's business.

A bigger contracting force will require institutional support to make sure it's effective. That means restructuring organizations so that personnel get the training, education, practical experience, and support tools they need (such as up-to-date information systems) and that lines of responsibility are clear.

The recommendations of the Gansler Report parallel many similar recommendations made by the Special Inspector General for Iraq Reconstruction and the Government Accountability Office. In short, they all conclude that when the people, resources, and institutions required to do the job right are lacking, no one should be surprised when the people, resources, and institutions available fail to do the job well.

"Get the job done right" hardly sounds like battling an evil military–industrial complex or unmasking a political conspiracy, but it is nevertheless the heart of the problem. For example, because the military cannot keep track of its contractors, it hands out an estimated $43 million in free meals every year to contractors who also receive an annual per diem allowance.[26] If Washington seriously wants to deal with the real problems of fraud, waste, and abuse then it will have to start dealing with the real problems that cause them.

WINNING

It will be easy to tell when Washington gets contracting in combat right. There will be experienced and capable contracting officers at *all* deployed locations. They will have all the support tools and authorities they need to do their job. They will be responsible for all the contracting in their areas of responsibility. They will work closely with all the military forces and other interagency representatives in their area of responsibility. They will be supervising contracts awarded under a contingency contracting process capable of matching the needs of the force when the force needs them with contractors who are qualified and equipped to do the job. The work of the contracting officer and the contractors will be overseen by an integrated, qualified team of auditors and inspectors who provide real oversight and accountability but do not interfere with the ability of the force to do its job. They will be accompanied by criminal investigators in sufficient numbers, and with sufficient support, to go after the bad apples in any barrel. All work (both of contractors and overseers) will be part of a system that provides visibility and transparency so that everyone who needs to understand what is being done, and why, has access to needed information. Most important of all, the contracting team will be supporting a U.S. team trained, organized, equipped, and led in ways designed to get the job done right.

That is what contracting in combat in the twenty-first century ought to look like.

Epilogue   The Future of War

On September 10, 2007, six years after America's last day without the war on terror, General David Petraeus, the senior U.S. military commander in Iraq, and Ambassador Ryan Crocker, the American ambassador in Baghdad, confronted a Congressional committee to report on the state of the U.S. effort to stem the violence across Iraq. It was a date to remember.

Few experiences equal a high-profile Congressional hearing. Observers pack the gallery. Photographers formed a carpet in front of the witness table, sitting cross-legged on the floor snapping pictures. Television camera lights painted the room with a harsh glare. Every committee seat was full—and every member was anxious to make his or her opening remarks.

On that day in September, everyone was there—press, people, and the people's representatives—even though everyone pretty much knew that both Petraeus and Crocker were going to issue guardedly positive reports. Still, because they were all there, news would be made.

All waited to hear what the general and the diplomat had to say. "As a bottom line up front," Petraeus started, "the military objectives of the surge are in large measure, being met." Digital cameras flashed.

That was the news.

By now that news is old news. Progress had been made. Four months later, as the surge in the number of U.S. combat troops sent to Iraq came to a close, trends proved still positive. Even the administration's harshest critics could not argue that things were worse than the year before. In fact, by every measure in December 2007 levels of all kinds of violence in Iraq were as low as they had been in 2004.

The reasons for the decline in the violence and the long-term impact on Iraq, the region, and the future of U.S. foreign policy are hotly debated and will likely remain so for sometime. In thinking about the future of war, however, that debate can be put to the side.

Everyone in the room missed the real news.

The real news came in the last paragraph of the general's prepared statement. "In closing," Petraeus finished, "it remains an enormous privilege to soldier again in Iraq with America's new 'Greatest Generation.'" This was the most important statement of all—a reaffirmation that this generation of soldiers is no different than any other. In this statement, Petraeus confirmed that, in his view, every generation of American soldiers is the greatest generation. Today's force is no different. The transformation of war into a new age when the public and private sphere serve as more equal partners on the battlefield matters not a whit to the nature of American soldiering.

American soldiering has not changed. It is in the character of the American soldier to face adversity on the battlefield and to adapt to the challenges at hand. Part of the process of fitting the force to the fight has been, and will always be, taking the best of the American citizen and putting it into the fight. Sometimes that will mean adapting civilian practices to military uses, but other times the military will just take civilians into the fight.

Whatever the final outcome of the American adventure in Iraq, American soldiers proved once again that they are up to any challenge when given the resources and the leadership to do the job right. America's citizen-soldiers and citizens will always answer the call to arms and prevail as long as America gives them the support they need.

However, as America looks to the future, there is much to be done. Washington has an enormous obligation to improve the factors that impact on contractor performance. These factors range from keeping the economy competitive, so that America has access to a robust private sector, to structuring government so it is a better consumer of private services. The military has an equally important part in fulfilling these obligations.

The military has a mission. It is the military's job to think about the future of war. And it has to do a lot better at its job. Although Washington failed the military in preparing for contractors in combat, the military failed Washington in not anticipating the requirements for contracting for combat. Because the unique and exclusive purpose of the military as a professional institution is to be Washington's bridge between the aspirations of government and the realities of the mud, blood, sweat, stink, refuse, and horrors of war, failure is not an option. If the military does anything less than its fundamental duty, it puts itself and the entire nation in jeopardy.

Among the tasks the military cannot contract out is the responsibility for facing the future of war. It already takes this job very seriously, but that is not good enough. Intentions mean nothing in war—only results matter. The military must start getting the future right more than wrong.

The military's failure to lay the intellectual groundwork for contractors in combat in Iraq illustrates how serious such shortfalls can be. That failure not only threatened success in Iraq and Afghanistan, it helped create the conditions that allowed the public debate over the private sector's role in public wars to descend into the frivolous and outrageous. It allowed shaky scholarly claims to go unchallenged and fueled diversions that sidetracked public policy debates.

The military must do better.

DARK HORIZON

The military fights the future. Today, there are more men and women on operational missions around the world than at any time since the end of the Cold War. Still, the majority of the military spends its days preparing for the next battle, not fighting the one at hand. Cadets study. Troops train. Some stateside commands develop new requirements for new equipment; others refurbish equipment the military already has. Military scientists push the envelope, applying new knowledge to combat capabilities. Few organizations spend more time and other resources worrying about what challenges and pondering what possibilities tomorrow will bring.

Far too often, and far too glibly, pundits accuse the military of preparing to fight the last war. Nothing could be further from the truth. Few organizations are more adept at learning and adapting to new requirements than are the American armed services. That said, the military is hardly immune from the effects of the historical, intellectual, and cultural forces that filter how institutions see the challenges ahead.

The Army's Training and Doctrine Command (TRADOC) musings on the future national security environment in 2007 offer a case in point. PowerPoint slides now assume that the Army will have to participate in "persistent" operations requiring years of effort and at least tens of thousands of boots on the ground. The Army slides draw an all-too-obvious lesson from the current conflict, but they are no more insightful than are the briefings of a few years ago that trumpeted the need for an "expeditionary Army" such as the forces that were needed to win the first conventional battles in Iraq and Afghanistan. In contrast, new Navy and Air Force briefings highlight the potential for conflict with China—a mere coincidence that this theater places a higher premium on air and sea forces. All these "death by PowerPoint" presentations suffer from the tendency to envision the future as expected or desired rather than to prepare for the uncertainty ahead.

Perceptions of the future often contain impressionable impulses from the past that skew thinking about how next chapter of war will unfold. There are no better examples of this tendency than the first TRADOC efforts to come to terms with the impact of ubiquitous computing on the battlefield in the 1990s. When TRADOC commanders articulated their vision of how proliferating computers would change combat and what future warfare might look like, their notions sounded an awful lot like Captain Kirk fighting from the command deck of the *Starship Enterprise*, the formative "television show of imagination" from the days of their youth. One senior TRADOC commander even confessed to owning a pair of the rubber ears worn by Spock, Kirk's trusty alien sidekick. Science fiction from the past formed their vision of military science for the future.

The greatest danger about thinking about the future of war is the danger of outsourcing imagination to others. Hollywood in particular is not the best source for science or deep thinking about war. The military services must become adept at "thinking outside the TV box.'" Military imagination is more than aping what soldiers saw on television or played in video games. It requires intellectuals skilled in science and technology, popular culture, history, politics, religion, and many other disciplines as well.

Military imagination also demands "thinking outside the geographical box." America does not need a military full of Lawrences of Arabia, but it does need an intellectual corps that knows what is going on across the world wide stage. It would, for example, be a mistake to think about concepts for future war and ignore the trends in the third world to employ children as warriors. There could well come a day when U.S. soldiers routinely go toe-to-toe with children in combat.

AFTER CONTRACTORS

The military, and pretty much everybody in Washington, now understand that contractors are an important part of combat. They might ask themselves, however, what else they are missing—what else is on the dark horizon.

That is a question Eisenhower asked in his farewell address to the nation. He did not fear that the military–industrial complex was about to engulf the nation, but he did worry about the consequences of an unexamined future. In large part because his administration and those that followed in its wake worried about the greatest generations to come, the futures we fear never came close to becoming the futures we had to endure. This generation could do far worse than to match that legacy.

The future is a foreign country. America's unpreparedness for many of the challenges of the long war against terror is a reminder that the route is fraught with intellectual obstacles—and that hard thinking is the best preparation for the fight.

Notes

PROLOGUE

1. P.W. Singer, "Outsourcing the War," Salon.com (April 16, 2004). (http://dir.salon.com/story/news/feature/2004/04/16/outsourcing_war/index.html).

2. David Zucchino, "Army Stage-Managed Fall of Hussein Statue," *Los Angles Times* (July 3, 2004), 1.

3. Dwight D. Eisenhower, *The White House Years, Waging Peace: 1956–1961* (Garden City, NY: Doubleday, 1961), 614.

4. Office of Management and Budget, *Budget of the U.S. Government: FY 98* (Washington, D.C.: U.S. Government Printing Office, 1997), table 6.1. From 1962 to 2000 defense spending dropped from 9.3 to 3.0% of GDP. James Jay Carafano and Paul Rosenzweig, *Winning the Long War: Lessons from the Cold War for Defeating Terrorism and Preserving Freedom* (Washington, D.C.: The Heritage Foundation, 2005), 139.

5. Quoted in Charles J.G. Griffin, "New Light on Eisenhower's Farewell Address," in Martin J. Medhurst, *Eisenhower's War of Words: Rhetoric and Leadership* (East Lansing: Michigan State University Press, 1994), 275.

6. For the evolution of the final address, see Griffin, "New Light on Eisenhower's Farewell Address," in Medhurst, *Eisenhower's War of Words*, 274–277.

7. Martin J. Medhurst, "Eisenhower's Rhetorical Leadership: An Interpretation," in Medhurst, *Eisenhower's War of Words*, 294.

8. The writing and reception of the Gaither Report are described in David L. Snead, *The Gaither Committee, Eisenhower, and the Cold War* (Columbus: Ohio State University Press, 1999).

9. Eisenhower, *Waging Peace*, 615–616.

10. Dwight D. Eisenhower, *At Ease: Stories I Tell My Friends* (Garden City, NY: Doubleday, 1967), 40. Eisenhower added, "[Washington's] Farewell Address, his counsel to his countrymen on the occasions such as his speech at Newburgh to the rebellious officers of his Army, exemplified the human qualities I frankly idolized."

11. Kerry E. Irish, "Apt Pupil: Dwight Eisenhower and the 1930 Mobilization Plan," *The Journal of Military History* 70(1) (January 2006): 37.

12. Andy Rooney, "Ike was Right About War Machine," CBS News (June 18, 2006). (www.cbsnews.com/stories/2005/09/30/60minutes/main892398.shtml)

13. Aaron L. Friedberg, *In the Shadow of the Garrison State: America's Anti-Statism and Its Cold War Grand Strategy* (Princeton, NJ: Princeton University Press, 2000), 341.

14. Theodore O. Windt, *Presidents and Protestors: Political Rhetoric in the 1960s* (Tuscaloosa: University of Alabama Press, 1990), 3.

CHAPTER 1

1. J.G.A. Pocock, *The Machiavellian Moment: Florentine Political Thought and the Atlantic Republican Tradition* (Princeton, NJ: Princeton University Press, 1975), 183–218.

2. Isaiah Berlin, "The Originality of Machiavelli," in *The proper Study of Mankind: An Anthology of Essays, Isaiah Berlin,* eds. Henry Hardy and Roger Hausheer (New York: Farrar, Straus and Giroux, 1997), 301.

3. Ibid., xxvi.

4. Niccolló Machiavelli, *The Art of War,* ed. and trans. by Christopher Lynch (Chicago: University of Chicago Press, 2003), 73. Machiavelli failed to acknowledge the long-term implications of gunpowder technology, invalidating many of the practical recommendations in *The Art of War.* Nevertheless, like the translators' overstated opposition of Machiavelli to contractors in combat, interpreters misrepresented his distaste of artillery. He did not dismiss the role of firepower entirely but merely thought it of significantly lesser importance in offensive situations. See Ben Cassidy, "Machiavelli and the Ideology of the Offensive: Gunpowder Weapons in the Art of War," *Journal of Military History* 67(2) (April 2003): 381–404.

5. Philip Bobbitt, *The Shield of Achilles: War, Peace, and the Course of History* (New York: Alfred A. Knopf, 2002), 86.

6. Historians still debate whether the officers intended an outright coup. See C. Edward Skeen and Richard H. Kohn, "The Newburgh Conspiracy Reconsidered," *The William and Mary Quarterly* 31(2) (April 1974): 273–298.

7. Excerpts from George Washington's address to the officers at Newburgh, New York, March 15, 1783.

8. Paul A. Rahe, "Machiavelli at War," *Claremont Review of Books* (Winter 2004): 43.

9. Ibid.

10. Orville Prescott, *Princes of the Renaissance* (London: George Allen and Unwin, 1970), 35.

11. Edwin S. Hunt, "A New Look at the Dealings of the Bardi and Peruzzi with Edward III," *The Journal of Economic History* 50(1) (March 1990): 149.

12. David Potter, "The International Mercenary Market in the Sixteenth Century: Anglo-French Competition in Germany, 1543–50," *The English Historical Review* 111(440) (February 1996): 24–58.

13. For the life and times of Hawkwood, see William Caferro, *John Hawkwood: An English Mercenary in Fourteenth-Century Italy* (Baltimore: Johns Hopkins University Press, 2006).

14. Michael Mallett, "Mercenaries," in *Medieval Warfare* (Oxford: Oxford University Press, 1999), 209.

15. Thomes Ertman, *Birth of the Leviathan: Building States and Regimes in Medieval and Early Modern Europe* (Cambridge, UK: Cambridge University Press, 1997), 63.

16. Walter Raleigh, *The Works of Sir Walter Ralegh, Kt* (Book V) (Oxford 1829), 136.

17. Robert Lacey, *Sir Walter Ralegh* (New York: Atheneum, 1973), 341.

18. Ibid., 66.

19. David S. Bachrach, "The Military Administration of England: The Royal Artillery (1216–1272)," *The Journal of Military History* 68(4) (October 2004): 1104.

20. Brian Downing, *The Military Revolution and Political Change* (Princeton, NJ: Princeton University Press, 1992), 164.

21. Gervase Phillips, "To Cry 'Home! Home!': Mutiny, Morale, and Indiscipline in Tudor Armies," *Journal of Military History* 65(2) (April 2001): 317.

22. John S. Nolan, "The Muster of 1588," *Albion* 23(3) (Fall 1991): 391.

23. See, for example, P.K. O'Brien and P.A. Hunt, "The rise of the fiscal state in England," *Historical Research* LXVI(160) (June 1993): 129–176.

24. Charles Oman, *A History of War in the Middle Ages,* vol. II (London: Greenhill, 1998), 432.

25. D.C. Coleman, *Myth, History and the Industrial Revolution* (London: Hambledon Press, 1992), 69.

26. Janice E. Thomson, *Mercenaries, Pirates, and Sovereigns* (Princeton, NJ: Princeton University Press, 1996), 22–24.

27. Adam Smith, *An Inquiry into the Nature and Causes of the Wealth of Nations,* ed. E. Cannan (New York: Modern Library, 1937), 460.

28. Coleman, *Myth, History and the Industrial Revolution,* 161–162.

29. Stephen Ambrose, *Undaunted Courage: Meriwether Lewis, Thomas Jefferson, and the Opening of the American West* (New York: Simon and Schuster, 1996), 451, 461.

30. For a discussion of Pinkerton's agency and private security firms, see J. Anthony Lukas, *Big Trouble: A Murder in a Small Western Town Sets Off a Struggle for the Soul of America* (New York: Simon & Schuster, 1997), 74–84.

31. In practice, however, the law has never precluded the government from hiring private security firms or military service companies. For detailed analysis of U.S. law governing private security, see Charles P. Nemeth, *Private Security and the Law* (Cambridge, MA: Elsevier, 2004).

32. Joseph W.A. Whitehorne, *The Inspectors General of the United States Army* (Washington, D.C.: Center of Military History, 1998), 420–422.

33. Ricardo A. Herrera, "Self-Governance and the America Soldier, 1775–1861," *Journal of Military History* 65(1) (January 2001): 24–25.

34. See Theodore J. Crackel, *Mr. Jefferson's Army: Political and Social Reform of the Military Establishment, 1801–1809* (New York: New York University Press, 1987).

35. Described in Barry M. Stentiford, *The American Home Guard: The State Militia in the 20th Century* (College Station: Texas A&M University Press, 2002).

36. John Whiteclay Chambers III, *To Raise an Army: The Draft Comes to Modern America* (New York: Free Press, 1987), 9–11.

37. For a contemporary discussion of the politics surrounding Nixon's decision, see Congressional Quarterly, *U.S. Draft Policy and Its Impact* (Washington, D.C.: Congressional Quarterly Service, 1968), 7–9, 25–32.

38. Gus C. Lee and Geoffrey Y. Parker, *Ending the Draft—The Story of the All Volunteer Force,* Final Report 77-1 (Washington, D.C.: Department of the Army, April 1977): 37.

39. See, for example, Tim Kane and James Jay Carafano, "Whither the Warrior: The Truth About Wartime Recruiting," *Army* (May 2006).

40. See Robert W. Coakley, *Role of Federal Military Forces in Domestic Disorder, 1789–1878* (Washington, D.C.: Center of Military History, 1988) and Clayton D. Laurie and

Ronald H. Cole, *Role of Federal Military Forces in Domestic Disorder, 1877–1945* (Washington, D.C.: Center of Military History, 1997).

41. John R. Groves, "Crossroads in U.S. Military Capability: The 21st Century U.S. Army and the Abrams Doctrine," *Land Warfare Paper* No. 37, Association of the United States Army (August 2001): 2. (www.ausa.org/PDFdocs/lwp37_groves.pdf)

42. James Jay Carafano, "The Army Reserves and the Abrams Doctrine: Unfulfilled Promise, Uncertain Future," (April 18, 2005). (www.heritage.org/Research/NationalSecurity/hl869.cfm)

43. Eliot A. Cohen, *Supreme Command: Soldier, Statesman, and Leadership in Wartime* (New York: Free Press, 2002), 227.

44. H.R. McMaster, *Dereliction of Duty: Lyndon Johnson, Robert McNamara, the Joint Chiefs of Staff, and the Lies That Led to Vietnam* (New York: HarperCollins, 1997), 324–325.

45. See, for example, Edward M. Coffman, "The Long Shadow of The Soldier and the State," *The Journal of Military History* 55(1) (January 1991): 69–82.

46. The Human Security Centre, *The Human Security Report 2005: War and Peace in the 21st Century* (Oxford: Oxford University Press, 2005). (www.humansecurityreport.info/content/view/28/63)

47. Fareed Zakaria, *The Future of Freedom: Illiberal Democracy at Home and Abroad* (New York: Norton, 2003), 76.

48. The list was adopted from James Jay Carafano and Paul Rosenzweig, *Winning the Long War: Lessons from the Cold War for Defeating Terrorism and Preserving Freedom* (Washington, D.C.: The Heritage Foundation, 2005), 88–89.

CHAPTER 2

1. Robert H. Scales, *Certain Victory: The U.S. Army in the Gulf War* (Washington, D.C.: Brassey's, 1998), 63.

2. Anthony H. Cordesman and Abraham R. Wagner, *The Lessons of Modern War: The Gulf War*, vol. IV (Boulder: Westview Press, 1996).

3. Steven Weingartner, ed., *In the Wake of the Storm: Gulf War Commanders Discuss Desert Storm* (Wheaton, IL: Cantigny First Division Foundation, 2000).

4. These efforts are best described in John L. Romjue, *The Army of Excellence: The Development of the 1980s Army* (Fort Monroe: Office of the Command Historian, United States Army Training and Doctrine Command, 1993).

5. George B. Dibble, et al., *Army Contractor and Civilian Maintenance, Supply, and Transportation Support During Operations Desert Shield and Desert Storm*, vol. 1 (Bethesda, MD: Department of Defense, 1993), 2-1 to 2-2.

6. In 1980, Army Chief of Staff General Edward C. Meyer used the term "hollow Army" in congressional testimony to describe the shortage of soldiers available to fill the service's field units. The term is now widely used to characterize shortages of personnel, training, and equipment that significantly impinge on military readiness. U.S. Department of Defense, *CJSC Guide to the Chairman's Readiness System* (September 1, 2000), 3. For an illustration of the "hollow force" and its impact on the Korean War, see William W. Epley, "America's First Cold War Army, 1945–1950," Association of the United States Army, Institute for Land Warfare Studies *Land Warfare Paper* No. 32 (August 1999). (www.ausa.org/PDFdocs/lwp32.pdf). A similar pattern of neglect occurred after the Vietnam War. For example, see U.S. Department of the Army, Historical Summary FY 1989, updated May 19, 2003, 4. (www.army.mil/cmh-pg/books/DAHSUM/1989/CH1.htm)

7. U.S. Defense Science Board, *Report of the Defense Science Board Task Force on Outsourcing and Privatization* (August 1996).

8. George P. Sigalos, "The Mother of All Service Contracts," *Linkage: Contractors Servicing Government* 1 (Summer 2001), 10.

9. J. J. Messner and Ylana Gracielli, *State of the Peace and Stability Operations Industry: Second Annual Survey 2007* (Washington, D.C.: Peace Operations Institute, 2007), 46.

10. Richard G. Schenck, "Contractors: A Strategic Asset or Achilles Heel?" Strategic Research Paper, U.S. Army War College (April 10, 2001), 7.

11. Sarah E. Mendelson, "Barracks and Brothels: Peacekeepers and Human Trafficking in the Balkans," Center for Strategic and International Studies (February 2005), 35–37. (www.ceu.hu/polsci/Illicit_Trade-CEU/Week10-Mendelson.pdf)

12. Marc Lindemann, "Civilian Contractors under Military Law," *Parameters* (Autumn 2007), 83–94.(www.army.mil/usawc/Parameters/07autumn/lindeman.htm)

13. Lorna S. Jaffe, *The Development of the Base Force, 1989–1992* (Washington, D.C.: Joint History Office, 1993), 21, 37.

14. Eric V. Larson, et al., *Defense Planning in a Decade of Change* (Santa Monica, CA: 2001), 41–42.

15. Department of Defense, *Quadrennial Defense Review Report* (Washington, D.C.: Department of the Army, 1996), 75.

16. The discussion on entitlement spending is adapted from James Jay Carafano, "Sustaining Military Capabilities in the 21st Century: Rethinking the Utility of the Principles of War," *Heritage Lecture #896* (September 6, 2005). (www.heritage.org/Research/NationalSecurity/hl896.cfm)

17. See, for example, Mackenzie Eaglen, ed., "Four Percent for Freedom: The Need to Invest More in Defense—Selected Writings," *Special Report #18* (September 25, 2007). (www.heritage.org/Research/NationalSecurity/sr18.cfm)

18. Herbert Howe, "Private Security Forces and African Stability: The Case of Executive Outcomes," *The Journal of Modern Africa Studies* 36 (June 1998): 311–313.

19. Fred Schreier and Marina Caparini, "Privatising Security: Law, Practice, and Governance of Private Military and Security Companies," Geneva Centre for the Democratic Control of Armed Forces, Occasional Paper No. 6 (March 2005), 150.

20. Ibid., 80–86 provides an excellent overview of the arguments for and against the use of private military contractors.

21. P.W. Singer, *Corporate Warriors: The Rise of the Privatized Military Industry* (Ithaca, NY: Cornell University Press, 2003), 126.

22. Ibid., 133.

23. The Industrial College of the Armed Forces, "Final Report: Privatized Military Operations," *Spring 2007 Industry Survey* (Spring 2007), 3.

24. Matthew Uttley, "Contractors on Deployed Military Operations: United Kingdom Policy and Doctrine," Strategic Studies Institute (September 2005), 3. (www.strategicstudiesinstitute.army.mil/pdffiles/PUB624.pdf)

25. See Michael Page, et al., *SALW and Private Security Companies in South Eastern Europe* (Belgrade: South Eastern Europe Clearinghouse for the Control of Small Arms and Light Weapons, 2005).

26. Daniel L. Byman, "Uncertain Partners: NGOs and the Military," *Parameters* 43/2 (Summer 2001), 99, 104.

27. Messner and Gracielli, *State of the Peace and Stability Operations Industry*, 20–21.

28. *Final Report: Privatized Military Operations* (Washington, D.C.: The Industrial College of the Armed Forces, 2007), http://www.ndu.edu/icaf/industry/reports/2007/pdf/2007_PMOIS.pdf, 4.

29. Ibid.

30. Jennifer Elsea and Nina M. Serafino, "Private Security Contractors in Iraq: Background, Legal Status, and other Issues," Congressional Research Service (May 8, 2004), CRS-4.

31. Lexington Institute, "Contractors on the Battlefield: A Support Force to Manage," (February 2007), 3–4.

32. John M. Broder and James Risen, "Death Toll for Contractors Reaches New High in Iraq," *The New York Times* (19 May 2007), A1.

33. See Elsea and Serafino, "Private Security Contractors in Iraq: Background, Legal Status, and Other Issues."

34. David Isenberg, "A Fistful of Contractors: The Case for a Pragmatic Assessment of Private Military Companies in Iraq," British American Security Information Council, Research Report 2004.4 (September 2004), appendix 2.

35. Elsea and Serafino, "Private Security Contractors in Iraq: Background, Legal Status, and other Issues," 8.

CHAPTER 3

1. See Kevin M. Teevan, *A History of the Anglo-American Common Law Contract* (Westport, CT: Greenwood, 1990).

2. The government defines a contract as "a mutually binding legal relationship obligating the seller to furnish the supplies or services (including construction) and the buyer to pay for them. It includes all types of commitments that obligate the Government to an expenditure of appropriated funds and that, except as otherwise authorized, are in writing. In addition to bilateral instruments, contracts include (but are not limited to) awards and notices of awards; job orders or task letters issued under basic ordering agreements; letter contracts; orders, such as purchase orders, under which the contract becomes effective by written acceptance or performance; and bilateral contract modifications" (Federal Acquisition Regulation) (acquisition.gov/comp/far/current/html/Subpart%202_1.html#wp1145507).

3. See, for example, Office of the White House, Executive Order 12352—Federal Procurement Reforms (March 17, 1982).

4. General Accounting Office, "DOD Competitive Sourcing: Results of A-76 Studies Over the Past 5 Years," GAO-01-20 (December 2000), 4–5. (www.gao.gov/new.items/d0120.pdf)

5. Susan M. Gates and Albert A. Robert, *Personal Savings in Competitively Sourced DoD Activities* (Santa Monica, CA: RAND, 2000); R. Derek Trunkey, et al., "Analysis of DoD's Commercial Activities Program," Center for Naval Analyses (1996). (handle.dtic.mil/100.2/ADA362379)

6. General Accounting Office, "Greater Emphasis Needed on Increasing Efficiency and Improving Performance," GAO-04-367 (February 2004). (www.gao.gov/atext/d04367.txt)

7. Ibid.

8. General Accounting Office, "Defense Management: DOD Faces Challenges Implementing Its Core Competency Approach and A-76 Competitions," GAO-03-818 (July 2003). (www.gao.gov/atext/d03818.txt)

9. U.S. Department of Defense, "Competitive Sourcing Program Policy During Times of Mobilization and Declared War" (March 2002). (www.amc.army.mil/amc/rda/rda-ac/a76/a76-mob-policy.pdf)

10. Valarie Bailey Grasso, "Walter Reed Army Medical Center (WRAMC) and Office of Management and Budget (OMB) Circular A-76: Implications for the Future," Congressional Research Service (August 21, 2007).

11. *Federal Procurement Report FY2005*, Section III, 3. (www.fpdsng.com/downloads/FPR_Reports/2005_fpr_section_III_agency_views.pdf)

12. General Accounting Office, "Contract Management: Contracting for Iraq Reconstruction and Global Logistics Support," GAO-04-869T (June 15, 2004), 11–12.

13. Minority Staff, Special Investigations Division, House Committee on Government Reform, "Dollars Not Sense: Government Contracting Under the Bush Administration" (June 2006), 8, 13. (www.oversight.house.gov/Documents/20060711103910-86046.pdf); Minority Staff, Special Investigations Division, House Committee on Government Reform, "Halliburton's Iraq Contracts Now Worth Over $10 Billion" (December 9, 2004).

14. Valarie Bailey Grasso, "Defense Contracting in Iraq: Issues and Options for Congress," Congressional Research Service (January 26, 2007).

15. Minority Staff, Special Investigations Division, House Committee on Government Reform, "Dollars Not Sense: Government Contracting Under the Bush Administration" (June 2006): 8.

16. General Accounting Office, "Contract Management: Contracting for Iraq Reconstruction: Contracting for Iraq Reconstruction and Global Logistics Support," GAO-04-869T (June 15, 2004), 2.

17. Special Inspector General for Iraq Reconstruction, "Iraq Reconstruction: Lessons in Contracting and Procurement" (July 2006), 63–64. (www.sigir.mil/reports/pdf/Lessons_Learned_July21.pdf)

18. Government Accountability Office, "Actions Needed to Improve Use of Private Security Providers," GAO-05-737 (July 2005), 4–5.

19. Memorandum from Thomas E. White, Secretary of the Army, to Undersecretary for Acquisition, Technology, and Logistics, et al., dated March 8, 2002.

20. Federal Acquisition Institute, *Federal Acquisition Institute Workforce Report: Fiscal Year 2006* (May 2007), 13.

21. Government Accountability Office, "Military Operations: DOD's Extensive Use of Logistics Support Contracts Requires Strengthened Oversight," GAO-04-854 (July 2004). (www.gao.gov/htext/d04854.html)

22. Valarie Bailey Grasso, "Defense Contracting in Iraq," CRS-10; Government Accountability Office, "Defense Acquisitions: DOD Needs to Exert Management and Oversight to Better Control Acquisition of Services," GAO-07-359T (January 17, 2007), 10. (www.gao.gov/new.items/d07359t.pdf)

23. Government Accountability Office, "Military Operations: DOD's Extensive Use of Logistics Support Contracts."

24. Stuart W. Bowen, Jr., Testimony before the United States House of Representatives, Committee on the Budget, July 31, 2007, 5.

25. Special Inspector General for Iraq Reconstruction, "Iraq Reconstruction," 108–109.

26. Federal Acquisition Institute, "Report on Competitive Sourcing Competencies" (February 12, 2004). (www.fai.gov/pdfs/cscrfinal02-12-04.pdf); Federal Acquisition Institute, "2007 Contracting Workforce Competencies Survey: General Analysis" (October 2007).

27. Special Inspector General for Iraq Reconstruction, *Report to Congress* (July 2007), 195.

28. Bowen, Testimony before the United States House of Representatives, Committee on the Budget, 2–3.

29. Government Accountability Office, "Information on False Claims Act Litigation," GAO-06-302R (January 31, 2006), 2.

CHAPTER 4

1. James Jay Carafano, *GI Ingenuity: Improvisation, Technology, and Winning World War II* (Westport, CT: Praeger Security International, 2006), 65–67.

2. Gerald Schumacher, *A Bloody Business: America's War Zone Contractors and the Occupation of Iraq* (St. Paul, MN: Zenith Press, 2006), 60.

3. Robert Pelton Young, *License to Kill: Hired Guns in the War on Terror* (New York: Crown, 2006), 72–73.

4. Ibid.

5. U.S. Special Operations Command, "USSOCOM Posture Statement 2007," 12. (www.socom.mil/Docs/USSOCOM_Posture_Statement_2007.pdf)

6. Ibid., 14; see also 13.

7. Young, *License to Kill*, 168.

8. Richard J. Griffin, testimony before the House Committee on Oversight and Government Reform, October 2, 2007, 5. (oversight.house.gov/documents/20071002145249.pdf)

9. Messner and Gracielli, *State of the Peace and Stability Operations Industry*, 47.

10. Ibid., 14.

11. "War by the Numbers" is adapted from James Jay Carafano, "War by the Numbers," October 15, 2007. (www.heritage.org/Press/Commentary/ed101507a.cfm)

12. Griffin, testimony before the House Committee on Oversight and Government Reform, 5.

13. Debirah C. Kidwell, "Public War, Private Fight? The United States and Private Military Companies," Occasional Paper 12, Combat Studies Institute, 1.

14. Government Accountability Office, "Defense Base Act: Review Needed of Cost and Implementation Issues," GAO-05-280R (April 29, 2005), 5 (www.gao.gov/new.items/d05280r.pdf)

15. Ben Murray, "American, British civilian contractors honored for work in Iraq," *Stars and Stripes* (UK Weekly Edition), June 28, 2006. (www.estripes.com/article.asp?section=144&article=37652&archive=true)

16. Paul Christopher, "Civilian Contractors: Ethical and Legal Parameters," *Journal of International Peace Operations* 2(2) (September 2006): 9.

17. See Charles R. Shrader, *Amicicide: The Problem of Friendly Fire in Modern War* (Fort Leavenworth: Combat Studies Institute, 1982). (www.cgsc.army.mil/carl/resources/csi/Shrader/shrader.asp)

18. Described in James Jay Carafano, *After D-Day; Operation Cobra and the Normandy Breakout* (Boulder: Lynne Rienner, 2000), 109–121.

19. U.S. Department of Defense, Office of Assistant Secretary of Defense (Public Affairs), "Military Probes Friendly Fire Incidents," News Release No. 504-91 (August 13, 1991).

20. U.S. Department of the Army, *Regulation 27-20, Claims*, (July 1, 2003), para. 10-2a. For a description of Foreign Claims Commissions operations in Iraq, see Karin Tackaberry, "Center for Law & Military Operations note from the field: judge advocates play a major role in rebuilding Iraq: the Foreign Claims Act and implementation of the Commander's Emergency

Response Program—CLAMO," *Army Lawyer* (February 2004). (findarticles.com/p/articles/ mi_m6052/is_2004_Feb/ai_115695637)

21. ACLU, "U.S. Army Documents That Depict American Troops' Involvement in Civilian Casualties in Iraq and Afghanistan," Press Release, September 4, 2007. (www.aclu.org/natsec/31540prs20070904.html)

22. "A Fractured Band of Brothers" is adapted from James Jay Carafano and Dana R. Dillon, "Winning the Peace: Principles for Post-Conflict Operations," Backgrounder #1859 (June 13, 2005). (www.heritage.org/Research/NationalSecurity/bg1859.cfm)

CHAPTER 5

1. The introduction to Chapter 5 is adapted from James Jay Carafano, "Breaking and Remaking Paradigms Past and Present: Rethinking International Relations Theory for the Post–Cold War World," H-Net (June 1999). (www.h-net.org/reviews/showrev.cgi?path= 5125932488225)

2. See, for example, Paul Schroeder, "Historical Reality vs. Neo-realist Theory," *International Security* 19 (Summer 1994): 108–148.

3. See, for example, Immanuel Wallerstein, "Liberalism and the Legitimation of Nation-States: An Historical Interpretation," *Social Justice* 19(1) (Spring 1992): 22–33.

4. Peter J. Katzenstein, ed., *The Culture of National Security: Norms and Identity in World Politics.* New Directions in World Politics (New York: Columbia University Press, 1996), 16–17.

5. Parts of "Brave New World" are adapted from James Jay Carafano, "After September 11—More Observations Than Insights," H-Net (January 2004). (www.h-net.org/reviews/ showrev.cgi?path=312111079074579)

6. Justus D. Doenecke, "William Appleman Williams and the Anti-Interventionist Tradition," *Diplomatic History* 25(2) (Spring 2001): 284.

7. Joseph E. Stiglitz, *Globalization and Its Discontents* (New York: W.W. Norton, 2002), 20, 67, 81.

8. Carafano, "After September 11."

9. James Jay Carafano, "The Real Islamic Threat," (September 23, 2006). (www.heritage.org/Press/Commentary/ed092506b.cfm)

10. Pradeep P. Barua, *The State of War in South Asia* (Lincoln: University of Nebraska Press, 2005), 116.

11. For an overview, see Robert B. Ekelund, Jr., and Robert D. Tollison, *Politicized Economies: Monarchy, Monopoly, and Mercantilism* (College Station: Texas A&M University Press, 1997), 185–220.

12. Mark L. Montroll, "Maintaining the Technological Lead," in Hans Binnendiijk, ed., *Transforming America's Military* (Washington, D.C.: National Defense University Press, 2002), 349–350; Nathan Rosenenberg, "A Historical Overview of the Evolution of Federal Investment in Research and Development Since World War II," in *Papers Commissioned for a Workshop on the Federal Role in Research and Development* (Washington, D.C.: National Academy of Sciences, National Academy of Engineering, Institute of Medicine, 1985), 1–36.

13. Alexander Bolton, "Sens. Cochran, Stevens lead in earmark tally," *The Hill* (December 3, 2007). (http://thehill.com/leading-the-news/sens.-cochran-stevens-lead-in-earmark-tally-2007-12-03.html)

14. American Association for the Advancement of Science, *AAAS Report XXXI: Research and Development FY 2007* (Washington, D.C.: American Association for the Advancement of Science, 2006). (www.aaas.org/spp/rd/07pch1.htm)

15. International Monetary Fund, *World Economic Outlook* (September 2002), 132. (www.imf.org/external/pubs/ft/weo/2002/02/index.htm)

16. U.S. Department of Commerce, "Manufacturing in America" (January 2004), 25. (www.hongkong.usconsulate.gov/usinfo/2004/doc_mfg_report.pdf)

17. John Steele Gordon, *An Empire of Wealth: The Epic History of American Economic Power* (New York: HarperCollins, 2004), 417.

18. See Jack Spencer, *The Military Industrial Base in Age of Globalization* (Washington, D.C.: The Heritage Foundation, 2005), (www.heritage.org/Research/NationalSecurity/industrial_base_book.cfm)

19. Pierre A. Chao, "The Future of the Defense Industrial Base: National Security Implication in a Globalized World," 32–33.

20. Committee on Prospering in the Global Economy of the 21st Century, *Rising Above the Gathering Storm: Energizing and Employing America for a Brighter Economic Future* (Washington, D.C.: National Academies Press, 2005), 60; National Academy of Engineering, *The Engineer of 2020: Visions of Engineering in the New Century* (Washington, D.C.: National Academies Press, 2004), 14.

21. Pierre A. Chao, et al., "The Structure and Dynamics of the U.S. Federal Professional Services Industrial Base, 1995–2005," Center for Strategic and International Studies (May 2007), ix. (www.diig-csis.org/resources/view.asp?RESOURCE_ID=86)

22. Suzanne D. Patrick, "The Defense Industrial Base: Myth vs. Reality," *Aviation Week & Space Technology* (September 13, 2004), 86.

23. Chao, "The Structure and Dynamics of the U.S. Federal Professional Services Industrial Base," 44.

24. Gordon, *An Empire of Wealth*, 419.

25. For an introduction to the debate about Kennan's place in Cold War historiography, see John Lamberton Harper, *American Visions of Europe: Franklin D. Roosevelt, George F. Kennan, and Dean G. Acheson* (Cambridge, UK: Cambridge University Press, 1996), 183.

26. Bosley Crowther, "Gary Cooper Plays an Idealistic Architect in Film Version of 'The Fountainhead,'" *The New York Times*, July 9, 1949. (http://movies.nytimes.com/movie/review?res=9902E7DA113EE03BBC4153DFB1668382659EDE)

27. U.S. Department of Labor, Bureau of Labor Statistics, "The Employment Situation, June 2004," USDL 04-1170 (July 2, 2004). (www.bls.gov/news.release/empsit.nr0.htm)

28. U.S. Department of Labor, Bureau of Labor Statistics, "Extended Mass Layoffs Associated with Domestic and Overseas Relocations, First Quarter 2004" (June 10, 2004). (http://bls.gov/news.release/reloc.nr0.htm)

29. Organization for International Investment, "The Facts About Insourcing" (April 2004). (www.ofi.org/insourcing)

30. See, for example, Haynes Johnson, *Sleepwalking Through History: America in the Reagan Years* (New York: W.W. Norton, 2003), 178–179.

31. James Jay Carafano, testimony before the House Armed Services Committee (March 3, 2006). (www.heritage.org/Research/HomelandSecurity/tst030306a.cfm)

32. Daniella Markheim and James Jay Carafano, "After Dubai Ports: Getting CFIUS Reforms Right," *WebMemo #1081* (May 17, 2006). (www.heritage.org/Research/NationalSecurity/wm1081.cfm)

33. Parts of "Fiscal Policies" are adapted from Carafano and Rosenzweig, "Winning the Long War," chapter 5.

34. Robert Bartley, "Thinking Things Over: Does Spending Stimulate? Do Deficits?" *The Wall Street Journal* (February 4, 2002), A17.

35. Frank G. Steindl, "Money and Income: The View From the Government Budget Restraint," *The Journal of Finance* 29(4) (September 1974), 1143–1148.

36. Amity Shlaes, *The Forgotten Man: A New History of the Great Depression* (New York: HarperCollins, 2007), 11.

37. J.D. Foster, "Taxpayers, Beware: Record Tax Burden Is Rising," *WebMemo #1639* (September 26, 2007). (www.heritage.org/Research/Budget/wm1639.cfm)

38. Shlaes, *The Forgotten Man*, 20.

39. Committee on Prospering in the Global Economy of the 21st Century, *Rising Above The Gathering Storm*, 1, 14; National Academy of Engineering, *The Engineer of 2020*, 24.

40. Committee on Prospering in the Global Economy of the 21st Century, *Rising Above The Gathering Storm*, 15-16.

41. Robert F. Brunner, "The Brush Strokes of Business," *The Washington Post* (December 24, 2007), D3.

42. Quoted in U.S. Department of Education, *Meeting the Challenge of a Challenging World: Strengthening Education for the 21st Century* (Washington, D.C.: U.S. Department of Education, 2006), 14. (www.doleta.gov/wired/files/Meeting_The_Challenge_of_a_Changing_World.pdf)

43. Committee on Network Science for Future Army Applications, National Research Council, *Network Science* (Washington, D.C.: National Academies Press, 2005).

44. James Jay Carafano, "Better, Faster, Cheaper Border Security Requires Better Immigration Services," *Backgrounder #2011* (February 28, 2007). (www.heritage.org/Research/Immigration/bg2011.cfm); James Jay Carafano, testimony before the Committee on Government Reform, Subcommittee on National Security, Emerging Threats, and International Relations (September 13, 2005). (www.heritage.org/Research/Homeland Security/tst091305a.cfm)

45. David Henderson, *The Role of Business in the Modern World* (Washington, D.C.: Competitive Enterprise Institute, 2004), 18.

46. Ibid., 17.

47. Mike Moore, *A World Without Walls: Freedom, Development, Free Trade and Global Governance* (Cambridge, UK: Cambridge University Press, 2003), 89.

48. Michael J. Ferrantino, "International Trade, Environmental Quality and Public Policy," *The World Economy* 20(1) (January 1997), 43.

49. Committee on Prospering in the Global Economy of the 21st Century, *Rising Above The Gathering Storm*, 14.

CHAPTER 6

1. Washingtonpost.com, "Day One Transcript: 9/11 Commission Hearing" (March 23, 2004). (www.washingtonpost.com/wp-dyn/articles/A17798-2004Mar23.html)

2. See Nathalie Bastin, "Revisionism Post-9/11," European Strategic Intelligence and Security Center (December 13, 2007). Post–September 11 conspiracy theories are not confined to the United States. They are rampant in the Islamic world. See "Unraveling Anti-Semitic 9/11 Conspiracy Theories," Anti-Defamation League (2003). (www.adl.org/anti_semitism/9-11conspiracytheories.pdf); "9/11 Conspiracy Theories on Arab and Iranian TV Channels 2004–2005," The Middle East Media Research Institute, Special Report—No. 38 (September 9, 2005). (www.memri.org/sr.html)

3. See, for example, Chris Suellentrop, "Sy Hersh Says It's Okay to Lie (Just Not in Print): The runaway mouth of America's premier investigative journalist," *New York* (April 11, 2005). (nymag.com/nymetro/news/people/features/11719)

4. See Mark Fenster, *Conspiracy Theories: Secrecy and Power in American Culture* (Minneapolis: University of Minnesota, 1999).

5. William G. Palmer, "The Burden of Proof: J.H. Hexter and Christopher Hill," *The Journal of British Studies*, 19(1) (Autumn 1979), 122–129.

6. P.W. Singer, *Corporate Warriors: The Rise of the Privatized Military Industry* (Ithaca, NY: Cornell University Press, 2003), 97–100, 136–148.

7. Ibid., 141, 146.

8. Richard Lacquement, "Cooperate Warriors by P.W. Singer," *Naval War College Review* (Summer/Autumn 2004), 159–160.

9. See, for example, U.S. Department of Defense, "Background Briefing on Investigations on Abu Ghraib" (August 25, 2004). (www.defenselink.mil/transcripts/transcript.aspx?transcriptid=2694)

10. In addition to the government studies in Chapter 3 that cite cost savings from outsourcing, academic researchers have examined the issue as well. A 2001 study estimated Pentagon annual savings at $1.46 billion per year with a potential to reach $5.74 billion per year. See Christopher M. Snyder, Robert T. Trost, and R. Derek Trunkey, "Reducing Government Spending with Privatization Competitions: A Study of the Department of Defense Experience," *The Review of Economics and Statistics* 83(1) (February 2001), 108–117.

11. P.W. Singer, "The Contract the Military Needs to Break," *Washington Post* (September 12, 2004), B3.

12. Deborah D. Avant, *The Market for Force: The Consequences of Privatizing Security* (Cambridge, UK: Cambridge University Press, 2005), 2.

13. Ibid., 6.

14. Bruce L. Benson, "The Market for Force," *The Independent Review* XI(3) (Winter 2007): 452, 453.

15. Richard Sklar, *Movie-Made America: A Cultural History of American Movies* (New York: Vintage Books, 1975), 250.

16. Sudhir Muralidhar, "Why Are Iraq War Movies Box-Office Flops?" *The American Prospect* (November 27, 2007). (www.prospect.org/cs/articles?article=why_are_iraq_war_movies_boxoffice_flops)

17. Mary Corliss/Cannes, "A First Look at 'Fahrenheit 9/11,'" *Time* (May 17, 2004). (www.time.com/time/arts/article/0,8599,638819,00.html)

18. Christopher Hitchens, "Unfairenheit 9/11: The lies of Michael Moore," *Slate* (June 21, 2004). (www.slate.com/id/2102723)

19. Sklar, *Movie-Made America*, 214.

20. Although some individuals may indeed join the armed forces for that reason (during peace and wartime), statistical evidence argues conclusively that poverty and desperation are not widespread motives for enlistment. For recent studies, see Congressional Budget Office, "The All-Volunteer Military: Issues and Performance," Pub. No. 2960 (July 2007). (www.cbo.gov/ftpdocs/83xx/doc8313/07-19-MilitaryVol.pdf); Tim Kane, "Who Are the Recruits? The Demographic Characteristics of U.S. Military Enlistment, 2003–2005," Center for Data Analysis (October 27, 2006). (www.heritage.org/Research/NationalSecurity/cda06-09.cfm) For contrasting conclusions, see the analysis of military recruiting in 2005 by the National Priorities Project. (www.nationalpriorities.org/Publications/Military-Recruiting-2005.html)

21. Walter Addiego, "Iraq for Sale: The War Profiteers," SFGate.Com (September 15, 2006). (www.sfgate.com/cgi-bin/article.cgi?f=/c/a/2006/09/15/DDGSEL4J9M1.DTL#flick4)

22. Jeannette Catsoulis, "Deep Pockets in Iraq," *New York Times* (September 8, 2006). (http://movies.nytimes.com/2006/09/08/movies/08prof.html?ex=1315368000&en=b62e6 7ca30a6e91e&ei=5090&partner=rssuserland&emc=rss)

23. For the interview, see "Robert Greenwald's Interview with Peter Brooks." (iraqforsale.org/doug_brooks.php)

24. Amy Menefee, "Movie Review: 'Iraq for Sale: The War Profiteers:' Election-season release from Wal-Mart film's director is latest documentary that attacks businesses," Business and Media Institute (September 20, 2006). (www.businessandmedia.org/ commentary/2006/20060920155617.aspx)

25. Steve Johnson, "Greenwald's 'Iraq for Sale' Veers Off the Small-Film Path," *The Chicago Tribune* (September 8, 2006).

26. Bruce V. Bigelow, "Iraq documentary latest to use Web, new technologies to sway the debate," *San Diego Union-Tribune* (September 23, 2006).

27. *Iraq for Sale.* (http://iraqforsale.org/facts.php)

28. Gerald Schumacher, *A Bloody Business: America's War Zone Contractors and the Occupation of Iraq* (St. Paul, MN: Zenith Press, 2006), 12.

29. Robert Young Pelton, *License to Kill: Hired Guns in the War on Terror* (New York: Crown, 2006), 107.

30. Ibid., 107–109.

31. Ibid., 116.

32. John Freeman, "'Blood Money': The trouble with 'outsourcing' in war-torn Iraq," *The Seattle Times* (September 29, 2006). (http://seattletimes.nwsource.com/html/ books/2003279796_bloodmoney01.html)

33. David Isenberg, "A Fistful of Contractors: The Case for a Pragmatic Assessment of Private Military Companies in Iraq," BASIC Research Report 2004.4 (September 2004); David Isenberg, "A government in search of cover: PMCs in Iraq," paper prepared for "Market Forces: Regulating Private Military Companies," March 23–24, 2006, conference, Institute for International Law and Justice, New York University School of Law. (www.basicint.org/pubs/Papers/pmcs0603.pdf)

34. Sarah Percy, "Regulating the Private Security Industry," Adelphi Paper, International Institute for Strategic Studies (2006). An expanded version of her analysis can be found in Sarah Percy, *Mercenaries: The History of a Norm in International Relations* (Oxford: Oxford University Press, 2007).

35. Matthew Uttley, "Contractors on Deployed Military Operations: United Kingdom Policy and Doctrine," Strategic Studies Institute (September 1, 2001). (www.strategicstud-iesinstitute.army.mil/pdffiles/PUB624.pdf)

36. Frank Camm and Victoria A. Greenfield, *Civilian or Military? Assessing the Risk of Using Contractors on the Battlefield* (Santa Monica, CA: RAND, 2005).

37. Robert L. Borosage, Eric Lotke, and Robert Gerson, "War Profiteers: Profits Over Patriotism in Iraq," Campaign for America's Future (September 2006), 17.

38. Maureen Dowd, "Sinking in a Swamp Full of Blackwater," *The New York Times* (October 3, 2007). (www.nytimes.com/2007/10/03/opinion/03dowd.html)

39. "Billions Wasted In Iraq? U.S. Official Says Oversight Was 'Nonexistent,'" CBS.com. (www.cbsnews.com/stories/2006/02/09/60minutes/main1302378_page3.shtml)

40. Walter Pincus, "Power of the Pen: A Call for Journalistic Courage," *Frank* (Fall/Winter 2007), 16.

41. "Dollars, Not Sense," 57–58.

42. Borosage, Lotke, and Gerson, "War Profiteers," 17.

43. Memorandum to the Members of the Committee on Government and Oversight Reform, RE: Additional Information About Blackwater USA, October 1, 2007. (http://oversight.house.gov/documents/20071001121609.pdf)

CHAPTER 7

1. Fareed Zakaria, *The Future of Freedom: Illiberal Democracy at Home and Abroad* (New York: W.W. Norton, 2003), 13.

2. Ibid., 17.

3. There is a reason Andrew Roberts starts his excellent history of the English-speaking peoples at the turn of the twentieth century, when the United States and its principle allies shared nearly equal political systems, a condition that occurred over the last half of the nineteenth century. Andrew Roberts, *A History of the English-Speaking Peoples Since 1900* (New York: HarperCollins, 2006).

4. Portions of "An Affair to Remember" are adapted from Alex Douville, "Breaking Ranks—Breaking Rules: The Iran-Contra Scandal," in James Jay Carafano and Richard Weitz, eds. *Mismanaging Mayhem: How Washington Responds to Crisis* (Westport, CT: Praeger, 2008), 130–148.

5. "Address to the Nation on the Iran Arms and Contra Aid Controversy," The Ronald Reagan Presidential Library. (www.reagan.utexas.edu/archives/speeches/1987/030487h.htm)

6. "Excerpts from the Tower Commission's Report," The American Presidency Project. (www.presidency.ucsb.edu/PS157/assignment%20files%20public/TOWER%20EXCERPTS.htm)

7. The White House response to the Iran–Contra affair is well described in David M. Abshire, *Saving the Reagan Presidency: Trust is the Coin of the Realm* (College Station: Texas A&M University Press, 2005).

8. Pelton, *Licensed to Kill*, 107.

9. For criticisms, see B.G. Burkett & Glenna Whitley, *Stolen Valor: How the Vietnam Generation Was Robbed of Its Heroes and Its History* (Dallas: Verity Press, 1998). For a defense of the project, see Gerald Nicosia, *Home to War: A History of the Vietnam Veterans' Movement* (New York: Carroll & Graf, 2004).

10. "Blackwater Chief Welcomes Extra Oversight," CBSnews.com (October 14, 2007). (www.cbsnews.com/stories/2007/10/13/60minutes/main3364195.shtml)

11. The nature of the terrorist surveillance program controversy is described in K.A. Taipale and James Jay Carafano, "Free the Hostages: Continuing FISA concerns," National Review Online (October 24, 2007). (http://article.nationalreview.com/?q=Y2VjNzQzYWU1Mjc4ZWI4ZjkyNzMyNjNmYjUyODBjYTY=)

12. See, for example, the argument made about enduring alliances in James Jay Carafano and Sally McNamara, "Enduring Alliances Empower America's Long-War Strategy," *Backgrounder #2042* (June 15, 2007). (www.heritage.org/Research/NationalSecurity/bg2042.cfm)

13. James Jay Carafano and Paul Rosenzweig, "Protecting Privacy and Providing Security: A Case of Sensible Outsourcing," *Backgrounder #1810* (November 5, 2004). (www.heritage.org/Research/HomelandSecurity/bg1810.cfm)

14. See, for example, Reinhold Wagenleitner, *Coca-Colonization and the Cold War: The Cultural Mission of the United States in Austria after the Second World War* (Chapel Hill: University of North Carolina Press, 1994).

15. See, for example, Stuart D. Brandes, *Warhogs: A History of War Profits in America* (Lexington: University of Kentucky Press, 1997).

16. Curtis L. Gilroy and Cindy Williams, eds., *Service to Country: Personnel Policy and the Transformation of Western Militaries* (Cambridge, MA: The MIT Press, 2006), 22.

17. The influence of civilian attributes on wartime service is described in James Jay Carafano, *GI Ingenuity: Improvisation, Technology, and Winning World War II* (Westport, CT: Praeger, 2006).

18. Robert A. Griffin, ed., *School of the Citizen Soldier* (New York: D. Appleton-Century, 1942).

19. Lori Lyn Bogle, *The Pentagon's Battle for the American Mind: The Early Cold War* (College Station: Texas A&M University Press, 2004), 134–163.

20. The effort to institute Universal Military Training is well described in Michael J. Hogan, *Cross of Iron: Harry S. Truman and the Origins of the National Security State, 1945–1954* (Cambridge, UK: Cambridge University Press, 1998).

21. Friedberg, *In the Shadow of the Garrison State*, 156.

22. Robert Jervis, "The Impact of the Korean War on the Cold War," *The Journal of Conflict Resolution*, 24/4 (December 1980), 565.

23. Carafano, "The Army Reserves and the Abrams Doctrine."

24. Dennis J. Reimer, *Soldiers Are Our Credentials: The Collected Works and Selected Papers of the Thirty-Third Chief of Staff, United States Army* (Washington, D.C.: The Center of Military History, 2000), 10.

25. John A. Lynn, *Battle: A History of Combat and Culture from Ancient Greece to Modern America* (Cambridge, MA: Westview Press, 2003), xv.

26. For an elaboration of this thesis, see Carafano, *GI Ingenuity*.

27. The section "I Robot" is adapted from James Jay Carafano and Andrew Gudgel, "The Pentagon's Robots: Arming the Future," *Backgrounder #2093* (December 19, 2007). (http://author.heritage.org/Research/NationalSecurity/bg2093.cfm)

28. Antulio J. Echeverria II, *Imagining Future War: The West's Technological Revolution and Visions of Wars to Come: 1880–1914* (Westport, CT: Praeger Security International, 2007), 95–96.

29. Associated Press, "Explosive-Sniffing Robots Headed to Iraq to Help U.S. Military Counter Deadly Roadside Bombs," *Niagara Gazette* (March 29, 2007). (www.niagara-gazette.com/newtoday/gnnnewtoday_story_088144250.html)

CHAPTER 8

1. See Carafano and Weitz, *Mismanaging Mayhem*. This work includes a collection of historical cases analyzing the effectiveness of interagency operations since World War I.

2. This proposal is detailed in James Jay Carafano, "Missions, Responsibilities, and Geography: Rethinking How the Pentagon Commands the World," *Backgrounder #1792* (August 26, 2004). (www.heritage.org/Research/NationalSecurity/bg1792.cfm)

3. For the genesis and explanation of the Goldwater–Nichols reforms, see James R. Locher III, *Victory on the Potomac: The Goldwater-Nichols Act Unifies the Pentagon* (College Station: Texas A&M University Press, 2002).

4. Proposed reforms are described in James Jay Carafano, "Missing Pieces in Homeland Security: Interagency Education, Assignments, and Professional Accreditation," *Executive Memorandum #1013* (October 16, 2006). (www.heritage.org/Research/HomelandSecurity/em1013.cfm)

5. "Fighting with Friends" is adapted from James Jay Carafano and Sally McNamara, "Enduring Alliances Empower America's Long-War Strategy," *Backgrounder #2042* (June 15, 2007). (www.heritage.org/Research/NationalSecurity/bg2042.cfm). This paper includes more detailed recommendations.

6. For example, see Elke Krahmann, "Conceptualizing Security Governance," *Cooperation and Conflict* 38(1) (March 2003): 5–26.

7. The White House, *The National Security Strategy of the United States of America* (September 17, 2002). (www.whitehouse.gov/nsc/nss.pdf)

8. James Jay Carafano and Janice A. Smith, "The Muddled Notion of 'Human Security' at the U.N.: A Guide for U.S. Policymakers," *Backgrounder #1966* (September 1, 2006). (www.heritage.org/Research/WorldwideFreedom/bg1966.cfm)

9. "Learning How to Win the Peace" is adapted from James Jay Carafano and Dana R. Dillon, "Winning the Peace: Principles for Post-Conflict Operations," *Backgrounder #1859* (June 13, 2005). (www.heritage.org/Research/NationalSecurity/bg1859.cfm)

10. James Jay Carafano, *Waltzing into the Cold War: The Struggle for Occupied Austria* (College Station: Texas A&M University Press, 2002), 11.

11. Erwin A. Schmidl, "The Evolution of Peace Operations from the Nineteenth Century," in *Peace Operations: Between War and Peace,* ed. Erwin A. Schmidl (London: Frank Cass, 2000), 7.

12. For more specific recommendations, see Carafano and Dillon, "Winning the Peace."

13. See Barry Machado, *In Search of Usable Past: The Marshall Plan and Postwar Reconstruction Today* (Lexington, VA: The George C. Marshall Center, 2007).

14. For one proposal, see John R. Boullé III, "Operational Planning and Conflict Termination," *Joint Force Quarterly* (Autumn/Winter 2001–2002): 99–102.

15. For specific recommendations, see James Jay Carafano, "Shaping the 21st Century National Guard and Reserves," Testimony (May 4, 2006). (www.heritage.org/Research/HomelandDefense/tst050406a.cfm)

16. "Four Percent for Freedom," is adapted from James Jay Carafano, Baker Spring, and Mackenzie Eaglen, "Four Percent for Freedom: Maintaining Robust National Security Spending," *Executive Memorandum #1023* (April 10, 2007). (www.heritage.org/Research/NationalSecurity/em1023.cfm)

17. William L. Megginson and Jeffry M. Netter, "From State to Market: A Survey of Empirical Studies on Privatization," *Journal of Economic Literature*, 39(2) (June 2001): 321–389, and Robert W. Poole, Jr. and Philip E. Fixler, Jr., "Privatization of Public-Sector Services in Practice: Experience and Potential," *Journal of Policy Analysis and Management* 6(4) (Summer 1987): 612–625.

18. "When to Rent" is adapted from James Jay Carafano and Alane Kochems, "Engaging Military Contractors in Counterterrorism Operations," in James J.F. Forrest, ed., *Countering Terrorism and Insurgencies in the 21st Century: International Perspectives*, vol. 1, (Westport, CT: Praeger, 2007), 190–207.

19. U.S. Department of the Army, *Risk Management Multiservice Tactics, Techniques, and Procedures for Risk Management*, Field Manual 3-100.12 (February 15, 2001), Glossary-4–Glossary-6.

20. Camm and Greenfield, *How Should the Army Use Contractors?*

21. Special Inspector General for Iraq Reconstruction, *Iraq Reconstruction: Lessons in Human Capital Management* (January 2006), 25. (www.sigir.mil/reports/pdf/Lessons_Learned_Feb16.pdf)

22. Ibid., xx–xxii.

23. See, for example, Jullian J. Ewell and Ira S. Hunt, *Sharpening the Combat Edge: The Use of Analysis to Reinforce Military Judgment* (Washington, D.C.: Department of the Army, 1974).

24. Special Inspector General for Iraq Reconstruction, *Iraq Reconstruction*, 25.

25. Commission on Army Acquisition and Program Management in "Expeditionary Operations," "Urgent Reform Required: Army Expeditionary Contracting" (October 31, 2007), 2. (www.army.mil/docs/Ganselr-Commission_Report_Final_071031.pdf)

26. Government Accountability Office, "High-Level DOD Action Needed to Address Long-Standing Problems with Management and Oversight of Contractors Supporting Deployed Forces," GAO-7-145 (December 2006), 4.

Index

About the Author

JAMES JAY CARAFANO is a senior fellow at the Heritage Foundation, specializing in homeland security, defense policy, military affairs, post-conflict operations, and terrorism. He is the author of four books on national security and military history and is a frequent guest on television and radio programs.

Recent Titles in The Changing Face of War

Mismanaging Mayhem: How Washington Responds to Crisis
James Jay Carafano and Richard Weitz, editors